NO BRIDGES BLOWN

No Bridges Blown

William B. Dreux

UNIVERSITY OF NOTRE DAME PRESS
NOTRE DAME LONDON

UNIVERSITY OF NOTRE DAME PRESS
Notre Dame, Indiana 46556

LIBRARY OF CONGRESS CATALOG CARD NUMBER:
72-165994

Manufactured in the United States of America by
NAPCO Graphic Arts, Inc., Milwaukee, Wisconsin

TO L. S.
AND THE OTHERS
WHO DID NOT MAKE IT

Grateful acknowledgment is made for excerpts from the following works:

"The Soldier" by Rupert Brooke. Reprinted by permission of Dodd, Mead & Company, Inc., from *The Collected Poems of Rupert Brooke*. Copyright 1915 by Dodd, Mead & Company; copyright renewed 1943 by Edward Marsh.

"Under Ben Bulben" by W. B. Yeats, from *Collected Poems* by W. B. Yeats, reprinted by permission of The Macmillan Company. Copyright 1940 by Georgie Yeats, renewed 1968 by Bertha Georgie Yeats, Michael Butler Yeats and Anne Yeats.

"A Rendezvous with Death" by Allan Seeger. Reprinted by permission of Charles Scribner's Sons.

Poem by Patrick Shaw Stewart reprinted from *Dialogue with Myself* by Martin C. D'Arcy, S.J., copyright © 1966, by Martin C. D'Arcy. Reprinted by permission of Simon & Schuster, Inc. publishers.

Contents

Nous n'irons plus au bois, les lauriers sont coupés.

Théodore de Banville

Preface

I was an infantry officer in July of 1943 when I joined OSS as a volunteer for missions in enemy-held territory. In the summer of 1944 two French paratrooper officers and I were parachuted behind the German lines in France. Our mission was to lead Maquis groups in the northwest sector of Brittany, coordinate their guerrilla operations, and radio back intelligence reports to headquarters in London. This story is about some of the things that happened during that period, and it is also about some of the people I knew.

I have included reminiscences of my boyhood in Paris during World War I, although this has nothing at all to do with the story, except perhaps in an indirect way.

This is not a blood and guts story. Of course there was fighting, but such things have been written of often, and sometimes by those who never saw combat and so perhaps could write more objectively about it. I have seen the look of pain and fear on the face of a young Maquis fighter right after he had been cut down by a machine gun burst. But it is just as well to leave some of this out, and I would rather write of other things.

Parts of my story may be hard to believe, but they are true nonetheless and told as I remember them. This story does not tell of stalking a German sentry at night and quietly killing him (if you did it right and were lucky) by jumping him from the rear, hooking your left arm tight around his neck and with your right hand sticking your commando knife deep in the small of his back and cutting the kidney artery. There was none of that.

There are no seductive women spies either, gliding around with their slit skirts in dimly lighted rooms. It is true that on several occasions we did use teen-age French girls as couriers. That was because we had learned that the Germans rarely stopped girls for questioning. So we would give the girls messages and send them off on their bicycles, skirts blowing in the wind, pedalling merrily past German control points. There was not a Mata-Hari among them, and judging from the old pictures of Mata-Hari I have seen, these girls were far fresher and prettier.

Nor does this story tell of blowing up bridges as in the dramatic episode in *For Whom the Bell Tolls*. This was a great disappointment to me. The two French officers and I were well trained in demolitions, and I had looked forward to setting time charges on a key bridge and then watching it go up with a magnificent bang, hurling a German convoy of tanks and trucks all over the countryside.

The only blown bridge that I saw behind the lines was a beautiful old stone bridge across the river Rance just outside Dinan, and the Germans had done that. They had dynamited the center arch as they retreated.

In movies and on television you sometimes see a tough American paratrooper knock out a German guard with a devastating karate chop or a swift judo throw. You will find none of that in this story. The closest any German ever came to me was when he was poking his submachine gun in my stomach as I sat trapped in a car. No karate or judo expert could have gotten out of that fix. I had to do it differently.

There are no great victories either. If anything, it was the other way around. Once I led a Maquis group and tried to punch a hole through the rear of the "Atlantic Wall" defenses on the Brittany coast. My group was made up of untrained young Frenchmen and some former Senegalese and Algerian soldiers. The Germans let me lead my men forward into a trap. Then they opened up on us; the Senegalese and Algerians panicked and ran. My young Frenchmen stood fast, but they took a beating. I had made a tactical error for which others paid the price. We were well clobbered that morning.

The people I knew in the Maquis were for the most part plain people, farmers, storekeepers, priests, mechanics, gendarmes, ex-soldiers, very young men and very old men, and the women.

There was a butcher and a veterinarian, and both of them were shot by the Germans for helping us. There was also an elderly aristocrat in whose château I spent a night between sheets for the first time in months. I remember that he suggested that I keep my pistol at hand on the bedside table, and I did.

As guerrilla fighters most of these people in our area of Brittany were half-trained at best. But they all had courage, sometimes reckless courage. They also had faith in themselves and in France, and they were sure that at last the long night of Nazi tyranny was ending.

When I told a friend of mine that I was going to try to write this story he smiled a little and replied that if I did it would be because I wanted to re-live the war days and that evidently I missed the adventures, the hopes and fears, the camaraderie, the sense of achievement, and also the conviction, beyond any doubt, of having a cause. He said that perhaps I had a nostalgic feeling for what was and now is not, and that I would be writing to please myself. My friend is unusually perceptive, sometimes uncomfortably so. What he said may well be true and perhaps I am really writing for myself. But then it has been said that a writer should first of all try to please and satisfy himself, and that he should think of himself as playing to an audience of one. And yet here something else should be mentioned: the story which I tell is, in some ways, the story of a failure.

In writing this story I realize that I now see what happened in 1944 through the mellowing filter of time, and that I, the writer, am no longer the same person who jumped into France. Some of the things I saw have acquired a richer meaning which I then saw only dimly, if at all. Time is a kind friend in those lonely hours when you start dredging up a part of your life, and the past becomes a constant companion, a sad one at times and a gay one at others, but always someone who is at your side and is, indeed, part of you.

Sometimes when I was asked after the war what it was like to be behind the lines and what I did, I would be reminded of the old story of the French nobleman who was asked what he had done during the French Revolution. And his reply was, "I survived."

CHAPTER I

The Decision

In June of 1943 I was stationed at the Infantry School at Fort Benning when I was asked to report to a lieutenant colonel from the Office of Strategic Services in Washington.

When I reported to the lieutenant colonel, a stout, bald man with horn-rimmed glasses, he told me that he was recruiting officers for missions behind the German lines in occupied Europe. Did I speak French? I did. Had I travelled in France? Very little. Would I be interested in volunteering for this type of mission? Maybe. Then I asked if this meant being a spy or secret agent. No, this kind of mission meant operating in uniform, at least most of the time, and directing and coordinating Maquis operations such as ambushes and sabotage.

"If you are caught," he said, "the Germans will treat you as a regular prisoner of war. Or at least they should."

"We are asking for volunteers," he went on, "because these will be hazardous missions. We expect maximum casualties."

I told him I would like to think it over and would let him know the next day. That night my wife and I held a council of war. What about this "maximum casualties" thing? "Maximum casualties" could mean one hundred percent. Is this what he meant? Were these to be one-way trips? Did I want to be a dead hero? The next day I told the lieutenant colonel that the phrase "maximum casualties" left me a little uneasy. Were these suicide missions?

"No, no, Lieutenant," he said. "Nothing like that at all. You will be well trained, and if you're resourceful and have a bit of luck, why then you could easily come through without a scratch. We have to be realistic though. These will be hazardous missions so we use that Army jargon about 'maximum casualties.' Don't let those words bother you too much."

It occurred to me that since he was a recruiting officer and would not be going on these missions it was easy enough for him not to be disturbed by those words. "Yes sir, all right," I said. "I understand." Then I told him he could put me down as a volunteer and he gave me a long questionnaire to fill out.

Within a few weeks, having been screened and investigated, I reported to OSS headquarters in Washington.

On the train ride to Washington I thought again of the reasons which led me to join OSS. Certainly memories of my boyhood in Paris during World War I had influenced my decision. My father was French, my mother an American of Irish descent, and I was born in Paris and lived there until the spring of 1919. What I saw and heard and felt then became completely a part of me. I was shaped in those years and made aware of France and her traditions, her rich history of triumphs and disasters. Many recollections of days long past flowed through my mind that night in June when I was considering the lieutenant colonel's offer. These memories were like an old, flickering movie which is still bright and sharp in spots.

Those were heroic times and I had my heroes such as Marshal Foch. However as a boy I went back much further than World War I for my French heroes. I started with Vercingetorix, the Gallic chieftain who fought for a lost cause against Caesar; then on to Roland with his sword "Durandal" cutting down Saracens at the Pass of Ronscevalles; Bayard, the Chevalier "*sans peur et sans reproches;*" and finally Marshal Ney, called by Napoleon "*le brave des braves.*" I had decided to eliminate Joan of Arc only because she was a woman and I felt that her success must have been largely due to the brave men she led.

Charles Guynemer, the ace fighter pilot, was my special favorite. After he was reported missing in action his first plane, the

"*Vieux Charles*," was put on display in the War Museum at the Invalides, and it is still there. My father had to take me there time and again so I could see this small, fragile fighter plane with its bright blue, white-and-red circle insignia. After these visits to the "*Vieux Charles*" I would go off in a corner of the living room, make a cockpit out of a stool and two upsidedown chairs, and play at being a fighter pilot. The living room didn't exist anymore. I was then truly a French ace in far-off skies, shooting down "Boche" planes by the score.

I know now that at the outbreak of the war there were military bands blaring out "*Sambre et Meuse*" and other martial tunes while the infantry in their baggy red pants marched gaily off to the front, and the crowds, especially the women, cheered and waved flags, but I remember none of this.

Yet although I was only three and a half years old at the time, I do remember the day war broke out in August of 1914. That night, as usual, the lamplighter had come by on his bicycle, carrying on his shoulder his long pole with a lighted wick, and he had stopped at our corner, turned on the gas at the street lamp and then stuck his pole up to the glass-enclosed top to light the lamp. On our corner there was a pastry shop run by a stout man with a German name. Although it later turned out that he was a Swiss, the German name stirred up an angry crowd which gathered outside the shop, and soon began screaming and hurling stones through the windows. I was watching wide-eyed from our second-floor balcony.

A few weeks later I noticed that my father and mother looked worried and would sometimes go off in a corner and talk in whispers. The next day a taxi pulled up in front of our apartment, my father got out, rushed upstairs, and he and my mother threw some clothes into a big suitcase. Then they grabbed me by the arm, shoved me and the big suitcase into the taxi and we sped off.

My father told me we were leaving Paris to visit his cousins in the Loire valley. Although I found all of this exciting, my parents looked grim. Only months later did I realize that we had left Paris so hurriedly because advance patrols of German Uhlans were then only twenty miles away, and the Germans were expected to goose-step into Paris within forty-eight hours at the most. Years afterwards I learned that Paris was then under martial law. Only military trains were moving out of Paris heading towards the front on the Marne, and the day after we left, General Gallieni, Military Governor of Paris, requisitioned all Paris taxis to rush troops to the front in a desperate effort to stop the relentless German advance. When we left Paris a military pass was required to leave the city and I still have the pass issued to my father authorizing the three of us to leave Paris by taxi.

After the Germans were stopped at the Marne we came back to Paris and stayed there throughout the war. The air raids had started when we got back. I remember watching Zeppelins gliding through the night while the bright arcs of the searchlights scanned the sky. The few field guns used as anti-aircraft batteries fired wildly and furiously.

Then the Germans stopped using Zeppelins and the bombers started coming, almost always at night. While of course these raids were nothing like the air raids of World War II, it was the first time that a city had come under air bombardment. It is true that the effect on morale was not what the Germans had hoped, yet bombs were being dropped, the upper stories of apartment buildings were being smashed, and civilians were being killed and wounded. One day after a raid my father took me to see a building in our neighborhood that had been hit. The top floor was wrecked and strewn with broken furniture. I remember vividly that a battered piano hung high over the sidewalk, hooked by one leg on the edge of the floor.

There were no air raid sirens in those days. The alert at night was given by fire trucks that would speed up and down the boulevards with their sirens giving a half-moan, half-screech. Then the people living in the top floors would go down to the coal cellars, or sometimes come down to our apartment on the second floor.

Through all this my mother, who had somehow mastered the technique of knitting in the dark, sat there calmly knitting as though nothing was happening. Early in the war she had decided that one of her primary missions was to knit gloves, scarves and socks for the men in the trenches. The living-room floor was always littered with balls of blue and khaki yarn. Another of her vocations was working for the Red Cross, where she made bandages by the hundreds and was learning first aid. Sometimes I would be hauled off to one of these Red Cross meetings and my mother and the other ladies would practice bandaging my arm or leg. When I would protest at this indignity my mother would tell me to play that I was a "little wounded French soldier." But I wanted to play at being a fighter pilot, and I would tell my mother so. "Then play that you are a wounded fighter pilot," she would tell me. That helped matters very little but I had discovered by that time that my mother, though gentle and outwardly meek, was also incredibly stubborn and when she had decided something, anything at all, it was completely useless to try to talk her out of it.

She also made frequent visits to the military hospitals. Occasionally she took me along, despite my vigorous objections. I had quickly learned that while war was fine when you were playing at being a fighter pilot, it was something else again to go through an old hospital ward reeking of antiseptic and filled with mangled and groaning soldiers. Mother tried to be cheerful as she visited the wards, tugging me by the hand and bringing little presents for the wounded, some of whom seemed beyond caring.

Since my mother was a small, frail person, and was not in the best of health, all of this activity was wearing her down. But she continued to throw herself into war work with furious energy. My father begged her to slow down. His pleas got him nowhere. She would listen to him patiently without seeming to hear. This infuriated my father. "I am talking to you," he would shout. "I am talking to you and not to the wall. Did you hear what I said?" "Yes," she would say. "I can hear quite well, thank you." Ten minutes later she would be off again to a hospital or to the Red Cross. It was obvious that my father found these encounters with my mother deeply frustrating. Matters got so bad that my father turned for help to a priest who was a close friend of the family. My mother was an ardent Catholic and especially devoted to Our Lady, so my father asked this priest to come see my mother and reason with her.

The priest came and did his best. Knowing that this should be interesting, I peeked around the living room door and took it all in. The priest reminded my mother that she had a solemn obligation to take care of herself so that she could care for her family, and that to continue to push herself as hard as she did might be a grievous mortal sin. He pointed to a small statue of the Virgin on the table and he eloquently invoked Our Lady. In addition he quoted one or two saints, and he also brought God in, although almost as an afterthought. My mother listened respectfully, nodding her head from time to time and saying, "Yes, Father." While she didn't argue with him it was plain that the priest was making no headway at all. Five minutes after the poor priest had left, looking like a thoroughly beaten man, she was back in the kitchen simultaneously cooking dinner and knitting khaki socks. My father gave up.

I think what particularly irked my father was the fact that, although the priest had passionately invoked the Virgin, he might in this one instance just as well have appealed to Mohammed. Throughout the war my mother's confidence in the Virgin remained unshaken. Sometimes when the news from the front was particularly bad my mother would quietly say that she was sure that Our Lady would see the Allies through. At these times my father knew better than to discount Our Lady and he would only mutter that the Virgin, with all due respect to her, could do with the help of a few brilliant generals rather than some of the imbeciles we had.

When the war dragged on month after month, with the Germans still occupying all of northern France, and the casualties mounting, my father, like many civilians, tended to blame certain French generals. With a few notable exceptions, he thought they were either butchers or idiots, and sometimes both. As to the British generals, they were all slow-witted and in some cases feeble-minded.

My father was a writer and professor. Since he was over military age and had bad eyesight, he was not drafted except towards the end of the war and then only for office work. By that time the French casualties were so high that, in many cases, the authorities were forced to waive physical fitness. Somehow I always felt it was regrettable that my father could not be a fighter pilot, or at least an officer in one of the crack infantry regiments such as the *Chasseurs Alpins*.

Another thing I clearly remember is the "*ventouse*," a home remedy consisting of a glass suction cup which was used for bronchitis. A burning wad of cotton was dropped into the cup which was then immediately applied to the chest, thus creating a vacuum and sucking up the skin. This was supposed to relieve congestion. Since all doctors, except the very old ones, had been called to active duty, it was extremely difficult to get a physician even in an emergency. So my mother bought a thick book for the lay practitioner. I suppose that medicine had then made one of its periodic great leaps forward, at least in France, and the big book recommended the suction cup for very severe chest colds. My mother believed firmly in this remedy—I think there was something Spartan about it which appealed to her—so I always got this therapy when I had any kind of chest cold, however slight. The flaming wad of cotton terrified me, but for some reason I didn't understand my chest was not burned. I have never seen *ventouses* since, so it must be supposed that medicine took another great leap forward and this cure became a thing of the past, like blood-letting.

Later in the war the Germans had a disagreeable surprise for the Parisians. One day there were explosions in various parts of the city as though bombs were falling. But it couldn't be an air raid for no bombers were in the sky and no alert had been given. These explosions caused great commotion and no one seemed to know what was happening. Could it be that the Germans had broken through the French lines but the Government was afraid to admit it? It was several days before an official communiqué was issued stating that the Germans now had an incredibly long-range gun, the "Big Bertha" which fired on Paris from a point seventy-five miles away, well behind the German lines and out of reach of the French artillery. If the Germans had that kind of gun, the people thought, what else might they do?

From then on the Big Bertha continued firing on Paris, a shell landing in widely scattered neighborhoods every twenty minutes or so. Sometimes there was an interval of a week or more because the Germans moved the big gun from time to time to hide it from aerial observation.

Once the Big Bertha scored a direct hit on a church not far from where we lived. Since it was Good Friday the church was filled and dozens of people were killed. My mother, who had been a block away when this happened, came home horrified. She was sure that the Germans had aimed for the church. Although my father was furious, he did try to explain that from that distance the Germans couldn't possibly aim for the church. My mother was unconvinced, which was not unusual for her. A few days later my father took me to see the church. Part of the roof had caved in, and half of a side wall was shattered. When we went inside we saw, in the midst of the rubble, a large statue of Christ which had toppled and broken. The head lay off to one side next to some splintered timbers. My father stood silently for a few moments gazing first at the gaping hole in the roof and then at the broken statue and the head. On the way home he didn't say a word, walking along slowly with his head down.

Like all children I was impressionable and all that I saw in Paris at that time left its mark on me. I remember that Paris was filled with wounded soldiers. When you went out on the boulevards or in the parks human wreckage was everywhere. Sad-faced men with both legs amputated were being pushed in wheelchairs. Others with one leg missing hobbled on crutches, while still others had lost an arm and the empty sleeves were pinned across their chests. Some were horribly mutilated and had scarred and twisted faces. With sardonic humor, and with pride too, they had nicknamed themselves the "*Gueules Cassées*," a slang term which cannot be properly translated but which means the "Smashed Faces."

The blind veterans—there were many—tapped their way along slowly with a cane or were led by a friend. Sometimes they wore dark glasses, or a bandage across their eyes. There were some who had neither, and as you passed them you saw an empty face with eyeless sockets.

My father did a great deal to help blind soldiers and often

went to the Association Valentin Haüy where blind veterans were taught to read Braille and to make brooms and cane furniture. One day he insisted on taking me with him, telling me that this was part of my education and that I had to realize that if you believed in something very deeply you would have to make sacrifices, and that the cost of courage could come high.

We entered the workshop, a large and dilapidated room, poorly lighted, its white walls dirty and stained. There were large spots in the ceiling and walls where the plaster had flaked off. Sitting on benches at long wooden tables the blind veterans were making brooms, cane bottoms for chairs and cane baskets. They all wore faded blue army uniforms, and some had their medals pinned on. There was little noise or talking. The men worked slowly and methodically, in a detached and melancholy manner, staring off into space that would remain forever blank.

We stopped by one bench. The man there was not only blind but half of his lower jaw had been shot away, leaving a gaping ugly scar, all like a hideous mask. My father told him he had brought his little boy to visit the soldiers. The man stopped working and said something to me. However the best he could do was mumble and I only half understood what he was trying to tell me. I wanted to say something to him, but instead I stared at him and tried to hold back my tears. The words wouldn't come out for me. My father explained to him that I was shy. I took my father aside and whispered that I would like to go home.

One day my mother took a blind infantry captain for a walk in the Luxembourg gardens and I was asked to come along. It was the custom then for civilians, invariably elderly men, to tip their hats when passing a badly wounded veteran. This was a quiet and solemn tribute to valor. We passed an elderly man who gravely tipped his hat. My mother turned to the captain and said that a gentleman had just tipped his hat to him. The captain smiled sadly, almost bitterly, and then, quickly catching himself, he answered with a sharp military salute.

The women in mourning were another depressing sight. When a close member of the family had been killed the women went into mourning and wore black, even to the stockings. As the war went on and on and the casualties mounted, it seemed as though most of the women I saw were in black. Their husbands or sons or fathers or brothers now lay in military cemeteries with their long straight rows of crosses, or perhaps they lay shattered and unrecognizable in the mud and debris at Verdun.

So my memories of Paris were not gay on the whole. I hardly remember Paris in the spring or summer with a bright blue sky, the chestnut trees in bloom and the neat multi-colored patterns of the flower beds in the parks. Children played then in the Tuileries and in the Luxembourg gardens. They sailed their toy boats in the ponds there as they do now. But my memory of such things is faint.

I remember much better the Paris of late fall and winter, with the trees brown and bare, the chill winds and cold rain, the wet glistening sidewalks, and a gray and overcast sky. My memory of Paris then is that of a somber city, whose people knew that at any time the plodding and ponderous mass of German infantry might engulf them. I thought it a sad place in which to live.

One of the reasons we left France early in 1919 was because my mother was determined that her son should not have to go to war. She had seen enough of other mothers' sons in the Paris military hospitals. So back in the States I grew up and became a lawyer, which should have been a safe occupation, except that Hitler came along.

Twenty-one years after we left, the Paris I knew had been captured. In World War I the French army had held out for four bloody years and left 1,300,000 dead on the battlefields. In this war the army had crumbled in a month. Now every day at noon a company of German infantry, led by a band, paraded down the Champs Elysées, goose-stepping proudly around the Arch of Triumph and the Tomb of the Unknown Soldier. Nazi officers with their rakish, high-crowned caps and polished boots were strutting arrogantly through the Tuileries and the Luxembourg gardens. A giant swastika flag flew from the Eiffel Tower. Humiliation sat on Paris like a huge toad.

So when the chance came to join OSS and go back to France, something was driving me on and I wanted to go.

CHAPTER II

The Congressional Country Club and Raleigh Manhattans

When I reported to OSS headquarters in Washington there was a guard at the entrance who checked my identity card against a list and then told me where to go. I walked down a long corridor crowded with men hurrying back and forth. Some were civilians, while others were in uniform, all kinds of uniforms, American and foreign. There were several British officers with their Sam Browne belts, and a Scot in kilts. A French officer wearing a light blue kepi rushed by. One of the civilians was olive-skinned and wore a turban. There were women too, civilian secretaries and WACS and WAVES.

The major to whom I reported had been expecting me. He looked at my papers and had me sign some others. He told me I was to report to the Congressional Country Club for training.

I thought I hadn't heard him right. "Did you say the Congressional Country Club, Sir?" I asked.

"That's right, Lieutenant. Very plush place. Herbert Hoover was one of the founders. It's about six miles out of town. We've taken over the whole club for training, golf course and all."

He looked at my papers again. "I see you did your basic training at Camp Wheeler and your Officer Candidate training at Fort Benning. You'll find the Club quite a change, quite an improvement. You'll get your parachute training in England. There will only be a few of you at first. You're in our first batch. Good luck."

When I got to the Congressional Country Club I saw that the major had been right. It was quite an improvement, even though the swimming pool had been drained. I had a fine room overlooking the golf course. There were two army beds in it, but I had the room to myself.

I went into Washington that evening and when I came in my room late I stumbled over a body on the floor. A voice said, "What the hell! Watch where you're going."

I switched on the light. A man clad only in his underwear was stretched out on the floor looking up at me with a grin. I didn't know who he was or what he was doing there but I thought maybe he was a little tight and I asked him if he was all right.

"Sure, sure," he said. "I was just doing my evening push-ups. My name is Farley, Bob Farley. I'm your new roommate."

"Hello, Farley," I said. "Nice to have you here. Do you always do your push-ups in the dark?"

"No, of course not. Just forgot to switch on the light."

Farley got up and flexed his biceps. He seemed to be in his early forties, with a brown, weatherbeaten face and sharp blue eyes. I thought he might be a little over age for our kind of active duty although he was lean and muscular, and he looked as if he had been doing push-ups all of his life. We said a few words and then turned in for the night.

The next morning five other officers had checked in at the Club and we were told to report on the grounds for physical training, including a run around the golf course. It was a blazing hot July day so we all turned out in shorts, except Farley who showed up in long winter underwear pants over which he had pulled on a pair of blue swimming trunks. He also wore two sweat shirts.

I looked at this strange costume and asked him if he had ever heard of heat stroke. "Don't be silly, old boy," he said. "I just want to work up a good sweat."

As we lined up for our run a tall, long-legged Danish officer introduced himself and told us he would teach us a new style of cross-country running called the "elastic stride." As Farley and I started jogging along in the usual way the Dane came bounding alongside like an antelope. "Not that way, not that way," he said. "You must s-t-r-e-t-c-h as you run. Do it like I do, s-t-r-e-t-c-h and l-e-a-p. So easy to do, so good." I told him to run his way and let me run my way and I would probably get around the course as well as he did, although not as gracefully. Farley ignored him. When we got back to the clubhouse the Danish officer looked exhausted. Farley came in, soaked with sweat, but breathing easily.

I asked Farley later what he thought of the "e-l-a-s-t-i-c s-t-r-i-d-e." "It's bloody stupid," he said. "Not my cup of tea at all, Pumpkin."

"No. Not mine either. Say, what's this 'Pumpkin' stuff?" I asked.

He thought about it for a few seconds. "Just a habit, I guess," he said. "Sometimes I call people 'Pumpkin' just for the hell of it."

I wondered how Farley, who didn't have a British accent, had picked up such British expressions as "bloody stupid" and "cup of tea" and "old boy" and yet coming from him it didn't sound like an affectation. When I asked him about this, he explained that he had gone to school in England for a few years. I asked him if he spoke French and he said yes, fluently, (this turned out to be a slight exaggeration) having lived in France for some time. He went on to tell me that while he had his master's degree in English he had never put it to any use, that he had been a hobo, a lumberjack, and had worked on a newspaper. During the Spanish Civil War he had fought against Franco in the International Brigade. When the war broke out in 1939 he had been a tennis instructor on the Riviera.

That evening Farley and I met two of the newly arrived officers who had the room next to us. One of them, Lieutenant Jack Cambray, had already qualified as a paratrooper at the Fort Benning Jump School and wore his silver parachute wings and brightly polished jump boots. He was slender, almost frail, and wore thick-lensed glasses which gave him a quiet, studious air. In civilian clothes you could easily have taken him for a young professor, which is what he was. After graduating from Yale two years before he had become an instructor in French at an Eastern prep school. He certainly didn't look like a tough paratrooper, but as is so often true of combat soldiers, his appearance was deceiving.

The other officer, Pierre Martel, was a young lieutenant of French-Canadian descent. When you first saw him you took him for a pink-cheeked, well scrubbed farm boy. But then you noticed that he looked trim and elegant in his well fitting uniform and that he wore it as though long accustomed to it. So it was no surprise to learn that he was a recent graduate of the Virginia Military Institute and that he held a regular commission as a second lieutenant. He had a gentle and almost constant smile as though he had found this to be the best of all possible worlds. Martel seemed shy and blushed easily. I found it strange that he treated Farley and me almost respectfully, addressing us as "sir" once or twice, evidently because we were older and, as first lieutenants, we outranked him. I soon realized that due to his cadet training, good manners and a sense of military courtesy were part of him.

I could see that Farley was looking Cambray over and wondering, as I was, how a man resembling a scholarly and effete college senior could have won his jump wings. Finally Farley asked Cambray how the hell he had been able to qualify as a paratrooper since obviously his eyesight was none too good.

Cambray explained that he knew he couldn't pass the eye test required for the parachute school, cursory as the test was, so he had managed to get copies of three eye charts, one of which was always used in an Army physical. Then he had spent hours laboriously memorizing the charts. When it came to the eye test he walked in without his glasses, sneaked a quick look to see which chart it was, and then rattled off the letters, being careful to make a few mistakes on the last line.

I told Cambray that I was a little near-sighted but that I had an easier system for beating the eye chart. I would walk in for the eye test wearing sun glasses with my correction. It had never occurred to the medical sergeants giving the test that my sun glasses improved my vision. They would invariably suggest that I take them off, saying that reading the eye chart would then be easier, and I would nonchalantly reply that I was so used to wearing sun glasses that it didn't make any difference.

We talked on and on that night. Martel had little to say, sitting on the edge of his bed with his little-boy grin. Farley was holding forth, giving his views on life in general and war in particular. He had great contempt for staff officers—especially those below the age of forty-five who had cozy posts in Washington—and for general's aides. We all knew that the post of general's aide was much sought after by certain officers who were attracted by its social prestige, and perhaps especially by the fact that the casualty rate among general's aides was not notoriously high. It wasn't high for staff officers either.

In a few days we were joined by a group of about fifty enlisted men, and more were to follow. The plan was to create Operational Groups of some thirty men to be dropped at strategic points behind the lines. We had more cross-country runs on the golf course and lectures on guerrilla warfare by senior officers who had never seen this type of operation, or combat either for that matter. They taught it by the book, apparently an old Army manual. These officers often assumed a superior air which irked Farley who felt that since he had been shot at many times during the Spanish Civil War this not only gave him special credentials which our instructors did not have but also made him an expert on warfare in general. After a few days Farley made it a point to correct our instructors with exaggerated courtesy—always prefacing his remarks with a respectful "Sir"—by saying, "Sir, that isn't the way we did it on the Ebro when I was in the International Brigade." Or, "Sir, outside Madrid we got shot up pretty badly trying that."

About a week later Farley came weaving into our room late one night. "Just got back from the Raleigh Hotel," he mumbled. "Great Manhattans there, absolutely great."

"I can see that," I said.

He walked slowly over to his Valpack and after fumbling around drew out a bottle which looked like Worchestershire

Sauce, explaining that it was Fernet-Branca bitters and that he would probably need some the next morning.

"It's a stomachic," he muttered. "Has alcohol in it. Nothing like it to settle the stomach. Tastes like hell. Trouble is if you take too much of the stuff it's like a strong laxative. Tears your guts out."

I steered him over to his bed and he flopped down. In a few minutes he was dead to the world.

The next morning Farley was singing loudly in the shower. I thought maybe he was one of those types who think that if they get up early after a bad night and manage to put on a good show of being chipper, then whatever happened the night before is all right.

That Saturday night I decided that a sortie to the Raleigh might be in order so that I could judge for myself whether the Manhattans there were as good as Farley stated. Farley said he would be glad to come with me, and Martel and Cambray said they would join us later.

So there we were at the Raleigh, having had Manhattans first, then dinner, and then back again to Manhattans. Admittedly the Manhattans were excellent, but I knew that having a flock of them before and after dinner was a mistake. The time passed and I lost track of how many Manhattans we had downed. Farley was puffing at his pipe and drumming his fingers on the table. There was a question I'd been meaning to ask him. "Tell me, Bob," I said, "why did you join the International Brigade?"

Farley took the pipe out of his mouth and looked at me thoughtfully for a few seconds. "Well," he replied, "it just seemed the right thing to do." He said this as though it were a complete answer. And I thought maybe that is the answer, simple and uncomplicated, like Thomas Mann's denunciation of his country's regime: "To be against a thing such as Hitler is always to be right, let matters turn out as they will."

At this point Jack Cambray and Pierre Martel walked in. Whatever else they had been doing it was clear they had not been fighting the battle of the Manhattans. Cambray sat down at our table as though he were joining a few faculty colleagues for some serious discussion.

Although I am hazy about the latter part of that evening I well remember the Churchill episode. Farley was looking at one of those bulldog jaw photographs of Churchill hanging on the wall when he suddenly launched into a rousing passage from one of Churchill's speeches, the one about the fate of nations overrun by Hitler and ending with "unless we conquer, as conquer we must, as conquer we shall!" He recited this in a loud voice, with a good imitation of Churchill's accent—except for a slight Manhattan slur—and roaring defiance at the end. People at other tables turned to stare at us.

"Oh Jesus!" Cambray said softly.

I tried to disassociate myself from Farley's performance by looking up fixedly at a spot on the ceiling. Cambray and Martel had a better idea; they vanished into the men's room.

Late the next morning I was awakened by Martel tiptoeing into my room. "Sorry I woke you up," he whispered. "How do you feel?" I thought he was being overly solicitous about the state of my health. I grunted that I felt fine.

A week later we were sent to a training area deep in the wooded, rolling country of Virginia. It was a restricted zone, miles from the nearest house, and except for an occasional weekend we spent the next two months there.

A few days after we got there a new instructor named Bolinsky arrived to teach us demolitions and the tactics of guerrilla warfare. He was a tough, grizzled sergeant from the regular army. He had trained with the British commandos where he learned how to use modern plastic explosives, called P.E. for short. Sergeant Bolinsky claimed that he had gone as an observer on several commando raids and he had wild stories to tell, none of which I believed.

But he did teach us a lot about the new explosives. A chunk of P.E. is soft and malleable, like ordinary clay, yet unlike dynamite, which is a very sensitive explosive, you could shoot bullets into it and nothing would happen. But once you inserted a primer and detonator, and attached a fuse (the fuses were of different colors for different burning speeds) and lit it you got a truly impressive and shattering bang. We practiced on trees, slabs of concrete and steel beams, and we used to explode craters in a road by tamping a small amount of dirt on top of the explosive so that the main force would be expended downward. This, Sergeant Bolinsky told us knowingly, was due to something called the "Munroe Principle."

Besides learning demolitions we spent considerable time on the range where we fired the submachine gun and carbines, especially at moving and bobbing targets. Cambray, glasses and all, turned out to be the best shot in our group. It was hard to believe, and yet you couldn't argue with the bullet holes he drilled through the cardboard targets time and again. This left Farley shaking his head.

After dark we executed night attacks. There was a small concrete dam out in the woods and at least twice a week we "blew" it up with dummy charges. One group of enlisted men led by their officers would attack, while a smaller group in charge of one officer would play the part of German sentries. When it was his turn to be the officer in command of the attacking group Farley went about it with great zest. Once he took a man out with a flying tackle and left him stretched out, half-conscious. The only trouble was that his victim was not one of the sentries but a staff colonel from Washington who was there that night only as an observer. Farley apologized for his mistake and explained that he wanted the rest of us to know, as he did from experience, how tough it could be to knock out a sentry. The colonel did not appear completely happy with this explanation or the apology. I had some reservations myself; there was a suspicious gleam of satisfaction in Farley's eyes. The colonel never came back to observe our maneuvers.

One night a senior officer from Washington headquarters came out to our camp to tell us that another plan was on tap. Teams of three officers, each team including at least one French officer, would be dropped behind the lines. The teams would be organized and trained in England, and if we wanted we could be re-assigned from the Operational Groups. He closed with the standard phrase, "Any questions?" We had plenty of questions to which he gave vague answers, and I decided that he wasn't being evasive but that, due to tight OSS security, he didn't know the answers and wouldn't admit it. He asked that we give him our decision the next morning.

So late into the night Cambray, Martel, Farley and I talked about this proposal and we all decided that we preferred this kind of mission to the Operational Group plan. Right or wrong, we thought this new venture promised more action and would be a greater challenge. Ten days later we were at Fort Hamilton, just outside New York, waiting to ship out.

CHAPTER III

How Sane Are Paratroopers?

On a bleak November morning we sailed out on the big four-stacked Cunard liner, *Aquitania*. Farley, Cambray, Martel and I were crowded into one small cabin with two tiers of bunks. The ship was not in convoy, for the *Aquitania*, like the Queens, was fast enough—at least theoretically—to avoid U-boat packs.

Within an hour a Navy blimp glided slowly out of the low-hanging clouds, her blinker light flashing signals. On the bridge of the *Aquitania* we could see her blinker light flashing off and on in response. Radio silence was on. During our first two days out either a blimp or a seaplane would come out of the overcast and circle the vessel again and again, blinker lights going furiously. Occasionally, after a pass over us by the blimp, the *Aquitania* would make a hard turn leaving a boiling, curved wake behind her.

At last we were on our way, and the sense of danger, an unseen and possibly remote danger, was a welcome change from training and blowing up the dam in the Virginia hills. Now we, the troops and officers aboard, were participating in a gigantic game of hide and seek, and while we were only interested spectators, with no part to play, we were vulnerable spectators. The prize was a forty-thousand-ton troopship and over ten thousand men. Up on the bridge the lookouts bundled in their greatcoats scanned the ocean with their binoculars. You could feel the tension in the crew but I hardly ever thought of a torpedo slamming into the ship and myself floundering in the cold waters.

Late one night I went out on deck which during the day was jammed with troops wearing orange life jackets. Now it was deserted and the ship was blacked out. I stood by the rail with the wind whipping and clawing at me. It gave me an eerie sensation, the great ship plowing ahead under a dark and stormy sky, the only sounds the steady whistling of the wind and the throbbing of the engines. Up on the bridge I could barely make out the figure of the officer on watch. What was he thinking about? At dawn would there be a submarine ahead, the U-boat commander squinting through his periscope? I had the odd feeling that the lookout and I were the only ones aboard and that the *Aquitania* was a ghost ship being swept along uncontrollably by some vast and sinister force.

Yet so far the voyage had been uneventful. The weather remained cloudy, with scattered rain squalls, and the gray ocean stretched out in an immense semi-circle, seemingly empty. The alert siren never sounded.

By now everyone was complaining about the meals dished out by the British cooks, particularly Brussels sprouts which were served both at lunch and at dinner swimming in a pale and scummy juice. During our next six months in Great Britain we had Brussels sprouts daily—they must have been grown in England and were perhaps the only fresh vegetable available—and I acquired a lifelong distaste for them. But Farley had another complaint. With the ship packed with men it was impossible to get a good workout by jogging around the decks or even walking briskly. And the *Aquitania,* pushing on at high speed through the mid-Atlantic swells, rolled and pitched so much that he found it difficult to go through with his varied repertoire of calisthenics.

Farley got more and more restless and he also became moody at times, sitting on the edge of his bunk while he puffed on his beat-up briar pipe and stared off into space. One afternoon when all four of us were in the cabin, I happened to remember the remark made by a psychiatrist.

"Listen you guys," I said, "let me tell you about an Army psychiatrist friend of mine at Fort Benning. Actually he was a pediatrician, but when he went in the Army they made a psychiatrist that, due to tight OSS security, he didn't know the answers and wouldn't admit it. He asked that we give him our decision the next morning.

So late into the night Cambray, Martel, Farley and I talked about this proposal and we all decided that we preferred this kind of mission to the Operational Group plan. Right or wrong, we thought this new venture promised more action and would be a greater challenge. Ten days later we were at Fort Hamilton, just outside New York, waiting to ship out.

out of him. He never could figure that out. Well anyway, he had to treat paratroopers once in a while and he told me he was convinced that anyone who volunteered for the paratroopers was either around the bend, or else he wanted the extra pay he got for jumping."

Cambray and Martel smiled a little, but Farley sat there brooding as though he hadn't heard. Then he slowly turned his head towards me.

"No, no," he said, speaking very deliberately, "there are a few crackpots probably, or some jerks who want the extra dough. But that doesn't get to the bottom of it. Sometimes I wonder. Maybe we're all glory hunters."

I saw Cambray and Martel watching Bob Farley with narrowed eyes. Nobody said anything.

Farley was still looking at me intently. "Or maybe it's a case of trying to prove something to yourself," he murmured. "But I don't know, some of those guys may have a subconscious death wish, and . . ."

"Oh for Christ's sake, Bob," Cambray interrupted, "knock it off, will you?"

Farley started to say something, then thought better of it and left.

"What the hell's gotten into Bob?" Cambray wanted to know.

"It's like that psychiatrist said," Martel grinned, "he's goofy."

"Oh sure, goofy as hell, but we're all a little goofy."

"Not me," I said. "I want that extra hundred bucks a month."

"O.K." Cambray replied. "Bill is a greedy bastard. Pierre, you and I are psychos. Come on, get the cards out. We'll play some three-handed gin."

There were no blimps or seaplanes the next two days for we were far out in mid-Atlantic and beyond their range. But after that British-based seaplanes flew around us often as they came out of the low-hanging clouds, blinkers flashing constantly. The *Aquitania* was approaching the northern tip of Ireland where stalking U-boat packs would try to intercept us and now the big ship was on an erratic zig-zag course.

Early on the morning of the seventh day out we reached Glasgow. Hours later we were taken off by tender and landed at the docks. Under the soot-covered train sheds stood row after row of grimy troop trains, their locomotives hissing clouds of steam. It was drizzling now as we shoved our way past masses of troops loaded down with their gear. Cheerful and friendly women in blue uniforms, broad of beam and their cheeks glowing with that English outdoor look, were passing out doughnuts and coffee and greeting us in their strange British accents.

Soon after we had jammed ourselves aboard our compartment we heard the squeaky, high-pitched whistle of a European locomotive and our train chugged out slowly. We went past the backyards of long rows of dirty brick tenements. The backyards were crisscrossed with clothes lines from which hung underwear, shirts, sheets, blankets, towels, handkerchiefs, socks, lots of socks, but no women's stockings. The open windows were crowded with many women, smiling and cheering and waving at us. Although it was truly a heart-warming welcome I thought there was something melancholy about it. It was as though all these women at the windows saw in the passing troop train, full of men going off to the wars, an escape from their drab lives and a hope, probably never realized, of brighter and happier days.

We spent all night on the train, dozing sitting up and talking a little, and the next morning we were in London.

CHAPTER IV

Jeds in the Highlands of Scotland

London looked as I had seen it in war pictures and in newsreels, scarred and dirty gray under leaden skies. The barrage balloons hung up in the sky like huge sausages. In the parks there were the anti-aircraft batteries, surrounded by sand bags, the helmeted crews standing by with bored expressions. Smashed buildings, piles of rubble, bleak empty spaces where buildings had stood, jagged skeletons of twisted steel beams, bomb-scarred facades, all this was as I knew it would be. And it was true, I thought, London does wear her scars proudly. Seeing London then you could hear again the beginning of a Murrow broadcast during the "Blitz," "This (pause) is London . . ." What struck me, what I was unprepared for, was that London gave one the impression of surging vitality and confidence. The city was bulging with men in uniform and the streets were clogged with army trucks, jeeps, motorcycles and command cars. The civilians looked out of place, like tourists in a strange land. London was a soldier's town and there was power in the air. And there were women in uniform too, WACS and WAVES and British Army and Navy girls, walking along briskly, but not alluringly, in their low-heeled shoes. The invasion of England by our Air Corps was well underway. The "fly boys" were everywhere, jauntily wearing their service caps crushed down at the sides, so that they had that carefully cultivated "out in the wild blue yonder" look. They all seemed very young, even the majors and colonels, and very eager.

At the OSS headquarters near Grosvenor Square we were greeted by busy-looking officers with preoccupied expressions. A dignified colonel stood behind a large desk cluttered with papers and gave us a little "Welcome to England" speech. He told us that the next day we would leave for Glasgow and from there we would go to the northwestern part of Scotland for commando training, and before leaving we would have a physical. A colonel addressing junior officers has certain advantages and therefore none of us asked him why we had been sent down to London from Glasgow only to be sent back, and no one pointed out that we had taken a physical just before leaving the States. He also told us that the code name of our operation was "Jedburgh," taken from the name of a small town in Scotland. So he supposed, he said, smiling a little, that we would be called the "Jeds." The Jedburgh operation was a joint Anglo-American project directed by OSS and its British counterpart SOE (Special Operations Executive). Our instructors would be British and the commandant at our base would be a British colonel. The French officers for the Jed teams would arrive shortly. He then nodded his head to show he was finished with us and he conveyed the impression that he had already given us more time than he really should. The name "Jedburgh" intrigued me, and a few weeks later I found it on a map and then looked it up in a big dictionary. This is what I read: "Small town in Scotland where in the 17th Century a band of marauders was summarily executed."

The next day we went back to Glasgow where we changed trains in the morning to go north to Fort William. Soon after leaving Glasgow our train started its climb into the Highlands. As I looked out the window I thought that some mountains, like our Rockies, are meant for bright sunshine and the splashes of colors on the rocks, but the mountains of Scotland were meant for the light mist which half swallowed them and softened their peaks and crags. The mist drifted down into the valleys and floated in wisps about the still waters of the lochs. There were only a few small villages, one on the edge of Loch Lomond, and occasionally a cluster of thatched cottages.

We reached the small town of Fort William about eleven o'clock and were met by six sturdy Scottish officers, the commando veterans who were to be our instructors. They were hearty and friendly and spoke with a rich, rolling brogue. From the station we were taken to a private estate, near the coastal village of Arisaig, which had been converted into the commando training headquarters for Jedburgh missions. We stayed in the main house at the foot of a tall mountain close to the sea. Supper that night was capped off by two big sardines on dry toast. Expecting a dessert, the Americans were astonished. We looked at each other, then down at our plates, glanced at the Scottish officers who were wolfing down the sardines, and finally we ate them, though with a noticeable lack of relish.

Later one of the Scots asked me if I'd enjoyed the "savory." I looked blank. He smiled a little and explained that the "savory" was the sardines on toast, considered quite a delicacy in these parts.

"Oh, I enjoyed it very much," I assured him. "I like sardines at the end of a meal."

I was relieved to hear from him that on occasion they varied the menu by having a "sweet," which was a pudding or a tart.

The next day one of the Scottish officers said we would go out on a field trip, a map exercise in which you moved across country by orienting yourself with a compass. He was in battle dress and carried a stout knurled walking stick. As we followed him we began to climb a high hill to the side of Arisaig. It was slow going because the ground, fed by many tiny springs, was boggy and our feet sank with every step. When we reached the top we looked out at the sea and the mountains around us.

"Look here," said our instructor in a heavy Scottish burr, "the schedule this afternoon calls for this map exercise. But I'm sure you buggers have done that sort of thing many times. So instead let's find a dry spot and we can sit down and I'll tell you a little about Scotland. That will be better."

We sat down not far away and he began to talk. He named some of the mountains and the lochs twisting in from the sea and the small offshore isles of Skye and Rum, pointing them out with his stick. Then he told us of the Highlands people and their clans, the customs and traditions, the kilts and bagpipes. He talked of the history of Scotland, of "Bonnie Prince Charlie" who had landed at a nearby loch in 1745 to carry on his gallant struggle against the English. As he spoke, gazing out at the open sea, his eyes had a far-off look and his quiet voice was deep with feeling. He made us aware of the proud and independent spirit of the Scots, and of his fierce love for Scotland, once free and now ruled by a government in London. It made me think of the powerful feelings generated by the glory of a lost cause. The ancient Scottish banners were forever furled, the clans no longer roamed boldly and freely in the Highlands, but for this Scot officer the memory of "Bonnie Prince Charlie" and the Scottish chieftains was like a religion. After he finished none of us spoke and we sat there for a long time, lost in reverie. In the half-light of the late afternoon the horizon of the sea and sky was a pale blur and the small islands were ghostly, shapeless patches in the haze. The wild and desolate beauty of the Highlands had a somber and mournful air, an air of loneliness, and you were caught by the spell and felt that perhaps if you could just soar up through the mist you might stretch a groping hand towards a mysterious presence, remote and unseen, far away at the end of the world. It was getting dark now and we climbed down the hill back to Arisaig.

After dinner that night we gathered in the drawing room of the main house of the estate. The Scots had changed from battle dress to kilts. To one who had only seen pictures of Scots in their native garb the effect was strikingly picturesque. They were a brawny lot with rugged faces, and the kilts, the plaids and tartans, the short ceremonial daggers they wore, all of this was straight out of a Scottish epic poem. One of the Scots, a chunky, deep-chested man, had bowed legs, hairy and knotted with muscle. You could understand why the Germans in World War I had called the Scots "the Ladies from Hell."

Whiskey was served and after a few drinks one of the Scots sat down at the piano and the others gathered around him and all began to sing. The first few songs were old Scottish folk songs which we knew. Then they swung into "The Ball of Kerrymuir," which none of us had heard. This is a magnificent, bawdy, rollicking song. It originated many years ago in the Medical School at Edinburgh and there is nothing in the world quite like it. The song has about one hundred and fifty verses and tells of a country dance and of the activities that took place there, quite apart from the dancing which, it turned out, was not the most fun. The song went on, verse after verse, sung each in turn by one of the Scots, then all joining in the chorus.

It was obvious that the Scots enjoyed singing the song. Their eyes twinkled and they smiled roguishly as they roared out the chorus. Finally they stopped and one of them turned to us and said, "Come on, you Yanks. Your turn to sing. You must have good songs in the States."

But we Yanks had no such songs and we couldn't come up with anything like "The Ball of Kerrymuir." I was surprised when I heard Martel say, shy and retiring as he was, that he would try a few songs. The whiskey must have loosened him up. He sat down at the piano and began to play and sing French folk songs and some French-Canadian songs. He sang very well in a clear and gentle tenor. The Scots applauded vigorously, for while they couldn't understand the words they could feel and appreciate the rhythm and cadence of folk songs and their age-old appeal. Martel's songs were gay, and when he sang "*Alouette, gentille Alouette,*" he had the Scots joining in the chorus, even though the French words as sung by them were hardly recognizable. It was all quite merry and jolly.

Martel said he would sing only a few more songs. But now his songs were no longer happy ones. What followed were sorrowful melodies expressing all the lonely solitude of the vast spaces of Canada. They made you think of Hemón's tale of Maria Chapdelaine, waiting month after month one winter for a lover who never returned from the snows of the wild north woods. He sang one more, "*À la Claire Fontaine,*" an old song which centuries ago had travelled with the French to Canada. It is beautiful and hauntingly sad. I can still hear Martel singing, "*Je voudrais que la rose fut encore à planter et que ma douce amie fut encore à m'aimer. Il y a longtemps que je t'aime, jamais je ne t'oublierai."* And when he got to the last line, his eyes dreamy and his voice dropping away softly, "I have loved you for a long time and never will I forget you," I sensed that Martel was no longer in Arisaig. He was far away and his song was meant for someone far on the other side of the Atlantic, perhaps someone dark and lovely, very much in love with her young lieutenant. By the time Martel had finished his last song the mood in the room had changed. Where there had been gaiety and smiles and ribald humor, now everyone was still. Each man in the room seemed to have been removed by Martel's singing to distant scenes, way beyond the bounds of sea and mountains, places and women and children he might never see again.

We spent the next week learning the advanced and highly sophisticated British demolition techniques. Their methods were far in advance of American ones for the British had been active in guerrilla warfare and military intelligence for a very long time. I thought of Henry Stimson, our Secretary of the Army, who had the distaste of an urbane man for that sort of thing and in speaking of spying once said that "a gentleman doesn't read another person's mail." The British not only wanted to read the German's mail; they wanted to blow up the post-office as well. They had ingenious devices, like the time-pencils—detonators resembling an ordinary mechanical pencil. Pinch off one end of the pencil and this would break an ampoule of acid inside. The acid would then eat through a thin metal wire, the strength of the acid determining the time: ten minutes, half an hour, an hour, two hours. When the metal wire was eaten through and broke, it released a spring which snapped a plunger into the detonating charge, in turn setting off the main explosive. The pencils came in various colors to indicate different explosion times. Thus you could set a charge with a time pencil and be long gone by the time the explosive went off. But if you weren't sure when you wanted your charges to go off, say blowing up a passing train or a convoy whose time of arrival was uncertain, then you would have to set the charge differently. There was also a limpet mine with a magnet which could be attached underwater to the hull of a ship. A piece of plastic explosive was made up exactly like a lump of coal and could be tossed in the coal tender of a steam locomotive. There were prepared charges made up ahead of time so they could be connected to train rails in only a few seconds. They would go off when the front wheels of the locomotive hit the detonator on the rails, the detonator being a converted British railroad fog signal. Our instructors called dynamiting a train a "real wizard prang."

Once during one of the lectures on demolitions the instructor was stressing the importance of keeping detonators waterproof and he asked unexpectedly if any of us had a "French letter." Martel said that he did and went up to his room to get it. He handed the letter to the instructor and said it was a letter in French from a Canadian relative. The instructor took the letter, looking most perplexed, and then he chuckled. It turned out that "French letter" was British slang for a rubber prophylactic device which, while intended for quite a different purpose, was ideal for keeping detonators dry. This slang expression amused me because the medical term for this contraption is the name of the 18th-century English physician who invented it. The French argot for it is *capote Anglaise*. And I thought that the British speak of someone taking "French leave" while the French turn this around and say "*filer à l'Anglaise*," all of which tended to show that since the Norman conquest of England, and maybe before that, the rapport between the two countries had not been all that could be desired.

While we were at Arisaig we were awakened every morning by a bagpiper, complete with kilts and his regalia, who solemnly marched up and down the corridors, tootling on his pipes and setting up a fearful din. We then turned out before breakfast for a two-mile run down the country lanes. Farley appeared for these runs in his *costume de rigueur*, two pairs of long winter underwear, over which he pulled on his blue swimming trunks, then two sweatshirts and a heavy woolen sweater. A physical training sergeant-major, rugged and tough as his boots, ran alongside encouraging us briskly. "Come along now, gentlemen, a little faster if you please. Righto!" It was still pitch black when we took these runs, and on the first morning Farley missed a sharp turn in the narrow country lane and went sprawling off in the underbrush. I heard him cursing and thrashing his way out and then the sergeant-major jogging along spoke up politely, "Now, now, sir, we mustn't miss the turn, must we?" This little incident delighted Cambray who, from time to time afterwards, would mimic the sergeant-major and warn Farley about a turn.

One night I was awakened by a strange sound and all of a sudden a girl burst into my room, whispered something I couldn't understand, and then raised my window all the way and leaped out in a flash of legs. A minute later I heard a slight commotion—then all was quiet again. Aha, I thought, Arisaig has possibilities I didn't know about. Could this be a quaint local custom, something the Scottish officer had failed to mention that first day on the hilltop when he was telling us about Scotland? If so, it should be investigated at once. I went out of my room and into the corridor where I ran into one of our instructors. I told him I would like to know what was going on because I felt I was missing out on something. He grinned. "You're not supposed to know anything about it," he said. "That was a French girl. There's a small training school for agents not far from here. Her mission tonight was to try to steal something or other from here and get away with it. It's all very hush-hush. Has to be, for security reasons of course. Eventually she'll be parachuted into France. We don't talk about it. So just forget all about it, will you now, like a good chap?" I said I would try.

Unlike our training grounds in Virginia where there was only one dam to attack, the Highlands near Arisaig had plenty of targets: railroad lines, tunnels, bridges, roads and isolated buildings. We attacked all of these, with the enlisted men of the training staff and one or two Scots officers taking the parts of German sentries, and other Scots officers serving as observers and umpires. Our commando instructors were casual with their comments of "good show, chaps" or "mucked this up properly, didn't you?" or the accolade, "wizard show that, wizard prang!" But the critique that followed each "scheme," as they called these training exercises, was complete to the last detail. They taught us the importance of careful planning and teamwork to achieve surprise and insure rapid execution of a hit-and-run raid. Each raid was preceded by a thorough reconnaissance called a "recce." One or two of us would study the target from a distance, often with binoculars, and then draw a sketch showing the possible approach routes and escape routes. Over and over again these veterans stressed that we had to be ready for the unexpected, and then react quickly, improvise, give clear and incisive orders, show leadership. Sometimes we found that the position of the German sentries had been changed between the time of the "recce" and the attack, or unexpected enemy reinforcements would roll up in a truck just before the attack. When the attack failed, the instructors would shake their heads and say, "Bloody poor show, that, you caught a packet from the Jerries on that one."

So up in the cold, wet hills and mountains we crawled in the bog on our stomachs, soaked and muddy. We crept through the heather, climbed ropes to reach cliff tops, hid in rain-soaked ditches, ran and slipped and fell as we lugged our equipment. It was all dirty and messy, but afterwards late at night, standing in front of a roaring fire with a large whiskey in hand, we felt that it had been great sport, especially if one of the commando officers had smiled and grunted, "You chaps did a first-rate job tonight, absolutely first-rate." Farley's favorite target was a tunnel which we tried to "blow up" twice. The first time was a complete failure when hidden German sentries pounced on us and, grinning derisively, said, "Sorry, Yanks. Not this time. Not tonight." The next time the umpires ruled the attack a success. The train had been "derailed" and the tunnel was blocked. Farley got a lot of satisfaction out of that second attack, and said he could truly see the charge going off with a roar, the locomotive hurtling off the rails, and crashing on its side, steam hissing out of the broken boiler in great clouds, and the panicked survivors of the German train crew scurrying helplessly in the dark and smoke-filled tunnel.

Firing the automatic pistol and hand-to-hand combat came next. Our instructors were two burly, big-fisted officers, grizzled men in their early fifties, who had served before the war with the International Police Force in Shanghai. I remember that one of them, Major Cairburn, had a thin, high-pitched voice contrasting oddly with his tough and weatherbeaten face. They told us to forget the American range style of firing, standing erect, pistol held at arm's length, as though you were engaged in the ceremony and punctilio of an 18th-century duel. The pistol, the four-five, as they called our .45 automatic, was a short-range weapon to be fired in a quick burst of two, in a half-crouch, pointing at the target without deliberate aiming. We were taught all about the various types of pistols—German, French, Belgian, Spanish—that we might find in occupied Europe. Then came karate and judo and knife fighting. No boxing, no left jab and then the right cross. Instead gouging, biting, knee or foot to the groin; the short, vicious karate chops to the neck; smash your boot down on the Jerry's face when he's down. Give no quarter. Cripple him, kill him. As they gave these savage demonstrations, using dummies, the instructors explained the techniques in quiet, matter-of-fact tones, much as a counsellor at a boy's camp teaches his little pupils to swim.

It was the demonstration of knife fighting that fascinated me. The commando knife was a stiletto, razor sharp, and tapering to a wicked point. When Major Cairburn showed us how to use the commando knife it was like watching a fighter shadow boxing and punching the big bag. He advanced on the dummy like a fencer, except partly crouched and half facing the dummy, left arm up as a shield. One threatening step followed the other in a deadly, purposeful pattern, the knife held out point forward and waving back and forth in short circular motions. There were feints, and then the sudden hard stab into the dummy, accompanied by a primitive snarl as the stiletto ripped into the fabric. We had to practice this many times and finally Major Cairburn and his assistant had us feeling that a karate chop which snaps a Jerry's neck, or a stiletto thrust which tears out his guts, was a sporting achievement from which one could derive much satisfaction, just as a golfer is pleased when he booms a long drive straight down the fairway. "Oh, good show, Lieutenant, good show." Even gentle-mannered Martel, the singer of sad and sentimental songs, tore into a dummy like a wounded tiger.

To me one of the intriguing things about all of this training was that the Scottish instructors made it seem as though it were all a game, a deadly serious one, but still a game. The Jerries had a team and we had a team. The game would be played somewhere in France, and while we might be on a sticky wicket now and then, still we had the better team and we would win the game and the trophy cup that went to the victors.

CHAPTER V

"Go Out Like a Guardsman, Sir!"

When our commando training at Arisaig was completed, the commandant told us we would be sent to a testing school in the southern part of England. This would take three days and include psychological tests, intelligence tests and physical tests for stamina and agility. What if you flunked out, we wanted to know. "Well, of course, that would be a pity, now wouldn't it?" he said. "Then you would be reassigned to other duties. But you chaps should have no trouble. Nothing to it really."

When we arrived at the testing school, a former country estate, we were given large white bibs with big block numerals, to be worn front and back at all times. A sharp-eyed "bird dog" English lieutenant followed us all over, except to the bathroom, occasionally jotting down something in a little blue notebook. It made us a little uncomfortable and we felt like poor tiny bacilli squirming under a microscope while a cold-eyed bacteriologist studied our behavior. First we took intelligence tests, then word association tests and the Rorschach ink blot test. We were given six abstract and rather meaningless pictures and told to pick three and write a paragraph about each one. This was tricky though, for after finishing we were asked to write why we had rejected the other three pictures. We were also asked to grade each other on personality traits such as leadership and tact.

The evening after we finished the intelligence and psychological tests we were brought into the drawing room of the manor and when we were comfortably seated the "bird dog" lieutenant casually told us we were now to discuss the future of post-war Europe and to please "carry on." He sat off in a corner with his little blue notebook. This form of test caught us by surprise, but I took charge of leading the discussion until Cambray came to my rescue. He acted as though this were a faculty seminar, quietly disagreeing at times, especially with Farley, on one occasion telling him that what he had just said was "nothing but a metaphysical absurdity." I could see that this baffled the "bird dog" who for once wasn't scribbling in his notebook.

The next day we had field tests. We were taken out into the woods of the estate and shown a big heavy box loaded with sand. This contained "highly secret Allied equipment." A German patrol was after us and we had half an hour to carry the box to a point about a mile away and marked on a map we were given. Again the English lieutenant said to "carry on, please." We moved out and were doing fine, with good teamwork, until we got close to the safe point and started to cross a small footbridge across a creek. The bridge collapsed and we and the box tumbled into the water. One of the bridge supports had been sawed through. Bad mark in the blue notebook; one man should have checked the bridge first. There were also individual tests for each man. Our group was out on the grounds when the lieutenant suddenly pointed a finger at me and said that I was now the leader of our team and I had five minutes to get my men across the narrow country road just in front of us. The road had been mined by the Germans. I solved that problem by using two nearby fallen trees. Good mark in the notebook for this was the better of two possible solutions.

The final test was a long obstacle course to test not only our stamina and agility but also our ability to make quick decisions. Making these decisions while running against time was the devilish part of it. For we were told ahead of time that this course, unlike the many other obstacle courses we had tackled, presented a choice. There was a hard way and an apparently easy way. You came to a deep ditch bridged over by two long planks. Of course you could use the planks, but what if they too had been sawed partly through? Or you could plunge down one side of the ditch and scramble up the other side, but then maybe you were stupid because you had not taken the easy way across. You had to take a quick look and make your decision. The course was also designed to detect a fear of height, and as I crawled along a rope stretched high between two trees I could see the lieutenant far below looking up at me to observe any sign of fear or hesitancy.

Finally all the tests were over and the next thing was an interview by a British Army psychiatrist. I was the first to report to him. He was a solemn, lanky major, with a thin wisp of a mustache, who slowly shuffled his papers as I sat across from him. He told me that he had gone over the results of my tests and that I had done rather well. I thanked him. Af first the major asked a few routine questions then suddenly went on the attack.

"Now, Lieutenant," he said, staring at me hard. "When did you stop wetting the bed?"

Immediately I knew that the question was meant to disconcert me and that he was watching me closely to see my reaction. I tried to keep a poker face and told him that I would like to think about that for a moment because I didn't want to give him a snap answer.

"Yes, of course, Lieutenant, take your time. No hurry."

"Thank you, sir." After several seconds I told him I thought this took place when I was about three years old.

"Hmm," he said, looking very serious. From the way he said "Hmm" I couldn't tell whether this was above average or below average. Could it be that English kids were champions at this sort of thing and stopped wetting the bed at the age of one, or even six months? I added that I was sorry I couldn't pinpoint the exact date, but unfortunately neither my parents nor I had kept records on this, not accurate records anyway.

"I see," he said, still very grave. He went through my papers and popped question after question at me. The interview lasted about a half-hour, and when it was finished he said, "Thank you, Lieutenant, I think you'll do."

We all passed the testing school and from there we went to Ringway, the British Parachute School outside Manchester. Since we were to jump into France out of converted bombers, using British parachutes and their jumping technique, all of us had to qualify at Ringway, including those American paratroopers who, like Cambray, had already gone through the Jump School at Fort Benning. American paratroopers jumped out of the door of slow-flying twin engine C-47's, called Dakotas by the British. British paratroopers jumped out of the bomb bay of faster flying four-engine bombers such as their Lancasters, or our B-24's which they called Liberators. There were several reasons for using bombers on these night jumping missions. The bomber, painted black to reduce visibility, was faster and could reach the dropping zone in less time. It was a sturdier plane and better able to withstand anti-aircraft fire. Since the bomber was armed it could try to fight off German night fighters whereas the C-47's used on mass jumps were sitting ducks and usually had fighter cover. Lastly, if German radar picked up an Allied bomber at night the enemy might be fooled into thinking the plane was only on a night reconnaissance mission or a lone straggler from a bombing raid.

Jumping out of a converted bomb bay, called the "hole" by the British, differed considerably from leaping out of the door of a C-47. During training we jumped as one of a group, or "stick" of six. The first man to jump sat on the floor of the plane, at the edge of the hole, legs stretched out in front of him. Behind him the other jumpers sat in the same position, waiting their turns. The first jumper tried—and seldom succeeded—not to look from time to time down the hole at the ground speeding by below him. He was watching the jump master who stood on the opposite side of the bomb bay, his earphones plugged to the intercom with the pilot. Next to the jump master was a small panel with a green light and a red light. When the pilot brought his plane into proper position and altitude over the drop zone (or rather what he thought was the proper position and altitude) he alerted the jump master and the red light flashed on. The jump master hollered, "Running in! Action station, number one!" and raised his right arm over his head. The first man then swung his legs out over the hole and sat on the edge, hands on the floor, legs hanging down into the bomb bay. When the pilot estimated that he was on target he flashed the green light on and the jump master yelled, "Go!" and brought his right hand down sharply. Number one then gave a quick shove with his hands and shot out and down into the hole and out of the plane. After he had fallen away far enough to clear the plane a static line hooked from the plane to his parachute jerked the parachute open. As number one went out, number two was getting into position and the jump master and the other jumpers repeated the same procedure. We had to scramble fast to get into position and hurl ourselves down the hole without any hesitation. When we jumped the bomber had throttled down, but it was still doing about one hundred and twenty-five miles an hour. Any delay by a jumper meant that not only he but the jumpers waiting behind him might overshoot the field.

The thing that really interested me was the startling difference between the American and British approach to parachuting. The Americans thought if you were a paratrooper you were a great, hairy-chested hero, for only the very tough and the very brave became paratroopers. The British point of view was just the opposite. As the instructors put it over and over, "It's a piece of cake, really. Just a piece of cake," a typical British understatement which was remarkably effective. The British convinced you—almost—that any able-bodied person, man or woman, could become a parachutist. It was all in the mind.

And so, unlike American paratroopers, British paratroopers did not carry a reserve chute. Aside from its function as an alternate chute, the Americans thought the reserve chute had a psychological value; even though you were a jumper and thus a hero it was reassuring to know you had a reserve chute, just in case. The British took a dim view of the reserve chute; since you would be jumping at an altitude of from four to six hundred feet, it was probably too late to be rescued by a reserve chute by the time you saw that your main chute wasn't opening, and as they put it, "You've had it, chum." There was also the danger—and this had happened to American paratroopers—that a jumper might panic when he thought his main chute wasn't opening and pull the rip cord on his reserve chute. As he did so the main chute was just opening, and thus the two chutes would tangle together. Scratch one paratrooper.

The first few days at Ringway were spent in preliminary drills. We jumped off high platforms and learned to land with our feet together, knees slightly bent, arms held against the chest, and then tumble forward to absorb the shock with our shoulders. One had to fight the instinctive urge to break the fall with one's arms out because this would probably mean a fractured arm or a dislocated shoulder. Still, despite all the instructions on how to land, our British sergeant instructors would tell us, "Any landing you can walk away from is a good one. Just think about landing like a sack of you know what, sir." The proper method of jumping through the hole, or "making a proper exit," as they called it, was most important. As you shoved yourself off and down you had to go out as though you were at attention, rigid, with your arms stiff down your sides, to cut down on wind resistance as you cleared the plane and prevent tumbling and flopping and getting fouled up in the "risers," the lines which attached you to the chute. "Go out like a Guardsman, sir!" the instructors would shout. A common fault in making an exit was called "ringing the bell." If you shoved off too hard you banged your head against the opposite side of the bomb bay. If you didn't shove hard enough and just slid down, the chute on your back caught the near edge of the hole and threw you forward so that again you cracked your head. You wore a steel jump helmet so that ringing the bell might only stun you momentarily. The danger was that if you "rang the bell" you would not "go out like a Guardsman," but would tumble out crooked and get tangled up in your risers. Several times I had to be cautioned during these drills, "Careful now, sir. Rang the bell that time, you did. Easy does it."

The British were exceedingly casual about what was called a "Roman candle," which meant that your chute didn't open at all and you went crashing down with your unopened chute trailing above you like a plume. The British mentioned a Roman candle in the same way that one might refer to the infinitely remote possibility of being struck by lightning. A Roman candle could be caused by what was called a "complete malfunction of your chute," possibly due to improper packing and folding by the chute packers, or due to a faulty exit and bad luck. Then there was a partial Roman candle, always due to a poor exit. In the latter case the risers were tangled and twisted together so that the chute only partially opened. This would result in a very hard fall, and the ambulance, or "meat wagon," would come roaring to the spot. In a combat jump at night behind the lines it would be different. No ambulance and no medics. Our British instructors conceded that if you got a Roman candle, "Why then, of course, you'd be properly squashed." But they added that it was most unlikely that the chute packers would pack a chute improperly. "They're bloody careful, you know. First-rate chaps, really. Some women packers too. And they're frightfully keen about their jobs." Finally there was a chute malfunction called the "Mae West." Due again to a faulty exit, one of the chute's lines would tangle and cut across the middle of the chute so that as the chute opened it was divided in half like a great voluptuous bosom. You came down very fast, dangling from the big white breast, and the "meat wagon" had a sure customer.

We were now ready for our first jumps. It was foggy on the day we were to jump and the bombers weren't flying, so we jumped out of a barrage balloon. Three of us and the jump master climbed into the balloon's gondola which had a hole in the center like a bomb bay. The balloon was released on its cable to a height of about six hundred feet and from up there you could barely see the ground through the fog. The three of us stood each in the corner of the gondola, inches away from the hole. There was barely room to stand and the side of the gondola reached below your waist. The gondola swayed gently up there in the fog and it was a spooky sensation. The jump master pointed to me and casually said, "You first, sir, on my signal." I remembered that some of the American paratroopers had a tradition of yelling "Geronimo!" on their training jumps. So when the jump master shouted "Go!" and swung his hand down I yelled "Geronimo!" as loud as I could and shot out and down through the mist. I could see the ground rushing up to meet me and still the chute hadn't opened. I had a panicky feeling. God, I thought, it's not going to open! But all of a sudden there was a hard jerk at my shoulders, the sound of rustling silk, and the chute was blossoming open in a beautiful pattern. Only then did I remember that when you jumped out of a balloon the chute opened more slowly because the balloon was stationary and there was no slip stream.

I tried to land as we were taught, but the ground was frozen and slippery and my feet went out from under me so that I hit very hard and was stunned for a moment. I unbuckled my chute to prevent being dragged along the ground and stood up, and as I ambled off I was filled with the magnificent elation of a successful jump, one that you could walk away from. But from the other side of the field the British ground officer was running towards me and he looked furious. "For Christ's sake, Lieutenant," he said. "What the bloody hell is the matter with you? Don't ever do that again!"

"What's that, sir?" I asked, feeling terribly let down all of a sudden.

"Yell 'Geronimo,' that's what! Use you head, man! You'll be jumping in behind the lines at night, remember? Maybe the Germans will hear the plane or even see it. Can't be helped. But then for you to yell 'Geronimo'—well now, Lieutenant, a bit silly, what?"

We went on to complete our training with four more jumps, one out of a balloon and three out of bombers, including a night jump. After the war I would sometimes be asked what it was like to jump and whether I was scared. I suppose that the true answer is that you get really keyed up before a jump, especially your first jump and a combat jump, but this is not the same thing as being frightened. You adopted a fatalistic attitude—"What will be, will be"—and you tried to concentrate on "going out like a Guardsman" and the other things you were taught. The gripping and intense satisfaction that you get from a successful jump is that of winning a gamble. When you jump out of the safety of the plane and into nothingness it takes only four or five seconds for your chute to open, and at the end of that time you know whether or not you have won the gamble, or really the most important part of the gamble. Then in another twenty seconds or so you find out whether you have won the second part and can get up and walk away. I was only scared once and then not for myself. In that training jump the jump master must have been mad, "jump happy" as we called it. He wore no chute and he kept hopping back and forth across the open bomb bay in a sort of dance of death. A lurch of the plane or the least slip on his part and he would have plunged straight down six hundred feet. I couldn't keep my eyes from him. It all had a horrible fascination. My palms were beginning to sweat and I was getting nervous. It was a great relief to jump out of that plane.

I would often be asked by friends how many jumps I had made, and when I would reply, "Seven, including a combat jump," I could see that my friends felt let down. I was expected to say fifty or maybe seventy-five. Sometimes I would mention the rule of thumb among paratroopers which is that when a jumper tells you that he had made a great many jumps, maybe forty or more, you divide that number by three and probably come close to the exact figure. I could also explain that our Jedburgh unit was a group of carefully screened and highly trained men and had one of us been injured on a training jump it would have been difficult to replace him, especially after he had formed a combat jump team with two other men. But whenever I tried to explain this I somehow sounded apologetic and the friends still seemed a little disappointed in me. I would also be asked how hard you landed and was it really like jumping off the top of a slow-moving train. And I would reply that sometimes this was true, but at other times you landed as easily as if you had jumped off your front porch onto the lawn. The wind makes a great difference in how hard a paratrooper hits the ground. Normally he won't be allowed to jump if the wind is too strong because it might carry him past the dropping zone, and even if he lands in the field the impact is jarring. Sudden and unexpected gusts of wind catching the paratrooper right after he jumps are also dangerous because they sweep him into the ground, or make him oscillate, swinging back and forth like a pendulum, then flinging him to the ground.

Then there would be the young woman who would flutter her eyelids at you and say, "My goodness, it must be simply terrible to jump at night!" But it wasn't. In a daytime jump we were not so much aware of falling; rather we saw the ground rushing up to meet us. We might get tense and unconsciously brace ourselves for the shock instead of landing "like a sack of you know what, sir." Once in a training jump I was caught by a gust of wind and, although I was completely unaware of it, I was pedalling furiously as though on a bicycle and only stopped just in time. The ground officer gave me hell for that. In a night jump you don't see the ground clearly until you have almost landed so there is less of a tendency to anticipate the landing and tighten up.

I did experience a partial "Roman candle" on a night jump during maneuvers shortly before we went into France. When my chute opened I looked up and saw that the risers were twisted all the way up to the canopy so that the chute wasn't fully opened. I was coming down fast and there was nothing I could do except watch the risers slowly unwind. I knew I would hit the ground before they untangled. When I landed I felt a sharp pain in my ankle and I knew right away that this was one jump from which I would not walk away. I had to crawl about two hundred yards to a road where one of our trucks was parked, and when the doctor checked me later he said it was a sprain and not a break. So he taped my ankle and told me that if I laced my boot tight I could hobble around, but no active duty for ten days. The trouble was that when I jumped into France shortly thereafter the bad ankle was still bothering me.

Paratroopers, as men who have mastered an unusual craft, had their own songs. So did the craftsmen of olden days, and sea chanteys have been sung ever since men first went down to the sea in ships. We learned some of these songs at Ringway. One of the British paratroopers' songs had a note of personal hygiene, the refrain being, "Going through the hole, going through the hole, oh we'll always keep our trousers clean going through the hole." The American paratroopers had a song, sung with fine bravado to the tune of "The Battle Hymn of the Republic," which told the sad and bloody story of a young paratrooper whose chute didn't open. The chorus, in which all joined with roaring enthusiasm, was "Gory, gory, what a helluva way to die! Gory, gory, what a hell of a way to die! And he ain't gonna jump no more."

After our training at Ringway we had a weekend leave in London. It was good to stroll in Picadilly Circus wearing the full regalia of the paratrooper: the silver parachute wings, the garrison cap worn at a cocky angle with its white and blue parachute patch, and the brightly shined parachute boots. Martel and I went into a pub swarming with "fly boys." Jammed next to Martel at the bar was a young colonel with his pilot's wings and three ribbons sprouting on his chest. He looked at Martel and said, "By God, Lieutenant, I'll fly the crates but I'll be goddamned if I want to jump out of one!" Martel gave him a shy smile and shrugged his shoulders.

CHAPTER VI

All the Jeds Get 'Married'

After our leave in London we reported to Milton Hall, a vast wooded estate requisitioned by the British Army as a training base for Jedburgh operations and located outside Peterborough, about ninety miles north of London. Milton Hall was set in a rolling countryside and although it was now winter and the cold was raw and penetrating, the meadows of the estate stretched out lush and green as fields in the States would be in the late spring. The huge and ancient manor house had brick walls nearly three feet thick, endless, dark corridors and many gloomy rooms. Coal was rationed and the fireplaces were used only in the mess hall and in the officers' mess so that in the rest of the mansion, including the bedrooms, it was as cold and damp as it was outside.

At Milton Hall we had our first experience with the admirable British Army practice of having officers served by batmen, or military orderlies. It was not long before that some of us had been plain GI's at a basic infantry training center. There you were awakened in what seemed the middle of the night by some sergeant or corporal, often a fugitive from the fourth grade, who routed you out of bed by raucously shouting four letter words. It worked, no doubt about that, but I preferred the Milton Hall method. Here a batman got you up by shaking you gently, handing you a steaming cup and saying quietly, "Here is your tea, sir. Time to get up, I'm afraid." What really made us laugh was that one British officer of the regular army apologized to us for the shortage of batmen. "Quite shocking, you know," he said, "only one batman for every ten officers or so. One batman for every two officers, maybe three, now that would be proper. Wartime, of course, still it's bloody rotten, I say." The batmen were most considerate and understanding. One night in the latter stage of our training when discipline had loosened up, a few British Jeds and I spent far too many pounds, shillings and sixpences in a Peterborough pub and when our batman came to wake me up the next morning I muttered that I was going to sleep late. "Are you now, sir?" he said. "Very good indeed, sir."

Shortly after our arrival at Milton Hall the American officers received promotions and Cambray, Farley and I became captains. The directive issued by our London headquarters stated in stilted Army jargon that while we were not yet due for these promotions, a higher rank would make it easier for us to issue orders to tough and possibly recalcitrant Maquis leaders.

Our training continued, much as at Arisaig. Within a few weeks other volunteers, American, British and French, had come to Milton Hall and now we had about two hundred officers and non-commissioned officers who had all been to Arisaig, passed the testing school, and had qualified as paratroopers at Ringway. There were more French officers than American and British because each Jedburgh team of three men had to have one French officer, aside from the radio operator who could be American, British, or French. The British and American radio operators were non-commissioned officers, but all of the French radio operators were second lieutenants. There were also a few Dutch and Belgian officers ready to team up for operations in those countries. Everyone got along very well, despite the marked national traits and the fact that most of the men were highly individualistic. We had a bond, a joint purpose, and while this may not have been a mystique, or esprit de corps, since we were not going into combat as a unit, still it was something very real. Each man had his own reasons for becoming a Jed, but in many cases the reasons were really the same, except for nuances. There was the camaraderie of men at arms, a companionship which is like no other. Sometimes in the evening while standing at the bar of the officers' mess a smiling British officer at your side raised his glass and said "Cheers!" looking you straight in the eye. And then, for a fleeting moment, you looked beyond and saw that for him, or for you, it might all end very soon, somewhere in France, when a German machine gunner, squinting through his sights, squeezed the trigger for a quick, sure burst.

Most of the British officers were jovial and carefree, joking easily with us, but I sensed that their casual ways masked feelings they didn't want to show. They all had a zest for adventure. Except for being a little older, they reminded me of the British fighter pilots in the 1940 Blitz, nonchalantly downing a pint of "mild" or "bitter" and then scrambling for their Spitfires and taking off to make wild and reckless attacks on the waves of German bombers roaring in across the Channel. Perhaps in imitation of the British air crews many of the British Jeds had adopted the cult of the mustache and you saw all varieties, including short, clipped military-style mustaches; wide, thin mustaches; and thick, bushy mustaches like those you see in portraits of middle-aged, dignified Victorian gentlemen. Until we got used to it the ones with the Victorian mustaches had an odd appearance because the mustache didn't seem to fit so young a face. There were British officers who had been in combat and a few of them wore the ribbon of the British Military Cross. These veterans were not quite so lighthearted. They never spoke of the past but they knew as we could not what lay ahead and perhaps they remembered all too vividly the bitter battles on the sands of Africa or the evaculation beaches of Dunkirk, and the pounding of German 88's or the sharp clatter of enemy machine guns.

Some of the British officers stood out as unusual, even among the Jeds. One was Major Hartwell of the Grenadier Guards. He was tall and slender, very erect, with a patrician face and he strolled around with his pet bulldog waddling and wheezing at his heels. Major Hartwell was distant and aloof and he seemed lost in thought most of the time. He was an excellent pianist and often would sit down at the piano in the officer's mess after dinner and, oblivious to the drinking and racket going on about him, would play Chopin nocturnes. I remember that one night as I sat in a pensive mood listening to him at the piano I thought of Rupert Brooke's "The Soldier," and although I had not read the poem for several years the first few lines came back to me very clearly:

> "If I should die think only this of me:
> That there's some corner of a foreign field
> That is forever England. There shall be
> In that rich earth a richer dust concealed;
> A dust whom England bore, shaped, made aware,
> Gave, once, her flowers to love, her ways to roam,
> A body of England's, breathing English air,
> Washed by the rivers, blest by suns of home . . ."

but I had forgotten the rest, except for bits and pieces, and then the mood left me and I went to the bar to have a beer with some of the American Jeds.

One evening Major Hartwell shed his reserve enough to say a few things about himself to Martel. He said that he had fought in a rear guard action near Dunkirk and was wounded and taken prisoner. He escaped and with the help of the French underground reached the Spanish frontier and got back to England. He spoke quietly but eloquently of the French people who had hidden him day after day, risking torture or death for an English officer they had never seen before and would never see again. He felt that he owed these people something and that it was his duty to make a payment on his debt to the French by getting a leave of absence from the Grenadier Guards and volunteering for the Jeds.

Major Hartwell had been allowed to bring his bulldog to Milton Hall, which he thought only natural. But he went much further than that. He wanted his bulldog to jump into France with him and he had it all figured out. He had a special parachute harness made for the dog and he planned to push the bulldog out of the bomb bay and then come leaping right after him. Hartwell was determined and when his project was turned down by the commandant at Milton Hall he went to headquarters in London to plead his case. The officer in London headquarters had been jocular at first and pointed out that the dog had really not been consulted, and while no one would doubt a bulldog's courage, still, "as a matter of propriety, proper military procedure, you know, Major, not quite the thing to do, really, to shove a dog or a man out of a plane without getting some kind of approval, now is it?" Major Hartwell gave the officer an icy look and informed him that he didn't appreciate having his request treated as a joke. The officer quickly realized that in dealing with this eccentric major of the Guards he needed reinforcements. He summoned two other staff officers and together they set aside their war maps and papers stamped "Top Secret" in order to talk a paratrooper out of jumping with his bulldog.

Major Richard Whitley, another British officer, was totally different from Major Hartwell. Whitley was the dashing, debonair type, handsome, always impeccably dressed, and he carried a swagger stick. I got to know him well during an air raid in London when we were on weekend leave. We were in a pub when the alert sounded and Whitley immediately said we should go to the roof of the building and "see the show." When we got to the roof entrance an air-raid warden barred the way, but Whitley waved his swagger stick at him imperiously and said he was Major Whitley making his inspection. The air-raid warden stood aside and we stepped out to watch the raid. Then we went back to the pub and as we got pleasantly potted I found that Whitley was very good company. After we got back to Milton Hall I learned more about him. He was married and he and his wife lived in a small town not far from Peterborough. Dick Whitley had a mistress, a charming, goodlooking woman, whom I met one night in a Peterborough pub. Her name was Rosalie and she lived in the same small town. Whitley saw no reason why the art of guerrilla warfare and the art of love should not be combined in a simultaneous operation, and so he asked permission from the commandant to set up a tent in a remote corner of the woods far away from the manor house. Whitley explained that this was a good idea because we would have to rough it when we got to France and he might just as well begin now. The commandant, favorably impressed by Whitley's zeal, allowed him to put up his tent.

But Whitley was roughing it like a sybarite. Of course the *raison d'être* for the project was that Rosalie frequently spent the night in the tent and "Whitley's Tepee," as the Americans later called it, contained a large camp bed, a small kerosene stove and a good stock of canned delicacies. Whitley had taken the precaution of setting up a perimeter warning system consisting of waist-high wires strung all around the tent area. Tin cans containing pebbles dangled from the wires. Thus if any intruder came within fifty feet of the tent Whitley would be alerted and he could take evasive action to avoid a contretemps. It was a cozy arrangement and I thought Major Whitley had gone a long ways towards proving his point about love and guerrilla warfare.

A few weeks later Whitley put on a superb performance. At the commandant's request Jack Cambray and I had reluctantly agreed that on our coming weekend leave in London we would stop by for tea on Sunday afternoon at the home of a retired Anglican minister, a vicar who wanted to show hospitality to the Yanks. That Sunday afternoon Cambray and I, and a few British Jeds who had been similarly dragooned into going to tea, were all sitting in the drawing room with the vicar and his wife. We were discussing whether this winter was colder than last winter, and various opinions had been advanced although apparently no satisfactory conclusion had been reached. I was facing the circular staircase which led from the second floor down to the drawing room when I heard an upstairs door slam, and then to my amazement I saw Major Whitley and Rosalie calmly strolling down the stairs. Whitley was smiling imperturbably, completely poised and relaxed. We stood up and the vicar's wife said, "And of course you know Major and Mrs. Whitley. So pleasant to have them spend the weekend with us." It went off nicely and then we got back to the weather. On the way back to Milton Hall that night Jack Cambray and I agreed that for Dick Whitley and Rosalie to shack up at the vicar's home was a tour de force the likes of which we had never seen. I ran into Dick Whitley the next morning at Milton Hall, and congratulated him on his aplomb.

"You were great yesterday, Dick," I said. "A 'wizard show' as you Limeys say."

He was pleased. "Took a bit of doing, that," he grinned. "Saves on hotel bills, of course. Actually, I didn't know you and the others were having tea there until a few minutes before you arrived. But I knew you chaps would carry it through all right. Might have been a bit sticky otherwise."

"Yes, I suppose so."

"I thought Rosalie carried off the thing rather well, didn't you?"

I agreed. Wondering about Whitley's peculiar marital situation, I added, "Tell me something, Dick. None of my business, of course. But with Rosalie living in the same small town as you and your wife, well, couldn't it get awkward? I mean, suppose she runs into you and Rosalie somewhere."

He laughed, and then he gave me an explanation which I still consider the most marvelous I have ever heard. "Not at all, old boy," he said. "You see, my wife is frightfully nearsighted."

The American volunteers who arrived at Milton Hall after us were a hell-for-leather bunch, gregarious, tough, unruly and very sure of themselves. The Americans were a mixed lot including another lawyer, two high school teachers, two insurance salesmen, a young bank vice-president, a Wisconsin dairy farmer, the assistant chef in a French restaurant in New York, and a stunt man who had once done a handstand on a ledge at the top of the Empire State Building. Some of the men had qualified as paratroopers back in the States and had left the 101st and the 82nd Airborne Divisions to join us. Highly individualistic as they were, I thought that probably these paratroopers wanted to be on their own, something they couldn't do in a regular outfit. There were also two Yale seniors—one of them now a celebrated columnist—who by special arrangement had been allowed to volunteer for the British Army before Pearl Harbor. Now they were second lieutenants in His Majesty's Army and on both sides of the Atlantic red tape was being cut to have them transferred to the Army of the United States.

The French officers, although pleasant and always extremely polite, were reserved and did not mix freely with us. They were career soldiers and combat veterans, including two Foreign Legion officers with their white kepis. We didn't know their real names because they had taken *noms de guerre* to protect their families in France. They would not talk to us about the 1940 Blitzkrieg in France and it seemed that their pledge was "Think of it always, speak of it never." It was not hard for me to understand why they felt this way. They were officers of a beaten army, a once proud and supposedly invincible army. These soldiers were the sons of men who had served with the French Army in World War I and who had fought and bled and won at the Marne and at Verdun. When history repeated itself and it was the turn of the French Army of 1940 to bar the way to another German invasion, that army, somehow, had failed, and because of that disaster the French flag had been hauled down in every city and village of France and had been replaced by the swastika of Hitler's conquering hordes. It had been a searing shame for these Frenchmen at Milton Hall, and what made the humiliation burn even deeper was that they were now on English soil, an England which for over a year and a half had stood alone, despite the odds, against the fury of the Luftwaffe and the power of the Wehrmacht.

Seeing these men I thought of the French military parade I had seen on July 14, 1934, when I was a college student on vacation. It had been a magnificent sight. Down the broad sweep of the Champs-Elysées marched battalion after battalion, file after file and rank after rank, stretching nearly two miles from the Arch of Triumph to the Place de la Concorde. First there were the *Chasseurs Alpins* stepping at their quick, brisk pace, then the *Tirailleurs Marocains* and the *Tirailleurs Algériens,* in their bright red and blue uniforms, and then the Senegalese Infantry, the Colonial Infantry, the *Fusiliers Marins,* all parading in perfect step with the rhythmic pounding of their boots on the pavement and their rifles with the fixed bayonets gleaming in the sun; and next came the long columns of the Foreign Legion and their bearded sappers, marching at the slow, steady cadence they had long used on the deserts of Africa; and finally the clatter of horses' hoofs and squadrons of Spahi cavalry galloping by with flashing swords, their white and red capes flowing behind them. It was all there in a dazzling show of military might, the bands playing the "*Mar-*

seillaise" and "*Sambre et Meuse*," the blaring of trumpets, the rolling beat of many drums, and the regimental battle flags carried proudly and dipped in sharp salute at the reviewing stand where the generals stood very straight with all their medals and their *fourragères*. But, I remembered, there were no tanks and there were no dive bombers winging past in tight formation. Thinking of these things I knew that, although they were much too proud to show it, these French officers had long been tormented by a gnawing pain, a passionate feeling that the bitter defeat of 1940 had to be avenged.

The first commandant at Milton Hall was a British colonel who had spent most of his career in India. He was a Pukka Sahib type in his early sixties with a craggy face and a bristling mustache. When he wasn't sure of what to say, which was often, he emitted a loud, prolonged grunt. The colonel had a mean black chow named "Mr. Wu" who often snarled at us and the Americans would growl back. This would bring on one of the colonel's grunts. The British officers seemed rather afraid of him and when they saw him in the officers' mess they would click their heels and say, "Sir!" The colonel often launched into long and tedious monologues, generally about his service in India, and the British listened deferentially. The Americans paid no attention, and neither did the French, but they had an excuse because few of them understoood English very well. During one of these interminable monologues one of the American officers, the stunt man, piped up that the colonel's story reminded him of his handstand atop the Empire State Building (it was difficult to see why) and he dashed up to his room, got a newspaper clipping about this exploit, and shoved it under the colonel's nose. The British were aghast. The colonel huffed and grunted dangerously, but with no appreciable effect on the stunt man.

While the rapport between the commandant and the Americans was poor at best, matters really came to a head with the battle cry of the American Jeds. This battle cry was brought by the American paratroopers from Fort Benning, and to my surprise it was Jack Cambray who started it up at Milton Hall. The story was that a captain attending the Parachute School at Fort Benning was a few minutes late reporting for one of the drills. As was the practice, the non-commissioned instructor barked at the captain to step out of the ranks and do fifty pushups in front of the men. The captain did so, counting out loud. He got to the end, "48, 49, 50," and then he stood up, red-faced and panting, and added, "Some shit!" Word of this incident spread fast and soon many American paratroopers adopted this unique method of expressing their displeasure or scorn. It was always done spontaneously, with a certain amount of dash, one paratrooper starting with "48," another chanting "49," a third calling out "50," and then all would join in the chorus. When the British Jeds first heard this battle cry they didn't understand it at all and being more staid and proper than their American confrères they had reservations about its propriety. However when it was explained to them they thought it very funny, ("Oh, I say, good show!") and some occasionally took part, though somewhat timidly. Once several of the French officers joined in, their French accents adding a nice Gallic touch. Although the commandant had no doubt been told about the battle cry he had never actually heard it. When he did a crisis was reached.

This occurred when a high-ranking American civilian in the OSS in Washington flew to London and then came to Milton Hall one Saturday for an inspection tour. We were told that this civilian wanted to review the Jedburgh unit at three o'clock, which meant delaying our weekend leave. At three o'clock sharp our detachment marched out in full uniform, the French with the few Belgians and Dutch in one group, followed by the British contingent and then the Americans. This was not an impressive display of military precision because each army has its own marching style and cadence and as a result each group was marching out of step with the other groups, and even some of the officers were out of step with their own group. Still we did manage to march past a small, hastily erected platform on which stood the British commandant and the OSS civilian. We stopped and left-faced towards the platform. The commandant introduced the civilian who, he said, wanted to say a few words to us. It took the civilian twenty minutes to tell us that he was much impressed by what he had seen. In closing, he told us that as he looked at our young, eager faces, and knowing how dangerous our missions would be, he just burned with fierce pride. There was a moment of silence as we stood there at attention then from the American ranks a voice rang out "48," and then all of the Americans joined in a loud chant of the battle cry. The effect was shattering. You could hear the silence. Everyone still stood at attention, straight-faced, eyes fixed ahead. Out of the corner of my eye I could see that the commandant's face was flushed. He opened his mouth to say something, changed his mind, and then emitted what was by far the loudest and most sonorous grunt I had ever heard from him. The civilian had dropped some papers and was down on one knee fumbling nervously to retrieve them. The commandant grunted again and, partially recovering his composure, ordered "Right face," then "Forward march!" and off we went, out of step as before.

The talented Major Hartwell decided to commemorate this occasion with a cartoon he drew and pinned on the bulletin board. The cartoon showed two polar bears sitting on a vast ice-field looking at a large hole in the ice between them. One polar bear asked, "What happened?" and the other replied, "I don't know. He just said he was burning with fierce pride and then he disappeared." After this near mutiny it was clear that something had to give between the commandant and the Americans. It was the commandant, and a few days later we had a new British commandant, a pleasant, friendly man whom everyone liked. In deference to him the Americans voluntarily curtailed the use of the battle cry and thereafter their discipline, while still leaving something to be desired, improved considerably.

Shortly after the new commandant arrived, our training in radio and code began. The radio operator tapped out dashes and dots on the sending key of the transmitter, which was powered by a hand-cranked generator. Of course the messages, called "signals" by the British, had first to be coded. The various codes and tricks used to fool German listening posts and their decyphering specialists were most ingenious. It was a matching of Allied wits against the cunning of enemy counterespionage. So we learned about such things as "one time pads," "five letter groups," "silk code sheets," and deliberate errors. Each team would be assigned its own designated mistakes.

All the radio operators had to do was polish up their sending and receiving and try to improve their speed. But the other officers had to learn how to send and receive well enough to take over if the radio operator got knocked off. We spent hours learning the dot-and-dash alpahabet of the International Code, and then more hours practicing. It was like being back in the first grade. A dash was called "da," while a dot was called "dee," except that at times, for no discernible reason, the dot became a "dit." Hence you had "da da dee da" for "Q" but "dee da dit" for "R." Our instructor, a grave and earnest sergeant, droned his "das" and "dees" in a high-pitched sing-song voice, covering each letter of the alphabet over and over again. As though he were teaching children, he had little phrases to help us remember the letters in code. Thus for the letter "Q" he told us to think of a queen being married, and he would solemnly croon "da da dee da" to the tune of "Here Comes the Bride." The sergeant had a pungent phrase as a memory aid for the "dee dee da dit" of the letter "F." He said it without cracking a smile, and that was one letter we had no trouble remembering. If you didn't do your lessons properly you were kept after school for more practice, the sergeant saying, "Sir, you were a bit slow this afternoon, you know. Made a few mistakes too, you did. Now, would you mind very much staying over and practicing a little more?" After a long afternoon session of radio training we invariably headed for the bar in the officers' mess to forget temporarily all those little "das" and "dees" which seemed to chase each other round and round in our heads.

In teaching the code, as in all other phases of our training, the British were very rigorous and tried to anticipate every contingency. At the end of our radio instruction each Jed recorded a taped message containing every letter of the alphabet. An expert can readily identify the touch, or "fist," of an operator, and by comparing a message received from behind the lines with the taped recording he can tell whether or not the message was sent by Germans who have captured the transmitter and the codes.

All the Jeds Get 'Married'

When we finished with radio training we had a lecture on D/F, the direction-finding techniques used by the Germans to locate secret radio transmitters. Our instructor was a French agent who had spent considerable time behind the lines. The Germans had discovered his identity and his "cover was blown" so that he couldn't go back. He told us how the German D/F stations, the listening posts scattered throughout France, used triangulation to locate the approximate area of a clandestine radio. Then a D/F vehicle, loaded down with special listening devices, was sent to the locality and could pinpoint the exact site of the radio. The French learned quickly and whenever a D/F truck was seen word went out immediately to the radio operator. The Germans countered this by disguising the D/F vehicle, for example as an ambulance. Again the French rapidly got wise. As our instructor described it, "Aha, a German ambulance mucking about our village, eh? Unfortunately all the Germans here look very healthy. They should. They are eating good French food and drinking our wines. So why is the ambulance here? And why does it have that long antenna, eh? It's a bloody D/F car, that's what. So the radio operator is warned and right away he shuts down his set and hides it, and tries to act like any ordinary farmer and he goes to a *bistro* and orders a cognac. No, I forget. You will be in uniform. You stay where you are, have a cognac brought to you, and you wait. If you are like me your heart pounds very hard and your palms sweat. But you haven't been on the air long enough for the D/F car to pick you up and it finally goes away. Good. Then first chance you get you bloody well better move your radio to another location."

He explained to us about changing the crystals in our sets so as to use a different frequency on alternate days, and also said that our schedules would call for our coming on the air at varying hours from day to day, all of which made it more difficult for the D/F to locate the radio accurately. The important thing was to be on the air for as short a time as possible. Hence the message must be concise, and you hoped that interference wasn't bad and that the home station in London wouldn't ask for a repeat of the message.

Then he told us about identification phrases. Since on a few occasions the Germans had successfully infiltrated Maquis groups it could well be that during our first few days in France some Maquis leaders might suspect that we were Germans passing as Allied officers. Therefore for three nights after the air-drop, the BBC, during the course of its regular evening program of French messages in the clear, would broadcast a phrase such as "The black cow has a broken left hind leg." As a guarantee of your identity you would tell the Maquis chiefs that this phrase would be broadcast that night and all they had to do was listen for it on their hidden sets. There would be another identification phrase for each man to use if necessary when he was overrun by the Allied forces. Possibly by that time you had been forced to disguise yourself as a peasant, a garage mechanic or even—though this was most unlikely—as a German soldier. It might then be rather difficult to convince the Allied lead patrol that you were actually an OSS paratrooper. Each Jed had chosen an identification phrase to cover this contingency, and at Corps headquarters the intelligence officers had a record of each man and his phrase. My phrase was, "My wife Nancy is a Kappa." In case of trouble when overrun you simply asked to be taken to headquarters. It amused me to foresee a ludicrous situation where, dressed perhaps as a pastry cook, I would salute the colonel at the Corps intelligence section and say, "Sir, I am Captain Dreux and my wife Nancy is a Kappa." And the colonel would check his file and then say, "Yes, very good, Captain. By the way, my wife Joan is a Kappa too."

One night the commandant got up at dinner and announced that neither he nor London headquarters would pick the officers for the three-man teams. We were free to choose our own partners, and as he said, smiling, "You chaps go ahead and make your own 'marriages.'" The wooing and pursuing started right after dinner. While this all may have seemed funny, I knew I had a real problem for obviously the choice of a partner was most important.

For two days I hesitated, doing nothing, and then the matter was quickly settled one morning before breakfast. The French officers had just gone through the Gallic tribal custom of shaking hands all around and saying "good morning," when Major Jeanpaul, whom I knew slighty, left his group and walked over towards me. He said "good morning" and, of course, we shook hands. Then speaking hesitantly—the only time I saw him do this—he said, "B-e-e-l," pronouncing my name as the French always did, "Do you think, well, do you think you and I could form a team?" And I said, "Yes, I would like to," and so we shook hands again. The "marriage ceremony" took place when we reported to the commandant, and consisted of his making an entry in his record and saying "Good luck, *bonne chance*, to you both."

Major Jeanpaul was a dark-complexioned man in his early thirties, sturdy and of medium height. He had piercing brown eyes and his firm-jawed face had a set look. He was a quiet man who seldom smiled, but when he did it was a brief, flashing smile and his eyes twinkled, and then just as quickly his face relapsed into that determined expression. One night in the officer's mess I had overheard French officers talking about him. They had said in French army slang that he was *un sacré baroudeur*, a hell of a fighter, and that in battle he was always up front, sometimes too much so. The ribbons on his battle jacket told part of the story: the Legion of Honor, the Croix de Guerre with four citations, and the British Military Cross. He had graduated from the Military Academy at St. Cyr a few years before the war, fought in France, was wounded and taken prisoner at Dunkirk, escaped to Africa and then commanded a battalion of Colonial Infantry against Rommel's Africa Korps. I had noticed him before, for he stood out and caught one's eye, and when stories about him reached me from the other officers I had said to myself he must be one of those officers for whom the military profession is like a faith, a way of life, and everything that is worthwhile. He is a definite type, I thought then, probably cast in the same mold as the French captain of World War I who, looking around at the shattered remnants of his infantry company as the shells rained down and the Germans swarmed forward, had shouted his last order, "*Debout les Morts!*" a ringing phrase which is impossible to translate adequately but which means, "You, the dead, on your feet!"

That afternoon I asked Major Jeanpaul what his first name was and he smiled briefly and said that this was his first name and also his *nom de guerre*. As to his last name, well, that could wait until after the war. So thereafter it was "Jeanpaul" and "B-e-e-l." Although we got to know each other very well, especially behind the lines, he always used *vous* in addressing me and not the more familiar *tu*. Once we even had to share a chamber pot in France, and you might think that if anything were to break down that mysterious French barrier between vous and *tu*, a brotherhood of the chamber pot would surely do it. Not at all. He just said, "*Vous cherchez le pot de chambre, B-e-e-l?*" and I said, "*Oui, où est ce que vous l'avez mis?*" The *vous* remained with us like an article of faith.

A few days afterwards we went out on maneuvers as a team for three days. We were to meet a "Maquis" group, composed of "unmarried" Americans led by Jack Cambray, also still "unmarried," and the "Maquis" band and our team were to attack an enemy supply dump. Jeanpaul was in command of the entire operation. We brought our radio and were in contact, by coded messages, with a transmitter back at Milton Hall. Everything was going smoothly, except that in making one of the rendezvous our team arrived too early because I misread the scale on our map and overestimated the distance we had to travel. Jeanpaul asked to see the map and then he said, "You made a mistake on the scale. It wasn't as far as you thought."

"Yes," I said. "That's where I made the mistake. Sorry." He gave me a hard, penetrating look and walked away. I felt as though I had been court-martialed.

I was curious to see how the American paratroopers of the "Maquis" force would take orders from Jeanpaul. These were tough and independent men, and discipline was not their strong point. But Jeanpaul, with that mysterious quality of leadership and a command presence, had won their respect right from the start. When he issued his orders they were crisp and clear, whether given in French or in his broken English, and the Americans reacted as though the orders had come straight from General Eisenhower. I noticed that he never referred to the "Boches," it was always the "Germans" or the "enemy." Throughout this maneuver Jeanpaul was deadly serious. He had his orders and he meant to carry them out, regardless of the cost, and despite "German" sentries, the rainy weather, the fatigue of his men or any other obstacle. Wiping out that supply dump was an obsession, and wipe it out he did. The umpires were impressed. Before the attack he joked on rare occasions, or made ironic comments about Larue, our French radio operator, who was an enlisted man recently promoted to second lieutenant and picked by Jeanpaul for our team. Larue was a huge, square-faced man with arms like a gorilla and, though an excellent operator, he was not too bright. Jeanpaul was amused by the sight of Larue, hunched over our radio, one big hairy hand rapidly yet gently tapping out Morse code on the sending key. Watching him, Jeanpaul chuckled and remarked, "Look at Larue. A real orang-outang. Straight out of the zoo. But he fingers that key like Paderewski at the piano."

In the meantime Bob Farley had "married" a Foreign Legion captain, a wiry and deeply tanned officer who looked as if he had spent most of his life leading patrols in the Sahara. Once I overheard him quietly telling Farley that bravery was not enough, things must be done "*avec chic et avec gout.*" I was reminded of the story from World War I about a second lieutenant who had just graduated from St. Cyr and immediately reported to the front at Verdun. Before leading a hopeless counterattack in which he was killed, he had put on the white dress gloves he had brought with him from St. Cyr. The Legionnaire unquestionably had an air about him, a sort of panache, which I'm sure appealed to Farley. Afterwards Jack Cambray and I were talking about Farley, and Cambray, while admitting that Farley was a damn good man, said, "But he's such a romantic bastard. He'll want to win the war all by himself. Horatius at the bridge. Cyrano against a hundred swordsmen."

A short time later Jack Cambray was "married" to a French first lieutenant, a young, studious-looking man who also wore glasses. Seen together they looked like a youthful professor and one of his disciples from post-graduate school. Bob Farley jokingly warned Cambray, "You know, Pumpkin," he said, "Those Krauts are going to play rough. They'll chew up a couple of Boy Scouts like you."

"Yes?" replied Cambray. "Well, we'll see. We'll see, Cyrano."

Then a few days afterwards Martel was successfully courted by a young French captain named Delbecq, a veteran of the African campaign. There was a rumor that Delbecq was a Count and his real name was that of one of the oldest families of France. He was a lean, graceful man, with an enigmatic smile and an aristocratic bearing. I thought that there might be some truth in the rumor. Delbecq had been wounded three times and his left arm hung down rigid at a crooked angle. I was surprised that he had passed the physical and qualified at the Ringway Parachute School. Like Jeanpaul, Delbecq wore the ribbons of the Legion of Honor and the Croix de Guerre, as well as the British Military Cross. He was invariably pleasant, but taciturn, and any discussions with him at the bar of the officers' mess were generally cut short with a slight smile and a courteous, "*Vous avez peut-être raison.*" Since Martel was not loquacious either, the dialogue between them was limited, but they got along very well and seemed happy with each other. Another thing they had in common was that they were both devout Catholics and early every Sunday morning they went to Mass in Peterborough, each carrying a thick missal. Sometimes in watching them leave, it occurred to me that I should be going with them instead of spending a lazy Sunday morning at camp.

During the last part of our training we learned about dropping zones, or "D/Z's" and "Reception Committees." The operation to drop a team was prepared by London headquarters who were in radio contact with the Maquis in that area. The Maquis picked out a D/Z. It was almost impossible to pick a perfect D/Z, a large flat, soft field, well away from roads, buildings, power lines, trees and other obstructions, and distant from any German installation. On the night of the drop a reception committee of at least four men came to the field. Shortly before the bomber was due, three men in line spaced a hundred yards apart stood in the center of the field, lit their flashlights and pointed them straight up. The fourth man stood to one side of the end man and flashed a blinker dash-and-dot identification signal agreed on by London and the Maquis. The position of the signalling man of the reception committee indicated to the pilot from which end of the field he should approach, that is from the end at which the signal man was stationed, so that the bomber would come in against the wind. Letters containing all dots or all dashes were not used because the pilot couldn't easily tell whether he was seeing flashes for three dots, as for "S," or three dashes, as for "O." The three dots and a dash for "V" was never used due to the danger that Germans, having previously seized the field, would flash the "V" for "Victory" and try to decoy the pilot into dropping his paratroopers in the arms of a German patrol.

Our D/Z instructor was an old hand at the game, and he was quite candid. "Mind you," he said, "I want to be honest with you chaps. You'll be bloody lucky if all three of you land in the D/Z. In fact I have a standing offer for you poor blighters. If any team here has all three men land in the D/Z—well, you come see me in London when your show is over and I'll buy you all the drinks you can stand in one night. That goes for you Yanks, too. The pilot can't very well circle around and around the field until he's sure that he's exactly on line and at the proper altitude, now can he? So he makes one pass at the field, and out you go, and you hope he doesn't drop you on top of a church steeple or some power lines. If you land in the next field, well, now, that's all bloody good, really. Now suppose after your bomber has left England the Jerries come buggering around the D/Z or a strong wind springs up, too much wind. Then the reception committee doesn't light up the field and the pilot turns around and comes home, and you chaps have a drink or so and then go nightie-nightie and try again the next night. O.K.? What if the pilot gets the wrong identifying letter flashed at him? Well that might mean the Jerries are having a bit of fun playing 'reception committee.' And the pilot has standing orders to get the hell out of there and back to base just as fast as he can. But really, there's not that much to this thing, you know. Been done many times. A little luck and all and then it's a piece of cake."

After our lectures on D/Z's we went out in the country to

reconnoiter for suitable D/Z's and practiced setting up reception committees. We had to be experts at this in case another team might be dropped in our zone, or we needed additional supplies parachuted to us in their containers. A few days of this and we saw why the Maquis frequently had to select D/Z's which, while suitable for a drop of containers, presented some hazards for paratroopers.

It was now late April and our training was completed, so we kept doing the same things over again. Every day we practiced unarmed combat, fired the .45 pistol, the carbine, and the Sten sub-machine gun. We went out on the range with the Bren light machine gun. Cross-country marches and runs were scheduled, but by now the Americans had become extraordinarily adept at avoiding these arduous exercises. It was no longer a case of outwitting "German" sentries; it became a game between the training staff and the ingenious Americans, and the Americans generally won. They would hitch rides to the destination, even steal staff cars, anything to avoid a long march or a run across the countryside. This was boring and we were getting restless. "D"-Day could not be far off, and while we knew that only one or two teams would jump in on "D"-Day, and that the other teams would be dropped in later as the tactical situation developed, still the sooner the better. In the meantime there were some diversions such as "Camerone Day" on April thirteenth when it is a tradition of the Foreign Legion to get truly potted in commemoration of the last stand of a Foreign Legion detachment at Camerone, Mexico, in 1863. We celebrated "Camerone Day" with our two Foreign Legion Jeds by taking over the Jolly Bull pub in Peterborough, somewhat to the annoyance of the regular English patrons. We got stoned. A few chairs were smashed, or, as Jack Cambray put it, "we made antiques out of them." Towards the end of that wild evening I watched in astonishment as Jeanpaul, with a lopsided grin, climbed unsteadily on top of a table to lead the singing of "*Auprès de ma Blonde.*"

To keep up the pretense that we were still undergoing training, a maneuver was set up including the night jump in which I had my partial "Roman Candle" and sprained my ankle. The commandant later admitted that it had been a mistake to lay on a jump at this late stage. Thereafter even running the obstacle course was eliminated to prevent last-minute injuries. I hobbled around for the next ten days and I thought it was rotten luck to have this happen now when we were bound to be going into France very soon. Jeanpaul was worried because now everyone was "married" and how was he to find another "bride" if my ankle didn't heal in time? June came and two teams were alerted and left Milton Hall. Then came June sixth and "D"-Day and within a week four more teams were alerted. We followed the invasion on the big war map in the commandant's office, each man speculating as to where and when his team would be parachuted. Most of the teams were still waiting at Milton Hall, and for us our base had now become a prison and the wardens were the officers in London headquarters. Every night we went pub crawling in Peterborough, but it was no longer fun, like the gay, rollicking evenings we had enjoyed in early spring. We drank morosely, saying little, staring at the walls with their prints of English hunting scenes. The days dragged on. We were like the fighter who has trained hard for a fifteen-round bout with the champion, and he knows that the champion is a great fighter and a hard puncher but he thinks he has an excellent chance. Then the fight is postponed indefinitely and the challenger is left feeling bitter and wondering if the fight will take place at all.

CHAPTER VII

"Running In! . . . Action Stations!"

On July tenth our team was finally alerted, as was the team led by Captain Drouant. The other members of Drouant's team were Captain Archie Truffington and Lieutenant Descartes, their French radio operator. Oddly enough, Truffington, an Englishman, was short and swarthy, whereas Drouant, a Frenchman, was a tall, very good-looking man, blond and blue-eyed. Although I knew Truffington only by sight, Drouant and I had already become good friends. André Drouant was reserved until you got to know him well and then he was gay, with a flashing wit and a boyish laugh. In this he was unlike Jeanpaul who was almost austere and nearly always kept his sense of humor submerged. But at times, if you were watching Drouant closely, you saw that his eyes were no longer laughing and instead they were somber and brooding, and then you knew that deep within himself he had the same fierce and relentless drive that motivated Jeanpaul. Drouant was popular with the British and American Jeds, and several times he had gone pub crawling with us in Peterborough. Once Dick Whitley was there, this time without Rosalie, who must have had the night off. Drouant had heard the stories about Whitley and his daring amatory adventures, and I could see that Drouant was observing Whitley with considerable interest.

After being alerted we got all our equipment together and tagged it so that what we didn't have on us when we jumped would go into containers to be dropped in with us. Then came the paperwork. We had to fill out and sign numerous Army forms, some of them very ancient, going back perhaps to the Colonial Wars, and of doubtful application in our case. I thought that some of these papers had a macabre note and conveyed the impression that your early demise was anticipated. It was like being in a hospital and having your doctor suggest that you should make a will. On a special OSS form I gave the name and address of my wife. The arrangement was that after you dropped in, London headquarters would send a weekly airmail letter to a designated relative stating only that London heard from you and that you were safe and well. We had been told of this plan before and I had written to my wife to tell her that soon, and for an indefinite period, I would be unable to write to her but that she would receive these messages regularly, and I added the usual idiotic phrase, "Please don't worry." Naturally this plan of sending messages back to the States was based on two suppositions: first, that radio contact between London and your team was being maintained, and secondly that, as indicated by these radio dispatches, you were indeed hale and hearty. This whole idea may have been good in theory—although this is debatable—but unfortunately within a week of our drop into France we had to cache our radio; consequently my wife received no letters from headquarters and was left wondering what had happened to me.

When we left for London the next day the other Jeds as well as the training staff and the administrative staff were all on hand to see us off and wish us luck. I stood off to one side with Farley, Cambray and Martel. We felt a little self-conscious and not sure of what to say, so we covered up with some bad jokes. Then I told them each "so long," shook hands, and when I got on the truck I waved back and said, "Be seeing you." As I said this I thought it was the last time I would see some of the Jeds, and this is how it turned out.

When we reached London our truck took us to an old area of the city, criss-crossed with narrow streets and winding passageways. London headquarters, we learned, had taken over an old apartment building to accommodate departing Jed teams, and there were bedrooms for us as well as separate briefing rooms and map rooms. We were milling about and talking while a Major Abernathy was trying to sort us out for room assignments. Major Abernathy was a warrior of the chairborne brigade and his martial duties included various administrative functions at Milton Hall and in London. He was a small, mousy man and we referred to him as "Mickey Mouse." We had always thought there was something irritating in his supercilious manner which clearly conveyed his opinion that staff officers were intellectuals and that jumpers, from the very nature of things, were not too bright. Major Abernathy was a Scot, though totally different from the rugged Scots at Arisaig, and at Milton Hall he frequently wore kilts and the British battle jacket. When I first met him I noted with some surprise that he kept his handkerchief daintily tucked into the left sleeve of his battle jacket. This struck me as being effeminate. And then there was the way he walked with light, mincing steps so that sometimes you wondered if he was about to take off on a trial flight. I had asked one of the British Jeds whether Major Abernathy was maybe a little bit that way, and I commented particularly on the way he carried his handkerchief. The reply, given after some deliberation, was that I might be right but then "Scots do not have proper pockets in their kilts, old boy." Sometimes Abernathy had a harassed expression as though the burdens of his high office were too heavy for one man to carry, no matter how capable that man might be.

Now he looked really worried, very much like a man who desperately wants to go to the bathroom but doesn't know where it is. He confided to me that one of his numerous problems on that day was to get currency for us. We were to jump in with a substantial amount of cash in dollars and francs which could be used as bribes or to purchase supplies if necessary. Much later I was to use some of this money behind the lines to buy an old touring car. Unfortunately, Major Abernathy had just discovered that the bank had given him the wrong amount. "You can't appreciate this," he told me, "but getting you chaps ready is a bit of a strain. And then for the bank to make that mistake, well, that really shook me, you know." I clucked my tongue and commiserated with him.

We were taken to an apartment on the third floor where we found Major Dillworth, who was to act as our conducting officer up to the moment we boarded the plane. We had known him before. Dillworth, who was an American mining engineer in civilian life, looked like a wrestler with his flat face, bull neck, and close-cropped hair. Although he didn't smoke he liked to chew tobacco so we had nicknamed him "Plug." Plug Dillworth had the interesting theory, which he said was confirmed by his dentist, that chewing tobacco was good for your teeth and gums whereas, of course, smoking was bad. When Dillworth had first disclosed this dental principle to me, I had expressed some skepticism and then in proof of his theory he had bared his teeth and I had to admit that they looked remarkably white and clean and in excellent condition. He was not chewing just then because the apartment lacked one necessary fixture, a problem he hoped to resolve shortly.

Plug Dillworth's job was to stay with us at all times, supervise our briefing and see that we got anything we wanted as a last-minute request. Especially he was to make sure that when we went out to our meals, or went to a pub afterwards, we wouldn't belt down too many drinks and get loquacious. Headquarters was very sensitive about maximum security. The nice part of that sojourn in London was that our conducting officer had a practically unlimited spending account. We ate at the best restaurants and had our choice of rare wines and the best in cognacs and liqueurs. The first afternoon we were told to take it easy because our briefing would not start until the next day. So we loafed, had an expensive dinner and came back to our apartment.

In the sitting room Dillworth found what he wanted, a large yellow flower bowl which he said would do nicely as a cuspidor, except that he preferred to call it a receptacle. He took a big bite on his plug of tobacco and sat down on the sofa to read a magazine. He put the flower bowl about three feet away, well within range of a marksman like himself. I could see that he wanted to put on a demonstration for the French officers and he succeeded. Apparently Jeanpaul and Drouant had never seen anyone chew tobacco and they appeared fascinated by this performance. Dillworth's superb accuracy especially impressed them. He was always on target with that yellow bowl. *"Formidable! Vraiment formidable!"* they said. Dillworth smiled appreciatively at this tribute. I thought he might get carried away by their compliments and move the bowl out farther so as to try scoring from long range, but he played it conservatively.

Dillworth did not want to be just an escorting officer and he was frustrated. He had volunteered for the Jeds, although about ten years older than most of us, but he had cracked four vertebrae on a training jump several months before and he still wore his cast. He was biding his time and was determined to go on a mission once that cast was removed. Later I learned that he did. Somehow he persuaded headquarters to let him join a group due to jump high in the French Alps. Because of the altitude it was decided to use a Flying Fortress, the first time this had been done for such missions. Something went wrong as two of the men jumped and their static lines broke and the chutes failed to open, or as they said at the Ringway Parachute School, "there was a total malfunction of the chutes." But Dillworth's chute opened, he came through his mission alive, and when I saw him afterwards in London he was in fine spirits.

As we sat in the apartment, talking idly, Dillworth said the weather reports had been good the last few days and the moon was just right, half full. This was a good time for an operation, enough light for the pilot to pick out his landmarks on the way to the D/Z and yet not the bright light of a full moon which made the bomber that much more visible and also made it more dangerous for the reception committee. "Your briefing officer," said Dillworth, "is Colonel Girard, a Frenchman."

"I remember him from Africa," said Jeanpaul. "He's an artillery officer, and a very good one. But he's a rather peculiar man. He was pretty badly wounded in Tunisia. Hit in the back by shrapnel. He has a stiff neck and his head is cocked off to one side."

Dillworth said that was the man, but that he was just filling in as a briefing officer. He added that Girard wanted to jump in, even though he was over fifty and had no jump training. "He's pestering the hell out of headquarters," Dillworth said, "pulling his rank and arguing. They'll let him go on a mission just to get rid of the guy."

I offered to bet Dillworth a buck that Girard wouldn't jump in, and Dillworth took me up on it.

Dillworth gazed off into space for several minutes. "You know," he finally said, "Girard had nothing to do with planning this mission. Our headquarters did that, working with Eisenhower's people of course. I think the mission . . ." He stopped and looked at me.

"What about it?" I asked.

"Never mind," said Dillworth, and he zeroed in again on the flower bowl and started to talk about a meal he once had at the Tour d'Argent in Paris.

I lost my bet to Dillworth. Girard did go on a mission and I got the story long afterwards in a roundabout way. After Colonel Girard's plane crossed the French coast the despatcher opened up the bomb bay even though the plane was still far from the D/Z. Immediately Girard moved right next to the bomb bay and sat there, his legs hanging over, staring down through the night at the ground far below. Even for seasoned paratroopers it is not recommended that you keep watching the ground long before jumping. The despatcher told Girard in broken French that they weren't near the D/Z yet and that he didn't have to sit there ready to jump. Colonel Girard blew up. "Not look at the ground?" he had said. "Of course I will! This is my first look at French soil in four years and I'm damned well going to look!"

Colonel Girard landed without injury and within a day they were overrun by an American armored column. Suddenly the Germans cut loose with a heavy mortar barrage and machine gun fire. Colonel Girard and an American officer dove for a ditch and crawled away to safety about a quarter of a mile away. When they got there Colonel Girard noticed he had lost his wristwatch. To the American's amazement Girard said he was going back after his watch. The American tried to talk him out of it. "For Christ's sake, Colonel, are you crazy? Why get your tail shot off for a forty-dollar wristwatch?" Colonel Girard didn't bother to answer him.

In a short time Girard came crawling back, triumphantly holding up his wristwatch and chuckling.

While we were in London many "V-1 buzz bombs" were coming over and you heard the wail of the air raid sirens at all hours. The buzz bombs came in at the speed of a fighter plane and high enough to fly over the barrage balloons. Their engines made a sharp puttering noise like an outboard motor. When you heard one overhead, and then the engine noise stopped, you knew the engine had cut off automatically and the bomb was gliding down somewhere near you. Instinctively you were trying to guess where the buzz bomb was when the engine cut off. Was it straight overhead? Had it passed beyond you, or off to one side? How close was it? It took from ten to twenty seconds from the time the puttering of the engine stopped until you heard the crash of the bomb. Some of the buzz bombs were shot down by fighter planes before reaching London, some by anti-aircraft, but many got through, sometimes singly, or in small groups, and sometimes in swarms. This went on night and day, sporadically at times and at other times heavy concentrations of them came through and crashed down at scattered points all over the city.

The buzz bombs were thick over London that night and you hardly knew whether a raid was on or not because a few minutes after the "all clear" sounded the alert came on again. We went out into the street to watch during one of the raids. Several times we spotted the red exhaust glow of buzz bombs streaking overhead and heard the puttering engines. We went into a pub on the corner. The barmaid had a thin, pale face and she looked nervous. When she put down my drink her hands shook and she spilled a little. She wiped the table and apologized. Talking very rapidly she said that she had been in London during the Blitz of 1940, but this was worse because at least during the Blitz the night raids only lasted a few hours—and it was really bad then—but when the German bombers left at dawn and the "all clear" sounded you knew it was over and you had lived through that night at least. Now it was almost constant and when you heard the "all clear" it might be only five minutes before another alert came on. She said that this was getting on her nerves in a way the 1940 Blitz never had, and that she thought all Londoners felt as she did.

She went back and began to wipe the top of the bar and I noticed that she kept wiping the same place mechanically, over and over again. Then we heard another buzz bomb, close this time, and when the engine noise suddenly stopped she looked up towards the ceiling as though trying to focus her eyes on that bomb dropping down somewhere in the blackness overhead. In a few seconds there was a loud crash and she hunched her shoulders and closed her eyes. Then she opened them and looked at us with a wan smile.

The pub was not a gay place that night and we went back to our apartment. The "all clear" sounded and we went to bed. There were several other raids during the night and some bombs came close. Once or twice, half awake during the night, I wondered how much more of this the pale-faced barmaid could take.

The next morning we reported to the briefing room on the top floor of our building. Two walls were covered with maps and aerial photographs. As we sat down to wait for Colonel Girard I looked out the window and saw that a helmeted air-raid warden was standing next to a flagpole on the roof of the building across the street. Dillworth explained to us that the air-raid warden was there to spot buzz bombs. When he saw one coming in his general direction he would run up a blue flag as a warning for the neighborhood. When the buzz bomb had passed, or there were none in sight, the warden hauled down his blue flag. I wondered how many people actually watched for the flag and Dillworth said this was mainly for morale purposes to give Londoners the feeling that the Civil Defense Authorities were taking every precaution. Just then the warden ran up his blue flag and faintly in the distance I heard the puttering of a buzz bomb engine, then the noise died out and in a few seconds, from far off, there came a dull crash. The warden hauled down his blue flag. I noticed that the air-raid warden ran up his blue flag and hauled it down in a slow, deliberate way as though he thought the whole thing tedious and unnecessary.

I was standing by the door when it flew open and Colonel

Girard charged in so fast that I had to jump out of the way. He was followed by a sad-faced little sergeant carrying a big briefcase. Colonel Girard was a man in his early fifties with a clipped mustache, big bushy eyebrows and three lines of ribbons on his chest. I noticed, as Jeanpaul had said, the stiff neck and the head tilted to one side. He shook hands all around, opened his briefcase, dumped some more maps on the table and immediately started talking French in staccato bursts, waving his hands in quick, chopping motions and occasionally punctuating his remarks by saying "*bien*" and "*très bien*." He said the zone of operations for both teams was the Ile et Villaine Department in Brittany, including the coastal section around St. Malo, Dinard and Dinan. This was a most important area. "*Bien*." Headquarters had lost all contact with the Maquis there since March because the Gestapo and the SS had picked up the leaders and that whole zone was "*grillé*," that is burned out. But when we jumped in we would re-establish contacts with the Resistance. "*Bien*." Ours was a difficult mission. "*Très bien*." Since there were no contacts in that region we couldn't be dropped there. A blind drop, without a reception committee, was considered too dangerous. So we would be dropped in the Mayenne area, near the little village of Courcité, about 75 miles east of our objective in Brittany. Headquarters had radio contact with a Resistance group there and they would have a reception committee waiting for us when we jumped. It would be difficult for us to get from Courcité to our area in Brittany. "Difficult? Yes. Impossible? No. *Bien*." He picked up a long pointer and banged with it on the wall maps to indicate key points. When he mentioned the port of St. Malo he gave the wall map a hard wallop and the pointer broke off at the handle with a sharp snap, but he kept right on talking, rattling off facts, using the handle as a pointer.

The V-1's were coming in during our briefing. I could see the blue flag going up and coming down and going up again. The V-1's puttered overhead, but Colonel Girard never stopped talking, intent on what he was saying, hitting the maps mighty blows with his broken pointer as though not only he wouldn't be interrupted but that he and his own noise would drown out the outside interference. Even Jeanpaul, cool as always, looked out the window now and then when a buzz bomb sounded a little closer, but not Colonel Girard. On and on he went. "You see these roads (crack went the pointer on the map), and now notice these bridges (again I could see the blue flag going up). We will blow these bridges (the puttering noise of a V-1 over head, then it cuts out), and when you blow those bridges (Crash! A bomb had landed nearby) you will have the Germans bottled up in that part of Brittany. *Bien.* There are twelve bridges to be blown. Major Jeanpaul, you and your team will take those six bridges in the northern zone (slap goes the broken pointer on the map) and Captain Drouant, your team has these six bridges in the southern zone (another sharp slap with the pointer). *Très bien.* (Crash! Another bomb, this time really close.) "Now, one very important point," he went on. "You know the French Army needs artillery. No one knows that better than I do as an old artillery man. How are we to get this artillery? Simple. Capture it from the Germans. Especially the 88's. *Très bien.* Now be very careful: You were in Tunisia, you know what happened there. We would capture artillery, and then what? The Americans would get it away from us some way or another. Not this time. Hang on to those 88's. The hell with the Americans. They have plenty of artillery, we don't. *Bien.*" For the first time in our briefing he stopped talking and looked at me for a moment.

"Excuse me, Captain," he said, and he put down the broken pointer. "I forgot we have an American here. I am sorry, but that's the way it is."

"Yes sir," I said. "That's all right. I understand."

"*Bien.*"

I glanced out and saw that the air-raid warden was hauling down his blue flag. Colonel Girard started in again and went on to other details of the operation. He stressed that when we jumped in our job was to get to Brittany first, then concentrate on organizing and equipping our groups. Weapons would be dropped in to us when we got to our zone. We were to harass the enemy, attack his lines of communication. The bridges were to be blown only when we got the signal. Full-scale operations by the groups we organized were not to start until we got a radio signal in the clear from London. He wanted no premature attacks. The radio signal would come over the BBC and consisted of the sentence, "Is Napoleon's hat still at Perros-Guirrec?"

Then Colonel Girard reminded us that Hitler had recently issued a strict order that all captured commando-type personnel were to be summarily shot, whether in uniform or not. Of course, as the colonel pointed out, this was a violation of the rules of war and the Geneva Convention. It was his opinion that most German commanders would obey this order, and as to the SS it didn't matter for they would have shot you even before Hitler's order. It was clear that Colonel Girard believed all of this was inconsequential and as far as he was concerned it was all very simple: don't get captured, and if you're cornered go down fighting. I thought he was right, and that it was not important, for it was a known risk we assumed. Yet when the Jedburgh operation was planned in 1943 the prisoner-of-war status had been one of the reasons why the teams were to jump in uniform. The other reason, and a much more valid one, was that, since the Maquis men were often a tough and headstrong lot, it would be easier to command these groups if you were dressed for the part, wearing your paratrooper's uniform, insignia of rank, and the winged Special Forces shoulder patch. As the commandant at Milton Hall had explained to us long ago, "Now look here, a bobbie in uniform can exert authority where the same poor chap in plain clothes could do no bloody good at all. Rather obvious, what?"

After his casual reference to Hitler's order Colonel Girard paused, put down his broken pointer, and said, "Now, any questions?"

"Yes sir," said Jeanpaul. "About those twelve bridges. That means we will need a lot of explosives. Can that be laid on?"

"Of course. No problem. You will pick out the dropping zones and we'll get the stuff to you. Besides some of those bridges are not big and a small charge of P. E. will do the job. Next question."

Then to my surprise, our radio operator, Larue, asked the question which I suppose had been in the back of our minds all along but which we didn't want to mention.

"Sir," he said, "moving from Courcité to Brittany in uniform, without any contacts at all, well, won't that be kind of difficult?"

Colonel Girard glared at him. "Lieutenant," he said, pronouncing the word "lieutenant" as though it referred to an obnoxious creature, "I have already said, have I not, that it would be difficult? Difficult but not impossible. Move at night, hide out in the day. Make your own contacts. Use your wits, Lieutenant. You're supposed to be picked men, trained for this kind of mission. *Bien*. Any more questions?"

There were none, so Colonel Girard again shook hands with all of us, wished us luck, said, "*Bien. Très bien,*" and tore out of the room, his sad-faced little sergeant behind carrying that big briefcase.

When he was gone Jeanpaul grinned at me. "I warned you that Colonel Girard was a little peculiar," he said. I told Jeanpaul that he was picking up the British habit of understatement.

We sat around for a while and Jeanpaul and Drouant speculated as to why our two teams had been chosen for this zone of Brittany. We had been told long ago that one of the factors that headquarters would consider in sending a team to a locality was whether the French officer of that team knew that part of the country. But neither Jeanpaul nor Drouant had ever been to this region. Months later I found out the answer. Colonel Girard had a high opinion of both Jeanpaul and Drouant and although he hadn't planned the mission he guessed it would be a hard one and he had insisted that our two teams be picked for it.

Plug Dillworth took us to lunch at the Mirabelle, and during the excellent meal served with vintage wines I was mulling over our briefing. The V-1's were still coming over but I was no longer thinking about buzz bombs or how close they might be. I was thinking of those twelve bridges to be blown, six by our team. Of course I could see, as Colonel Girard had shown on the map, that blowing those bridges could bottle up the Germans in that coastal district of Brittany, but wouldn't this also impede any Allied advance into that zone? Several months before a few of us had been sent to Cambridge for a special three-day intelligence briefing. One of the things we learned there was that after the Normandy beachhead had been established it was imperative that the Allies capture ports to handle the vast flow of supplies. St. Malo seemed to be one of those ports, and I asked myself if sealing off that zone wouldn't conflict with the seizure of ports such as St. Malo. Well, I thought, this is a matter of strategy and that is not my department. I was also thinking that blowing up twelve bridges was quite a project. I remembered Robert Jordan in *For Whom the Bell Tolls* and all the trouble he had dynamiting just one bridge. Before going behind the lines to blow up that one bridge he had been told that destroying that bridge was nothing in itself, blowing it at the right moment was everything. And then the coordination had failed. But I thought that after all this was a novel, and Hemingway was a writer and not a military expert. Here military experts had planned our mission. And yet a doubt persisted. Fine military minds had made blunders before. Was this to be another one, on a very small scale, of course, but involving me? True, I had been greatly impressed with the thoroughness and expertise of the British training staffs at Arisaig and at Milton Hall, but was the planning staff in London as thorough and knowledgeable? Oh to hell with it, I thought, the big thing is to jump in and get on with the show.

After lunch Dillworth got a phone call and then told us that we would not be going in that night. The planes weren't flying, but he didn't know whether this was due to weather over the D/Z or because the Resistance couldn't lay on the operation because of too much German activity or for some other reason. Later that afternoon officers from the Communications Section and the Code Section came over to brief us on our signal plan, schedules, and the frequencies to be used. We were given our code names: our team's name was "Gorin" and Drouant's team was "Gerbe." Whether due to a British weakness in logic, or for some obscure and devious reason, my code name was "Shilling," while Major Jeanpaul, the senior officer, only rated "Sixpence" as his code name. Our radio operator, Lieutenant Larue, became "Penny." We were told the identifying phrase that would be broadcast over BBC in the clear for three nights after our drop. It was "The wines of Anjou will be good this year."

When we finished with that last part of our briefing we went to call on General Pierre Koenig, the commander of the French Forces of the Interior, or FFI, composed of many Maquis groups scattered through all of France and operating under his direct orders. With his erect military bearing and penetrating eyes General Koenig looked like what he was, a soldier's soldier, and in meeting him you didn't feel that natural antipathy that so often exists between staff officers and combat men. The memory of General Koenig's gallant stand with his Free French Forces against the savage assaults of Rommel's Afrika Korps at Bir-Hacheim was enough to dispel any such sentiments. Jeanpaul and Drouant knew him well and after a sharp exchange of salutes they talked together as old friends. It was easy to see General Koenig's pride in these two comrades at arms, and while he was very courteous to both Captain Truffington and myself I could feel that he was really counting on these two French officers, and as far as he was concerned Truffington and I were just along for the ride. Before we left General Koenig he gave us each a "passport" with our name on it. The passport, issued by General Eisenhower and stamped and signed by General Koenig as commanding general of the FFI, was in French on one side and in English on the other. It stated that the named bearer was a regular member of the Allied Forces and requested that he be furnished any assistance possible, including food, shelter and transportation. I have kept it as a souvenir. But I only used it once and then to convince the suspicious commander of an American armored spearhead that I had indeed been behind the enemy lines and that I was not a German agent trying to pose as an American officer.

Early next morning word came through that the operation was set for that night. Late in the afternoon an unmarked Army station wagon took us out to an airport about fifty miles north of London. There we met Major Tomlinson, one of the British Jeds and a close friend of mine. His team had been alerted the day before we were. As always, Tomlinson was jovial and carefree. They were going in that night but to a different area. They had tried the night before but they had run into bad weather and a low ceiling at the dropping zone had forced them to turn back. Tomlinson asked me about our mission and I told him it looked rugged, at least to me if not to the planning staff. That brought a laugh from Tomlinson who described his mission with the standard British expression, "Piece of cake, old boy." It seemed London had received a radio message from the Maquis in his area stating they had even managed to get a few trucks and some gasoline. Tomlinson said he expected to be met by a truck at the dropping zone and taken to a château where he would establish his headquarters and also enjoy the wine cellar. He thought it unfortunate that in the meantime "you poor bastards will be mucking about and bloody lucky to find a barn to hide in." I thanked him heartily for his sympathy and wished him well in his château.

But when I got back to London after our mission I found out that things had not turned out at all as Tomlinson expected. The pilot of his plane had made a slight miscalculation so that when Tomlinson jumped the bomber was flying at an altitude of only about two hundred feet. The chute had barely opened when Tomlinson hit the ground and he had a compound fracture in one leg and a simple fracture in the other. On top of that, a German patrol reached the dropping zone a few minutes after Tomlinson's team landed, due either to bad luck or because they had been tipped off. Tomlinson's radio operator dragged him away and they hid in a swamp for twelve hours while the Germans combed the area. Eventually the Maquis managed to hide them, not in a chateau but in a barn. A French doctor made it to the barn the next night and did what he could for Tomlinson, and in the meantime the Maquis were able to make radio contact with London and report Tomlinson's injury. Two nights later, in a daring operation, a Lysander plane the size of a Piper Cub swooped into a nearby field, and Tomlinson was rushed aboard and flown back to London. When I saw Major Tomlinson months later he was on crutches but still in fine spirits. I thought it best not to ask him about the château and its wine cellar.

After supper at the airport we again went over our final instructions with Major Dillworth and checked our equipment for the last time. Dillworth insisted that we take dexedrine tablets, saying we had a long, hard night ahead of us. I told him I was charged up enough as it was and didn't need his tablets. We were taken to the dressing room where parachute fitters had our chutes out and were ready to help us put on our equipment and fit the chutes. I was jumping in with a lot of equipment, including my carbine strapped across my chest, the barrel pressing uncomfortably against my collarbone. On top of the carbine was my musette bag filled with emergency rations, a first-aid kit which included a small syringe of morphine, and extra clips of ammunition. A canteen full of water was hooked to my belt as was my .45 pistol and my commando knife. My binoculars were hung around my shoulders. Around my waist and under my shirt was my bulging money belt. An escape kit containing water-purifying tablets and an assortment of ingenious items such as a tiny compass made to look like an ordinary button was stuffed in one pocket of my jump jacket. In another pocket I had jammed my toilet articles, a flashlight, two pipes and a pouch of tobacco. Strapped to my back was a large map case, the size of a telephone directory, containing maps, code books and cypher pads. I even carried a mess tin and knife, fork and spoon, which was ridiculous, and a small flask of very strong rum, which was not. The rum was issued as standard equipment when you jumped in and it reminded me of the British practice aboard warships of giving seamen a tot of rum before battle.

I put on my camouflaged "strip tease" jacket over all of this equipment. The strip tease was a loose fitting smock with a zipper front, worn over your uniform and your equipment so as to cover any projecting parts of your gear which might otherwise get caught in your risers when you jumped and thus tangle your chute. The parachute fitter tugged and pulled and grunted and I was bending over and trying to make myself smaller as I tried to squeeze into the strip tease. It was exactly like a fat woman (or perhaps any woman) struggling to get into her girdle. I then put on my jump helmet, a regulation steel battle helmet with a special chin strap. Finally the parachute was attached to my back with its broad straps running tightly across my chest and through my legs and then hooked up in the back. When the parachute fitter and I got through I found that I could hardly walk, not because of the extra weight but because everything felt so tight and binding that I had to walk spread-legged, with short, jerky steps.

It was time to go out to the B-24 bomber on a runway at the far end of the field. Team "Gorin" was going on one bomber and team "Gerbe" in a second plane timed to arrive at the dropping zone a few minutes after we did. There was a station wagon ready to take us to our plane. Loaded down and bulging as we were, we had to get into the car backwards, the driver inside yanking on each man while the parachute fitters and Dillworth shoved from the outside. When we reached the plane we had to go through the same gymnastics to get out. The plane's crew was standing by the bomber and they laughed as they saw us squeeze slowly out of the station wagon and waddle towards them. The pilot came up to me and said, in the jargon of paratroopers, "Just three bodies, right, Captain? Plus your containers." I said, "Right." The pilot said he had carefully checked our course with his Air Corps briefing officer and we shouldn't have too much trouble on this run. We were avoiding the known flak areas, weather reports were good, and night fighters hadn't been spotted in that zone during the past week.

We smoked a last cigarette as the crew climbed aboard and started to warm up the engines. Dillworth shook hands, patted us on the back and said something which was impossible to hear over the roar of the engines. We got aboard the plane, with much tugging and pulling, and sat down on the floor, our legs stretched out, close to the bomb bay. The roar of the engines grew louder, died down as the pilot throttled down to check his instruments, then built up again as the plane taxied to the end of the field. The pilot gunned his engines and the big bomber shot down the runway, racing for the take-off and bumping slightly along the ground. Suddenly the jolting stopped. We were up and on our way. I looked at my watch. It was 10:45, exactly the time set for take-off. The plane climbed to 8,000 feet. I had stood up and was looking out the small window of the fuselage. It was not yet dark and the blackout curtain had not been pulled. We were flying over layers of white clouds and occasionally, through a break in the clouds, you could see the countryside far below, looking a dark grayish green in the twilight. Then we crossed the English coast, stretched out in a wavy line, and beyond that lay the Channel as far as you could see. When the sun went down it got dark very quickly. The despatcher blacked out the window and I sat down again.

Since our bomber would fly a zigzag course it would take perhaps an hour and a half to reach the dropping zone. There was nothing to do except sit there and let thoughts drift through your mind to the accompaniment of the loud, steady, monotonous drone of the engines. In looking back now I am surprised (perhaps I shouldn't be) at the unusual ideas and recollections that can flash unexpectedly before you at a time like this, and yet these things appear and reappear almost in rhythm, ebbing and flowing, with no conscious direction. I looked over at Jeanpaul sitting with his eyes closed. He could have been asleep, but I was sure he was not, that like myself he must be thinking. Thinking of what, I wondered? When we were packing to leave Milton Hall I noted with surprise that he had put all his medals in a leather case which was placed inside one of our containers. Why had he done that? He was certainly not a vain man. But just how and where did he ever expect to wear his medals behind the lines? I thought of the medieval knight going into a tourney with his plume proudly waving atop his helmet. Was it possible that in some curious way the medals replaced the plume, even though he would not be wearing them? But this was a romantic notion which didn't seem characteristic of Jeanpaul. Was it Napoleon who had said, "*On trouvera toujours des hommes qui se feront casser la gueulle pour un petit bout de ruban*"? (You will always find men willing to get shot up for a little piece of ribbon.) Yet this would be, as I well know, a somewhat cynical and unfair view of Jeanpaul's motivation. In the first place the reverse was certainly true: you could find many more men who had no desire whatever to get shot up for any piece of ribbon. What Jeanpaul had done, and what he would do, could never be due to a yearning for a "little piece of ribbon." But nevertheless those "little pieces of ribbon" were recognized—and by Jeanpaul himself—as badges of valor and honor.

Suddenly, although I had not read it in years, I remembered some lines from William Morris's poem "The Gilliflower of Gold," and I had a picture of the knight on his prancing horse, entering the tourney wearing upon his helmet the gilliflower given him by the woman he loved.

> "A golden gilliflower today
> I wore upon my helm away
> And won the prize of this tourney.
> Hah! Hah! *la belle jaune giroflée!*"

And as I watched the blackout curtain vibrating to the throb of the motors, the words of the refrain, "Hah! Hah! *la belle jaune giroflée!*" paraded in front of my eyes, over and over again as they did after each stanza of the poem.

Staring at the vibrating curtain, hearing the constant throb of the engines, produced almost a hypnotic effect. It was as though I were in a trance and one-half of myself, outside of me somewhere, were watching the other half inside the bomber, or maybe it was the other way around. From far back at memory's edge sharp pictures leaped back to me and I saw myself as a boy walking with my mother and the blind captain through the Luxembourg Gardens, and then I was standing again in the Invalides gazing up in awe at the suspended plane of Charles Guynemer. This reverie was shattered by a series of loud bursts from our bomber's machine guns. Larue jumped excitedly to his feet. He had apparently forgotten that we had been told the pilot would test his guns over the Channel. Jeanpaul opened his eyes, looked with amusement at Larue and told him something I couldn't hear. Larue sat down slowly, mumbling to himself and not appearing fully reassured.

Again I became locked in my thoughts. Between now and our drop many things might happen over which I had no control, and it was worse than useless to think of them. I was feeling fatalistic, "what must be, must be." Scattered lines from one of Shakespeare's plays came to me: "A man can die but once—we owe God a death—he who dies this year is quit for the next." But how did the whole passage go, and from what play was it? I couldn't remember. At least if I die in the great unknown that lies ahead, I have died for a purpose. That is stupid thinking, a part of myself told the other part, you are not going to die. That is the way to look at it, the only way.

Then I thought of how I had gone to Church and confession that morning in London. I had not been to Church in a long time. That was really hypocritical, I said to myself; you run to God when you think you may be in trouble. But the priest had been very understanding, and I imagined that he had a kindly smile as he sat there on the other side of the grille in the confessional. Surely he sounded like he had heard many such last-minute confessions. And anyway, if God was as merciful as we had been told—even though He must have a strong dislike for hypocrites—then He would make allowances for me. There you go, I thought, grade school theology. And besides this is anthropomorphism. But why would an odd word like "anthropomorphism" now jump out at me, seated in a bomber speeding through the night to a secret rendezvous in France? Never mind. The important thing, I thought, the all important thing, is that I do my best so that when it is all over, no matter how it ends, no one can rightly say I should have done more.

All of a sudden, my mood changed. And I smiled to myself as I thought of the nice touch of British humor in calling the men at the dropping zone a "Reception Committee." I remembered other reception committees, the men in formal attire, the white ties, the carnation boutonnieres. If I ever saw such a reception committee again I would always think of another kind, the kind now moving cautiously in the dark towards our D/Z. And still smiling inwardly, I gazed fixedly at the blackout curtain vibrating, vibrating, vibrating. What was the one thing I must remember now? "Go out like a Guardsman, sir!" Yes, that was it. That I had to do. One more thing: try to land relaxed and easy, "like a sack of you know what, sir!" Then an unwanted thought forced itself on me, although I tried to shove it back down and out of my mind. I was thinking of my bad ankle. The medics had taped it and I had put an elastic support over the tape before slipping on my jump boot and lacing it very tightly. I hoped the ankle would hold up, and also that in landing I wouldn't injure the good ankle by favoring the bad one. And then I looked back with amusement on one of the instructors at Ringway Parachute School telling us nonchalantly, "See here, this is the way you chaps should think about parachuting: it's just another way of getting from a plane to the ground, right? And any bloody fool who has jumped off a moving bus, or a streetcar, well, he ought to be able to do this, right?"

We flew on for about an hour and like Jeanpaul I had now closed my eyes and felt almost sleepy. When I opened my eyes again I saw that the despatcher was now standing. He was a lanky, freckle-faced kid and he was chewing gum as he listened to the pilot over his intercom headphones. "We ought to be getting to the dropping zone soon," he said, leaning towards us. "Pilot says weather is good, not too much wind, no sign of night fighters." The despatcher added, "I guess I'd better get you guys hooked up now." Half an hour before he had looked half asleep. Now he was wide awake and alert, darting sharp glances at us. We could feel the beginning of tension in ourselves and in the despatcher. He hooked us up each in turn to his own static line, carefully checking the lines. Automatically, as we had been trained to do, I watched him as he hooked me up and showed me the safety pin in proper position.

The long months of training were over; the moment of truth was almost here. I felt ready. The roar of the engines cut down a little. I could tell we were losing altitude steadily, and I could feel the change of pressure in my ears. The plane was beginning to bank and turn. Getting near the target the pilot was circling and looking for the pin-points of light which would show where the field was. Abruptly the despatcher walked to the bomb-bay doors and said, "Pilot says he's spotted the field. We're circling now and getting ready to come in." He opened the bomb-bay doors in the floor and that hole that we would have to jump through suddenly opened up beside us looking black and ominous. So here it was, any minute now. The despatcher looked back at us and shouted "Pilot says he's wishing you guys luck." He was getting excited now and chewing his gum furiously. Looking at me he yelled, "Give 'em hell when you get in there, sir, give 'em hell!" I said, "Good luck to you guys on the way back," but he didn't hear me. He was busy listening on the intercom and watching the panel of signal lights over the bomb bay. The plane was coming down lower and lower and losing speed. The throb of the engines had died down to a low hum. The plane was beginning to lurch a little and feel heavy as the pilot slowed down and headed for his run over the target. Suddenly the despatcher twisted around to face us. The red light on the panel had flashed on.

"Running in!" he shouted. Quickly we checked our jumping positions. "Action stations!" the despatcher yelled. Jeanpaul swung over with his legs dangling over the open bomb bay, watching for the final signal from the despatcher standing there, his right hand raised. The green light came on. "Go!" the despatcher shouted, chopping his hand down sharply, and Jeanpaul shot out through the hole. The despatcher yelled, "Go!" again, but by that time Larue was halfway out, and as the despatcher shouted "Go!" a third time and jerked his hand down I flung myself out of the hole.

I went out and down and into the darkness. And like a gigantic slap in the face the blast from the propellers hit me and I was tumbling down and down and then there was that violent jerk at my shoulders and the sound of rustling silk overhead and I looked up and saw that my chute had opened perfectly and the rigging lines weren't tangled and twisted. There I was, swaying gently, but it was the dark ground below that seemed to be swaying. Off in the distance I could hear the fading sound of the bomber's engines and see the four stabs of red light from the exhausts. And I thought here I am, coming down to God knows what, but my exit had been good and the chute had opened and developed as it should. Below me I could see the up-turned flashlights of the reception committee. They were well off to one side so the pilot had not made a perfect approach and I would not land in the field. Looking down it was hard to make out what lay below. Then I saw some trees and the corner of some woods, and I thought this looks as if it will be a tree landing. The ground, dark and obscure, still looked far beneath me as I drifted down.

All of a sudden, not twenty feet below me, there was the ground rushing up to meet me, and in the next second I hit. It was a very good landing, a soft landing, and immediately as I hit I knew that my bad ankle was all right.

As I got up I saw that I had dropped in a pasture off to one side of the landing field. I unbuckled my chute, and since there was no wind to carry it away I let it fall to the ground. I unzipped my strip tease and took it off. Now I could move freely. I crouched low, got out my .45 pistol, cocked it, and looked around. There was nothing to be seen, nothing moving. No sign of Jeanpaul and Larue. I felt fine and confident. Then off on a road close by I heard the sound of horses' hoofs and the rumble of wagon wheels. It sounded like many wagons. For a second I thought these were farmers, but of course that couldn't be, for with the German curfew on, farmers would not be out in wagons after dark. It had to be a German convoy. In the American Army, where everything moved by truck, we sometimes tended to forget that the Germans, short on trucks and especially on gasoline, sometimes had convoys of horse-drawn wagons. The Germans in the convoy must have heard our plane and even spotted our chutes as we came down. They would send out an alarm and we would have to move out very fast.

There was still no sign of any of the reception committee. I started to roll up my chute but then I stopped because I didn't want to be busy rolling up my chute if there were Germans around. It was very still now, a ghostly silence in the pale light of the half moon and yet as I crouched in the empty field I had the feeling that in those shadowy woods to my right someone was watching me. I remembered my flask of rum and I got it out and took a good swallow. It tasted strong and good and I took another big gulp.

Minutes passed and I had decided to look for the others when I heard noises in the underbrush about one hundred yards away. Then I saw two dark figures approaching very cautiously. Who were they? Maquis or Germans? I wasn't sure as I watched, half crouched, pistol in hand, but I decided they must be men from the reception committee. I stood up and gave a low whistle. They kept coming, still walking slowly, step by step. When they got closer I could see that they were dressed in civilian clothes and were carrying Sten submachine guns pointed straight at me. A Sten gun is treacherous and can easily go off accidentally. I hoped they knew how to handle their weapons and that they were not trigger happy.

When they got about fifty feet away I said, "I am Captain Dreux of the American Army," thinking at the time that never before had I introduced myself under such peculiar circumstances. One of them said, "All right, follow us." I asked what about my chute and he said orders were personnel first, the chute would be picked up later. As I was walking away the second plane made its run over the field. I saw the men jump and the three chutes opening. They had overshot the field and were also far off to one side.

I kept following the men who never spoke a word. After about a quarter of a mile we came to a small clump of trees and there were several men standing there, talking in whispers. One of them came up to introduce himself. His name was Raseur and he was the leader of the reception committee. When I asked where the other paratroopers were he said that one French officer was sitting down by a hedge a short distance away. They were still looking for the third man and for the containers that had been dropped in with us. He had sent men to try to find the men and containers that had come down from the second plane, but it wasn't going to be easy because there was a swamp in the vicinity.

I walked over to the hedge and saw Jeanpaul sitting there. He looked up and smiled, saying that he had landed very hard, his legs felt numb, but he thought he was all right. Larue walked up then, led by one of the resistance men. Larue had hit the ground so hard that he was dazed when he got up, and after shedding his chute he had galloped off into the woods, crashing through the underbrush. The Resistance men located him by the noise and corralled him. Now he had pulled himself together. In an intense, low whisper he started to tell us with vivid profanity exactly what he thought of our pilot for missing the field, and also in general what he thought of the Air Corps. Jeanpaul cut him off instantly and Larue subsided, muttering a few obscenities.

We waited for the others. It seemed a long time before Raseur came up with Captain Drouant and the other men of his team. They had been lucky, for although they had missed the field by at least three-quarters of a mile they had landed in another field and aside from contusions and bruises they were in good shape. Descartes told of his narrow escape. He had missed a high-tension line by inches as he came down, jerking his feet up desperately at the last second. As Descartes described this and his feelings about his pilot and the Air Corps, his obscenities were more varied than Larue's and he used a few words I had never heard. He too was told to shut up.

A few minutes later Raseur came up to us and said that we had to get out immediately, there were Germans prowling not far away. The Germans, he told us, probably knew about this field. It had been used before for drops of matériel but never for parachutists. Then there was the convoy that had passed who might have given the alarm. All the containers had been found except one, and the chutes and empty containers would be buried later. There was no time for that now. I thought then of how we had been trained at Milton Hall in the technique of burying chutes and containers, carefully cutting the sod in squares, removing and scattering the dirt, and then replacing the sod piece by piece so that no signs of digging were visible. This was just one of the skills we had learned but would not put to use.

When we got our equipment together from the containers the men had brought in we learned that the radio and extra weapons for Drouant's team had been smashed in the drop.

Raseur said he would hide us out that night in a nearby farmhouse. This was risky, he told us, because if the Germans suspected men had been dropped that night the first thing they would do would be to raid all the farms in the vicinity. But the two "safe houses" he wanted to use, one for each team, were not available that night. The next night one of his men would lead Drouant's team to a "safe house" on the outskirts of Courcité while he would take us to the church rectory in Courcité, also a "safe house." I wondered at the time just how "safe" the rectory would be in a German-held village, but Raseur seemed to know his business and he spoke with authority. We gathered up our gear to follow him.

One of the men who had led me in was carrying my chute. Like all paratroopers I wanted to cut off a large strip to keep as a souvenir, but the others were walking away fast so I yanked out my knife and quickly cut off a short piece from one of the risers. I caught up with the others and we moved away across the fields.

We soon arrived at a small farm where Raseur told us to climb up in the hayloft and have a man on guard at all times. After Raseur and the others had left, Jeanpaul said he would keep the first watch and I snuggled down in the hay. I tried to think of what we would do if an enemy patrol came but after a while I fell asleep.

It was early morning when Jeanpaul shook me awake to stand watch. I looked out and saw lush green meadows wet with dew, and hedgerows and patches of woods. Cows were grazing in the pasture and in the barnyard a few roosters strutted and crowed. It was such a quiet pastoral scene that for a moment I had difficulty realizing that we were behind enemy lines. What a strange way to come back to France, I thought. Yesterday I was enjoying the luxuries of London and now this. Suddenly I stiffened. From a distance I could hear the sound of motors, and as the noise grew louder it sounded like two or three staff cars. The cars came closer, heading down the road running past the farm. I could see a little cloud of dust above the hedgerows screening the road. The cars slowed down as they came opposite the farm and I was about to wake Jeanpaul. Then they speeded up again and I relaxed. A little later I heard a motorcycle going past, and then a convoy of trucks. This time there was a big cloud of dust which slowly settled.

During the day a plump farm girl brought us food and a big jug of cider. She did this very quietly, whispering a few words. It was long after dark when Raseur and one of his men came for us. Jeanpaul insisted on thanking the farmer personally so he and I and Drouant went inside. The farmer, an elderly and gaunt-looking man, was lying in bed with a comforter pulled up to his chin. He appeared sick, peering at us through half-closed eyes. When Jeanpaul thanked him, leaving some money on the bedside table to pay for our food, the farmer mumbled something I couldn't understand. We joined the others and set out for Courcité.

CHAPTER VIII

The Hideout in the Rectory

As we left the farm Raseur and one of his men carried part of our gear, but even so we all had heavy loads. In addition to the weapons and equipment strapped on us when we jumped, we were lugging the matériel from the containers, including Sten submachine guns, ammunition clips, the radio and generator, and our bulging rucksacks stuffed with a sleeping bag, extra clothes, concentrated rations and cartons of cigarettes. We looked like coolies as we followed Raseur across several plowed fields. I had not bothered to hook my rucksack on my back and I had it slung over my left shoulder so that I plodded with a hard list to port. We reached a narrow road, walking in single file, and after about a mile we came to an intersection. A tall stone Calvary stood at the crossroad and in the dim glow of the half moon the cross, with its arms stretched wide, cast an eerie and mysterious shadow on the white gravel road. We were at the outskirts of the village and as we moved quietly down the still and deserted street, half bent over with our loads, I hoped that Raseur knew what he was doing but I remembered what the OSS recruiting officer at Fort Benning had said about "maximum casualties." And now we might die stupidly because as we were trudging down the street of an occupied village we could suddenly run into German sentries and before being able to drop our gear and reach for our pistols or carbines they would open up with their quick-firing *Schmeisser* submachine guns and the adventure would end at its beginning.

But so far there had been no Germans. We arrived at a square and I could see a large church with a high steeple, pale gray in the soft moonlight, and I sensed rather than saw that it was very old and that with its worn and weathered stones it must have stood in the square for centuries, solid and firm. For a moment I imagined the bell tolling the Angelus in years gone by, and the peasants standing in their fields, heads bowed and caps off. Raseur took us to the side of the rectory where he knocked gently at the door. It was opened immediately by a sturdy, gray-haired priest standing in the poorly lighted hallway. As we came in he smiled and shook hands, looking us in the eye. He had a warm smile, and as I saw his strong, deeply lined face and his calm expression I felt that he must be a typical country curé, a man of deep and simple faith. He and his old church have lived together for a long time, I thought, and each in a way is part of the other. We dumped our equipment on the floor. When he saw this big pile and noticed our uniforms the curé stopped smiling. He frowned as he turned to Raseur. "Frankly," he told him, "I wasn't expecting anything like this. I thought I would be hiding three agents in civilian clothes. Instead I get three paratroopers in full uniform with pistols, carbines, Sten guns, knives, and the Good Lord knows what else. Probably a radio too."

"It's all right, Father," said Raseur. "It's going to work out fine. I assume full responsibility." He looked at his watch. "It's one o'clock," he said. "They will stay here today and I'll move them out tonight."

I had my first good look at Raseur then as he stood there, holding his Sten gun in the crook of his arm. He was about my age, with a flat nose and jutting chin, and he needed a shave. His trousers were baggy and muddy and his dark turtle-neck sweater was torn at the shoulder so that his skin showed. He looks tough all right, I said to myself, and not the type that the vicar in London would have invited for tea.

The curé was still frowning and said to Jeanpaul, "You know, there are a good many Germans around here."

"Yes, Father, we know that."

The curé smiled faintly. "You aren't planning on turning my rectory into a pillbox, are you?"

"No, Father, we don't want to be under siege any more than you do."

"Please come with me," the curé said and we picked up our equipment and followed him upstairs. He showed us our bedroom and said that it was away from the street and faced the back yard. We saw two bedrooms directly across the corridor from ours. Tacked on each door was a sign printed in French and German stating that the room had been requisitioned by the German Army for use as officers' billets. The curé saw us looking at these two signs. "Yes," he said. "A major came here some time ago to requisition both rooms. So it is possible that two German officers may show up to claim these rooms." Again he smiled briefly. "Of course if that happens while you're here, well, it could be embarrassing."

We sat down and the curé picked up one of the Sten guns, held it up to his shoulder, sighted along the barrel, then put it down and shrugged his shoulders. I looked around the room. A large wooden crucifix was above the bed, gaudy holy pictures hung on the walls, and an old, badly chipped statue of the Virgin stood on a table in the corner with a small vase of flowers beside it. There was something incongruous in the contrast between the religious atmosphere of the room, the priest sitting there, and ourselves with our arsenal. It was as though you saw three convicts in prison garb wandering around the lobby of a bank and chatting with the cashiers. The curé watched me as I got up to look at the two signs again and then he started to tell us about the major who had come about the rooms. "He was a real Prussian type," he said, "tall, ramrod straight, stern face, immaculate uniform and the Iron Cross medal on his chest, the gloves held in the left hand, everything but a monocle. When he called on me he clicked his heels, gave a stiff little bow and then talked French, slowly and with a heavy German accent, but good French just the same. After the papers were signed and the two signs posted on the doors he told me he hoped for more harmonious relations between the people of the village and the German troops. All he got from me was a cold look."

I was sleepy and did not feel like listening to what might be a long story, but the curé went on, "The major told me he had visited France before the war, and he loved France deeply. This infuriated me. 'That's the trouble with you Germans,' I told him. 'You love France so deeply that three times in the past seventy years you have made pilgrimages to France. But these pilgrimages have always been made by the German Army.' " The curé stopped and looked at us but we didn't say anything. "The major stared at me then," the curé continued, "and said something about history being a long record of wars and it was not easy to tell who was right and who was wrong, nor how right or how wrong. Well, naturally, I couldn't let that go and I told him history did not judge that it was Belgium which attacked Germany in 1914, nor would history report that Belgium attacked Germany in this war."

I started to yawn and the curé saw me. "I'm sorry," he said, "you need rest badly and here I am telling you about this German major. Good night. It is really good to have you here." He got up, shook hands with us, and left the room. The curé is just being polite, I thought, he doesn't like this one bit and I can't blame him. I flopped down on the big brass bed and Larue unrolled his sleeping bag on the floor and stretched out for the night.

Jeanpaul opened the commode by the bed and discovered a chamber pot which he held up for us to see. It was a beautiful chamber pot of shining white porcelain with a row of delicate pink cherubs chasing each other gleefully around the rim. The chamber pot amused Jeanpaul. He said it was a work of art, probably an antique, and an authority on the lore of chamber pots could undoubtedly trace it back to some medieval prince. In his opinion, this "*magnifique pot de chambre*," as he smilingly called it, belonged in a museum, maybe the Louvre, a point which I thought of relatively little interest. After putting it back in the commode Jeanpaul lay down on the other side of the bed. None of us undressed, only loosening the laces on our jump boots.

We awoke early the next morning and soon afterward our breakfast was brought to us by the curé's housekeeper, an elderly woman with a pleasant, crinkled face. There was coffee, surprisingly good even though it was ersatz, two long loaves of French bread, and lots of butter. The housekeeper seemed cheerful and unconcerned, as though serving breakfast to three Allied paratroopers in hiding was a routine matter. She was accompanied by a big Alsatian dog who sniffed us and wagged his tail. She told us that his name was Casablanca and that he was called Casa for short. The housekeeper gave no explanation for the dog's name but she said that Casa was a wonderful watchdog and that with him around we had nothing to worry about. The dog looked fat and placid and I didn't think her confidence was well founded.

After breakfast we found a staircase at the far end of the corridor. We climbed to an attic and decided to set up our radio there. A large window in the attic gave a full view of the quiet and peaceful square. But this was the battlefront for us now and tough *Wehrmacht* veterans and the Gestapo were ready to pounce if we made a false move. The day before yesterday in London, with the V-1's coming over, the war had seemed so much closer. A few farmers sauntered by and one of them stopped at a water pump in one corner of the square. It was an old-fashioned rusty-looking village pump, the kind you thought had gone out of existence long ago, and we saw the farmer work the long pump handle up and down to fill his bucket. We gazed for a few minutes when suddenly two German officers walked briskly into the square and sat at a café opposite the rectory. This was the first time I had seen German soldiers and a vague feeling of hate and curiosity came over me. The officers were served coffee and then one of them, a fat, red-faced man, leaned back and guffawed as he slapped his friend on the back. This made me mad, and for a second I had the wild impulse to unsling my carbine and pick him off. At that short range it would have been a cinch. Then I smiled and thought this was the kind of crazy idea that the impulsive Farley might have but even he would not have carried it through.

While Larue was getting the radio ready, Jeanpaul and I went down to our room and coded a short message for London saying that both teams had arrived safely, that the radio of Drouant's team had been smashed in the drop, and that we would leave Courcité that night and then try to make contact with the Maquis in Brittany. At nine o'clock sharp, right on schedule, we came on the air and sent our message, Larue tapping away at the key, earphones on, while I turned the crank of the generator. Reception was good at both ends and London did not ask for a repeat of any part of the message. Larue was elated at how well things had gone and he said the London operator must be a good man. Larue had a fixed idea that if he had trouble in getting a message through, as did happen a few days later, it was not due to atmospheric disturbances, and of course never his fault. It was always the fault of the London operator whom Larue cursed as an "*espèce d'imbécile,*" "*cochon,*" and "*couillon.*" "*Putain de putain*" he reserved for moments of real stress, but he could work up from this to a crescendo of colorful and truly impressive epithets. I enjoyed these episodes, and they enriched my French vocabulary which I felt was limited in such matters.

Larue and I hid our radio as best we could and went back to our room. Jeanpaul was sitting on the edge of the bed studying a Michelin road map of the region. Larue told him that he had sent our message, and the way he described it gave the impression that he and Marconi had much in common. We talked of the road network leading out of the Courcité area west towards Brittany. All of a sudden we heard knocking at the door downstairs, an excited, low-voiced conversation, then someone was rushing up the stairs. Larue and I grabbed our pistols out of their holsters, jumped to the other side of the room and stood half-crouched, covering the door and ready to fire. Out of the corner of my eye I could see Jeanpaul, still sitting calmly on the bed, looking at us with a sardonic smile as though we were putting on a silly Wild West display. Jeanpaul was right—the Germans would hardly have sent only one man after us like that—and it was Raseur who burst into the room looking very excited. Feeling foolish, I put my pistol back in the holster.

"For God's sake," said Raseur, trying to catch his breath, "are you using your radio? Shut it down! Shut it down! There's a D/F truck out there!"

Jeanpaul hadn't budged and his lean face was impassive except that his eyes now had a sharp glint. "Steady now, Raseur," he said, "we're not on the air. We got off the air at least five minutes ago."

"Holy God, Major! How long were you on? They must have picked you up!"

"We were on for only four or five minutes, probably less," I said. I felt fear twisting around in my guts but I was trying hard to appear imperturbable like Jeanpaul.

Jeanpaul was staring hard at Raseur. "Are you sure it was a D/F truck?" he asked.

"Good God, Major! Of course I'm sure. I saw what looked like an ordinary supply truck going up and down the street. Then it circled the square. I wondered why. The curtains on the back of the truck were closed. Then a German poked his head out for only a second. He was wearing earphones. Do you understand, Major? Earphones! What's a soldier in a supply truck doing with earphones, eh? *Nom de Dieu!* I'm sure!"

"All right," said Jeanpaul. "Wait here for me. Bill, Larue, up to the attic!"

Larue and I rushed after him and we looked out the attic window. No sign of the D/F truck, no unusual activity in the square. The two German officers were still at the café. Larue looked like a man in court who has just received the death sentence. Finally he said in a sort of high-pitched whisper, "*Ah ça alors, mon Commandant! Ah les salauds! Putain de putain!* What do we do now?"

"Right now, Larue, we do nothing," said Jeanpaul. "Now listen to me. You stay here and watch the square. Don't take your eyes off of it. If you see anything out of the ordinary, anything at all, report to me at once. Is that clear, Larue?" Jeanpaul had not raised his voice but it had a cutting edge.

"Yes sir," answered Larue. He stood facing Jeanpaul, his big powerful body very erect and his feet together as though he were at attention on the parade ground, but his eyes were darting back and forth between Jeanpaul and the window. When Jeanpaul and I got back to our room Raseur was pacing up and down. The curé was there now and he was sitting with his arms folded. He was tight-lipped and his expression was grave but he seemed calm.

"All right, Major," said Raseur, still walking back and forth. "Let's face it. Right now you're trapped here. You can't move."

"What about the back way?" asked Jeanpaul. "Going out through the backyard there?"

"No, no! You'd have to climb over that stone wall, then cross several streets before hitting the open fields. In those uniforms you'd be spotted right away." The curé nodded his head in agreement.

Jeanpaul sat down looking thoughtful. He was clenching and unclenching his right fist and I had never seen him do that before. "Let's summarize where we stand," he said, speaking rapidly, and he began ticking off the points on his fingers. "One, that D/F truck may not have picked us up at all, or anyway not enough to get any kind of a fix. Remember, we were only on the air for a few minutes. Two, they may have picked us up and got a fix. Then within a half hour—I'd guess an hour at the outside—our German friends will be here." He looked at his watch, and so did I. It was exactly nine twenty-five. "If that happens," Jeanpaul went on, "we'll have to try to shoot our way out and make a break out the back." Raseur started to say something but Jeanpaul impatiently held up his hand and cut him off. "Three, we can't go out the back way now, not from what you tell me. So we'll stay here and wait. Now four, we need lookouts. I have a man up in the attic watching the square. As to you, Raseur, I expect your men to act as lookouts in the village. Any suspicious movement, try to get the word to me as fast as you can. I think that covers it for now." Jeanpaul looked around at the curé and Raseur who like me had been obviously intrigued by Jeanpaul's matter-of-fact enumeration of his points. For although Jeanpaul had spoken quickly, it was done quietly, almost casually, like an instructor officer giving a resumé to a class of cadets.

"Bill," said Jeanpaul, "do you agree with me?" The question seemed to come as an afterthought and even though I had some reservations I said that I agreed completely.

"That's about it, Major," said Raseur. He was sitting now, tense but no longer excited. He had shaved since last night but he looked like he had then, the hard-faced leader of a Maquis group. "We'll try to get word to you," said Raseur. "Damn rotten luck, though. No D/F truck around here for months. Maybe they're after our radio. We used it the day before yesterday to contact London about your drop. What a mess! *Nom de Dieu!* Excuse me, Father."

"The Germans are incredibly methodical," said Jeanpaul thoughtfully, "so if the D/F truck got a good fix their report will probably have to go through channels—especially with a rectory involved—and it will take a little time before a raid is ordered. Otherwise, we could expect a little visit from *messieurs les Allemands* any minute."

"So what? That doesn't help matters," said Raseur.

"Of course not. I'm just gambling now that they didn't pick us up." Jeanpaul turned to the curé. "Father, I'm terribly sorry we've put you in this difficult position."

"Difficult position?" The curé had a half-smile. "Well, Major, it isn't the first time I've been in a 'difficult position' as you put it. I don't look terribly frightened, do I?"

"No, Father, you certainly don't. You're taking it better than our radio operator. He's a little upset. Acting as though it were his fault."

The curé and Raseur left the room and Jeanpaul and I went to the window to look again at the backyard. The housekeeper in her homespun black dress was in the vegetable patch picking string-beans. She kept turning her head and looking around and I decided she had been told by the curé to keep a close watch. I was thinking of Jeanpaul's decision to stay put and wait. One thing was sure: if the Germans came it would be impossible to hide ourselves and our radio in the rectory. This was no Gothic castle with secret rooms and passageways. Five hundred years ago we could have taken refuge in the sanctuary of the church and no one would have dared to touch us there for this was a holy place, but now it was 1944 and there was no sanctuary. Be that as it may, would it be better to try the back way now despite what Raseur had said? Or what about having a farmer with a big hay cart pull up next to the back wall? We would climb over, hide in the hay with our radio, and escape. I asked Jeanpaul but he shook his head.

"Neither one would work, Bill. Look, I can't be sure I've made the right decision," and he gave me a piercing look, "but I think I have."

We left the room and went to the head of the stairs, studying the layout of the corridor and the steps with their balustrade. He was thinking, as I was, of how we could shoot our way out, but neither one of us mentioned it. We went back to the attic, Jeanpaul whistling softly under his breath. Larue was watching the square intently and barely turned his head. He said there was nothing suspicious going on. We looked out on the square. The two officers at the café were still there. Four soldiers on bicycles pedalled by. Then three trucks loaded with troops drove rapidly through the square and after they had passed we could hear the rumbling noise fading away so we knew they had not stopped nearby and out of sight. We went back to our room and I looked at my watch. Nine thirty-five, exactly a half hour since we had gone off the air. Jeanpaul stood, hands on hips, observing the yard. I sat down and got out my pipe and tobacco and concentrated on filling the pipe slowly and deliberately instead of cramming it full quickly as I usually did. After lighting my pipe I took out my pistol, removed the clip, worked the slide back and forth, and snapped the trigger several times. The gun felt heavy and reassuring in my hand. I forced myself not to look at my watch again. Jeanpaul left the window and stretched out on the bed. Good Christ, I thought, I know he's a cool customer but this is too much. Then I noticed that as he stared at the ceiling his fist was clenching and unclenching again. In a few minutes he started to chuckle.

"What's the matter?" I asked him, not aware of anything particularly funny.

"I was thinking of Colonel Girard," he answered, "and his *idée fixe* about capturing artillery. We should have tacked another sentence to our message: capturing artillery unlikely today."

"Yes, that would have been good," I said, appreciating the humor but not enough to laugh at it.

Seeing Jeanpaul lying on the bed outwardly unconcerned, as though this were a lazy Sunday back in England, should have had a calming effect, and in fact I didn't feel that gut-twisting fear anymore. I did for a few seconds after Raseur had run into our room, but not now. During our training maneuvers we had done this before, a "Jed" team hiding in a farmhouse while "enemy" patrols scoured the countryside. Having lived this in my imagination, I felt as ready as I could be. But this was not like waiting for jump time when we flew in the night before. Then everything was out of our hands. Now we had options and decisions to make. Could we shoot our way out? Certainly.

Suddenly it was as on the plane last night and there were two of me and one said, in a small, flat voice, "You'll never make it and you know it. Not if the Germans do it right, and they will." And the other, the confident me, boldly said, "To hell with that kind of thinking. We can and we will. And maybe we won't have to." Then I thought perhaps the D/F truck didn't get a good fix but enough to know there's a radio near the square and the Germans will make a house-to-house search. Maybe so, but what good does it do to think of that now? I'll think of something else, anything else, think of that lovely chamber pot and its cherubs. That's ridiculous. All right, say a prayer. So I said a quick Hail Mary, looking straight at the old, chipped statue. Then a frightening picture jumped before my eyes and I saw a German patrol with their ugly battle helmets forming out of sight behind the square. The men all had those *Schmeisser* "burp-guns" and "potato-masher" grenades and they were listening to a lieutenant with the face of a busted-up prizefighter. He was giving his orders, very precise orders, for the attack on the rectory. I pushed that picture out of my mind. If this is it, I thought, I hope they come now, right now, and let's get it over with. We won't wait for them in the bedroom. We'll make our stand at the balustrade by the head of the stairs and gun them down as they come up the steps. But that's crazy thinking like Farley talking about death wishes. We don't want a gun battle in the rectory and a heroic death. And I sat back in my chair and re-lit my pipe.

So we waited, not talking, minute after slow minute. Finally I couldn't stand it any longer and I looked at my watch. It was now nine-fifty. I had hoped it was much later. Jeanpaul got up, stretched, and said we should go to the attic again. Same report from Larue: no suspicious activity. By now Larue, although he didn't look ecstatic, seemed to have himself well in hand. We watched the square for a few minutes. Except for some farmers, the café was deserted.

When we got back to our room we looked out the window again and saw the housekeeper still in the vegetable patch. We sat there and waited some more. We talked a little about Milton Hall, but in a desultory way, in detached phrases with long pauses, and our minds were not on what we were saying but it helped pass the time. After what seemed a very long interval we both looked at our watches again. It was ten-thirty, almost an hour and a half since we had shut down our radio. We both smiled at each other and although we didn't say anything we could feel the tension slowly ebbing and I knew then that inside of me, while that gripping, choking fear was long gone, I was like a tightly coiled spring and I would not uncoil all of a sudden but only very gradually. For until we got safely away from the rectory that night we could not be certain that we hadn't been picked up. And now that small flat voice of the other part of me, the pessimistic and perhaps realistic part of me, was quiet, and the confident part of me was saying over and over again, "We've made it. They didn't pick us up. We've made it. We've made it." Jeanpaul was whistling softly and walking up and down with his hands in his pockets, like a man leisurely stretching his legs.

About one o'clock the housekeeper brought our lunch, a rabbit stew cooked in cider. I told her it smelled delicious and we listened politely as she told us exactly how she fixed it. She sounded as though the proper preparation of a rabbit stew was more important than the Germans and their D/F truck. A few minutes later the curé walked in carrying two bottles of wine under his arm. He was smiling broadly and shook hands with us, saying, "*Dieu merci!*" and "*Quelle chance!*" several times and telling us those were probably the hardest hours he had ever spent. He was sure that everything was all right now, almost sure anyway. The German activity in the village was normal. Of course two German officers could come to claim the two rooms as billets but he could try to stall them and this could be handled some way or other, "*on se débrouillera,*" he said. I thought so too although I remembered he had said last night that "this could be embarrassing," or as the British would have said, "a bit sticky."

"A number of my parishioners called on me this morning," said the curé, "but my mind just wasn't there. I kept thinking of you and praying silently. Same prayers too, I just kept repeating them." We were all smiling now. "One of my parishioners was telling me about her little grandson," the curé continued, "and how he was very big for his age, and not thinking, I said, 'Oh God, help us! God help us!' and she thought this was a very odd remark—and of course it was—and she gave me a peculiar look and walked out in a huff."

We laughed and the curé uncorked a bottle and poured out three glasses. We touched glasses and said, "*Santé!*" It seemed to me that drinking each other's health was a most appropriate toast. The wine was excellent and when Jeanpaul asked the curé how he had gotten it he replied that when he heard about the landing on "D" Day he had taken a half dozen bottles of fine wine given him by a friend and buried them in the backyard.

"I thought this was a good idea," he said, "because if there was going to be heavy fighting around here and my church and rectory were smashed to rubble, well then, if I survived, I could dig up my wine and maybe it would cheer me up just a little bit." The curé looked wistful.

"Do you think there will be hard fighting here, Major?" he asked Jeanpaul.

Jeanpaul said no; the curé looked relieved and refilled our glasses. We began eating lunch and the rabbit stew was delicious. Again there were long loaves of French bread and we dipped chunks of it in the gravy. The curé said that food had been no problem here, despite German requisitions, that it was in the cities that things were bad because communications had broken down, especially with the Allied bombing before the invasion. We finished lunch and had more wine and then coffee. I got a pack of Camels out of my rucksack and gave it to the curé but he didn't want to accept it until I assured him that I had a whole carton and two pipes and tobacco. The curé thanked me profusely, lit a cigarette, inhaled deeply, and said that it had been such a long time since he had smoked that he had almost forgotten what it was like. Larue came in, reported that all was quiet, and went back to the attic taking a half-full bottle of wine, a heaping plateful of the stew and a loaf of bread which he stuffed inside his jacket.

We sat there a few minutes smoking and drinking our wine. "Father," said Jeanpaul, "I feel that I should thank you on behalf of all of us for willingly assuming this grave risk. Both the captain and I are most grateful." Jeanpaul had spoken stiltedly so that it sounded like a rehearsed speech and I was surprised.

The curé scowled and looked fixedly at Jeanpaul. "Thank you, Major. I am only doing my duty."

"You were going beyond that and . . ."

"Ah, yes, of course," the curé interrupted. "The military turn of mind. '*Honneur et Patrie*,' that's only for the military, eh?"

"No. I don't mean that," said Jeanpaul now looking embarrassed. "What I am trying to say is that as a priest you have a duty towards the Church. And towards your parishioners, the sick and the poor. You could easily go on saying your Masses and doing these other things and no one would blame you. With me it's different. I am a French officer with a duty to perform and this . . ."

"Oh, come now, Major," said the curé, waving his hand angrily, "Don't you think '*Honneur et Patrie*' can have a meaning for a country curé like myself? Well, Major, if you think it's only the Army officers, the St. Cyriens, who can feel that way and not a curé, or a farmer, or a mechanic—and the women too, for that matter—then Major, you are completely wrong. Then you do not understand the Resistance. And what is worse, terrible in fact, then you no longer understand France!" The curé had spoken very earnestly, jabbing his finger at Jeanpaul.

I could see that Jeanpaul was taken aback that he, of all people, should be told something about patriotism. "I'm sorry, Father," he said, "I did not express myself very well."

"You certainly didn't, Major," said the curé. He had smoked his cigarette to a nub and he lit another and poured more wine. "Now about this matter of duty. There's a veterinarian here. Takes care of cows, horses, pigs too. Well, he was on your reception committee last night. His name is Jaubert. And we have a doctor and the Germans let him use his car and give him a little gasoline. What they don't know is that sometimes when he uses his car at night it has nothing to do with his sick calls. Apparently he doesn't think his duty is limited to his patients. No, Major, you see, those people believe, and I believe, that what we do—it is for France, of course—but it's more than that. It's everyone's duty to rid the earth of a monstrous evil like Hitler and Nazism."

That last part, I thought, sounds Churchillian, and here it is again, the simple, uncomplicated answer, and maybe if you untangled the webs of individual motivation this hard-core principle would be revealed every time.

For a few minutes nothing more was said and Jeanpaul got up to look at the backyard. "You know," the curé said, "I don't have to sneak to my bedroom and listen to the BBC news to know that the invasion is going well. I can read defeat in the faces of the Germans right here. Before 'D' Day they were still confident. Now it's different. They know they're beaten."

"They may know they're beaten," Jeanpaul said, "but we're not fighting the Italians. The Germans will die hard, very hard."

We went on smoking our cigarettes and drinking the wine. What Jeanpaul had said about the Germans dying hard reminded me of an incident André Drouant had told me he saw during the Battle of France in 1940. He was then a lieutenant commanding a platoon and he and his men were defending the bend of a stream. On the opposite bank was a narrow clearing with woods on both sides. When the first Germans advanced into the clearing the French machine guns opened up and the German infantry broke and ran for cover. Through his binoculars Drouant thought he could see a German non-commissioned officer trying to rally his men. Nothing happened for a few minutes, then, as Drouant stared in utter disbelief, about twenty Germans came out of the woods in a column of twos, marching in step and in perfect formation, as though on parade, with the NCO at their head. They had marched half-way across the clearing before the French machine gunners recovered from their surprise and raked the open space. Some Germans were hit and fell, but the others did not break step as they marched across and reached the shelter of the woods. Evidently, as Drouant had told me, the German NCO, furious at seeing his men crack under the first burst of machine gun fire, had ordered them to follow him and march across. It was, Drouant had said, an amazing display of courage and discipline. After reaching the opposite bank wave after wave of Germans hurled themselves into the stream until it ran red with their blood. And then, half shattered by the steady, withering fire of the French machine guns, but still storming ahead, the Germans surged up on the French side of the water, firing their sub-machine guns in sharp bursts, until the French position was overrun. Drouant had told me that when he had read battle accounts telling of waters blood-red from bank to bank he had ascribed this partly to the imagination of the writer, but here he had seen it happen.

Now the curé was reminiscing about the Germans entering Courcité in 1940. "It is hard to realize that the Germans have been here four years," he said. "I remember only too well the day they came. The first Germans we saw were on motorcycles. There were two of them and they roared through the square without stopping. Then a command car came and stopped in the square. A few officers got out and spread some maps out on the hood of the car and they looked at their maps and waited. Not long after that a company of infantry marched in. The men looked dead tired, their uniforms were dusty and dirty, but they were singing, and loudly too. The Germans sing magnificently, you know. They came in as conquerors, and after all, that's what they were."

Jeanpaul was staring into space, his face grim. "Yes, they were," he said finally.

"What did the people do then?" I asked.

"Nothing," the curé said. "They just ignored the Germans. Naturally among themselves they gave way to their feelings, humiliation, despair, anger. They talked all the time about who was to blame for the defeat, rarely agreeing with each other, naturally. The Germans were arrogant, but I must admit they were scrupulously correct in their behavior. They didn't bother the women. You saw no drunken soldiers. Sometimes they tried to be friendly, with the children, for example, but that didn't work. Of course after the Resistance got started, things changed."

As he was telling us this I remembered a photograph which had appeared in *Life* magazine in 1940. It showed French people with somber expressions standing on the sidewalk watching the Germans march into their village. In the front row stood a middle-aged man wearing the rosette of the Legion of Honor. His face was contorted with grief and tears were streaming down his cheeks. I told the curé about this picture and he shook his head and frowned.

"That man should have kept his grief to himself," he said. And after a moment he added, "It reminds me of that passage in some old novel about Spain when the Moors had been driven out of the Alhambra and they were weeping and some woman seeing them said, 'They weep for the things they were not strong enough to hold.' "

Jeanpaul stiffened, his face flushed, and he opened his mouth to say something, but then he changed his mind.

Soon afterwards Larue came in, said the square still looked quiet, and helped himself to another glass of wine. As he left I told him I would relieve him shortly. We began to question the curé about the Resistance activities in the Courcité region and what he reported made the situation much worse than we had been told at our briefing. There were lots of Germans, including the Gestapo and the SS, and they had kept the Resistance down pretty effectively. The Maquis had carried out small-scale ambushes from time to time and they had been able to radio intelligence reports to London. But, as the curé pointed out, this was not good Maquis country, just a lot of small farms, and no mountains or hills or forests to hide in. I had taken off my paratrooper's jacket and hung it on the back of a chair. The curé picked it up and looked at the winged parachute patch on the sleeve. He asked what the letters "S. F." in the center of the patch stood for and I told him "Special Forces."

"If you will permit my saying so, I think it was a great mistake to send you here in uniform," he said. "And no doubt I shouldn't ask, but where are you going from here, Major?"

Jeanpaul hesitated. "To Brittany," he said, "to the St. Malo area. Do you know if the Resistance here has any contacts? Can they help us get there?"

"No," said the curé. "I'm quite sure they have no contacts there. From what I hear the Gestapo has been very successful in that part of Brittany. Resistance leaders have been arrested and the Resistance is practically non-existent. They were very active, but they've been all but wiped out now."

"How about civilian clothes?" asked Jeanpaul. "Could we get civilian clothes?"

"Oh, yes," the curé said. "We could do that. There might be trouble about shoes fitting properly though. And of course it's no good wearing civilian clothes and jump boots. But the real problem would be getting you identity papers."

"Why is that?"

"Well, we had a man here who was very good at it, but the Gestapo grabbed him a few months ago." The curé looked straight at Jeanpaul a moment. "Now he doesn't forge papers anymore."

"All right. How about someone else?"

"Major, we could get you forged papers. But they wouldn't be very good, and it would take at least two weeks. And as you know, even in civilian clothes, unless you have good forged papers and some kind of cover story, you're in trouble if the Germans stop you, even for routine questioning."

"We can't wait two weeks," said Jeanpaul.

"You can talk to Raseur and the others when you see them tonight," said the curé. "But getting from here to St. Malo in uniform, and with your radio and other gear, well, it's not impossible, I won't say that, but it will be extremely difficult. You could only move at night, of course."

Jeanpaul got up and started to walk up and down, head back and shoulders squared, as though he wanted to lead a charge right out of the room.

"Difficult or not," he said, "we have to do it and we will."

"Yes, of course," said the curé, but it was clear that he was unconvinced.

Jeanpaul stopped his pacing and asked the curé about the

Resistance leaders here and the curé replied that Raseur and the others were able and dedicated men. "It's a funny thing," said the curé. "Take some of the Resistance chiefs I know, well before the war you'd never have guessed they had it in them. Of course there are the others too, they were leaders in some way or other and now they're active in the Maquis. We did have some retired Army officers and their experience was invaluable, but mostly these are young men, and sometimes women too. And it's always the same ones who get the job done. *C'est comme au Bal des Pompiers, ce sont toujours les mêmes qui dansent.* (It's like at the Firemen's Ball, it's always the same ones who are dancing.) But all of them have one thing in common, Major. Perhaps you know what it is?"

"Yes, I suppose I do."

"It's faith. No, no! Don't get me wrong," said the curé, smiling a little as he saw Jeanpaul cock his head and raise his eyebrows. "I don't mean that kind of faith. I'm not talking about religion. Or maybe I am, but in a very broad sense. I am a Breton, Major, a Celt, and there is a Celtic blessing which says, 'And may the Lord hold you in the hollow of his hand.' I think He does. This is what I mean by faith now, let's say a belief in the eventual triumph of our cause, the victory of good over evil. I hope this doesn't sound naïve to you."

"No, I'm in accord with that," said Jeanpaul. "It's a consoling thought anyway." He grinned and added, "Some might say that's not a very realistic view."

"Well, realistic or not, that's the way these men feel, even though probably half of them don't realize it, and they might not admit it if they did." The curé poured out the last of the wine and lit another Camel. I noticed that he was not smoking the way the French usually do, with the cigarette dangling from the lips, but he was holding it in his fingers and taking deep puffs.

"You see, Major," the curé went on. "Even in the dark days of 1940 I believed that Hitler would lose in the end, come what may. My heart told me this when my mind was telling me the opposite."

"That's straight out of Pascal," replied Jeanpaul. "The heart has its reasons which the mind cannot comprehend."

"Right, Major." The curé smiled. "Now should I be surprised to hear this from a paratrooper?"

"No, you shouldn't. Not all paratroopers are ignorant or illiterate." Jeanpaul looked amused. "That's an unfortunate myth, probably started by staff officers." After looking out the window again Jeanpaul asked the curé about collaborators in the vicinity and the curé answered that there were none, or very few, but of course there was the Vichy *Milice*, and they were a great danger.

"Sometimes the men in the Resistance are a pretty rough crowd," the curé said. "They would kill a man for being a collaborator—a traitor really—and then discover that he wasn't a collaborator at all. In the Maquis, they hate collaborators far more than they do the Germans."

"They're right," said Jeanpaul.

"That goes for me too," I said.

"Oh, it's understandable," said the curé. "But sometimes that sort of thing, killing a man like that, well it can turn some of the people against the Resistance. Not that they become pro-German. They just won't help the Resistance. They do nothing. But we've had no trouble like that around here."

"It has to be done sometimes," said Jeanpaul.

"What has to be done?" asked the curé. "You mean killing a man in cold blood?"

"Yes."

"Would you do it?"

"With a traitor, yes. If I thought it was necessary."

"Ah!" said the curé, looking steadily at Jeanpaul. "The military turn of mind again. Major, let me tell you a story. It happened not long ago in a small town about a hundred miles away. A Resistance leader was picked up in a Gestapo raid and was held prisoner in this little town. The next day the Maquis pulled off a real coup. They stole a German car and made a surprise attack on the jail. They were lucky, there was only one guard. They slit his throat and freed the prisoner."

"All this in broad daylight?"

"Yes, in broad daylight. It was a daring raid—they had inside information, of course—and amazingly successful. As the men rushed out of the building they saw that the street was deserted except for a beggar on a bench who seemed to be watching them. As the men raced out of town they began to wonder about the beggar. He was the only eyewitness. There were reports that the Gestapo had been making good use of stool pigeons in that locality. Could the beggar have been one of them? That was it, they decided, he was an informer. He might be able to describe the men, maybe he even recognized some of them."

"That was a chance they took," said Jeanpaul. "They had accomplished their mission. They got away, didn't they?"

"Oh, yes, they got away. But they decided they couldn't take that chance. Remember these were tough, reckless men used to making quick decisions. So they drew straws. The three men who drew the short straws turned the car around and headed back down the main street. The beggar was still there. They gunned him down and left him dead in the gutter. And they were very lucky again. They made their getaway."

"That took a lot of nerve," said Jeanpaul.

"Yes. Very courageous," said the curé dryly. "But you see, later that night back in their hideout, the men found out about the beggar. He was not an informer at all. He was a harmless pauper, and they learned one more thing about this beggar, Major, and do you know what that was?"

"I have no idea."

"The beggar was blind, Major."

Jeanpaul stared at the curé, not saying a word. The curé was sitting motionless, his face fixed in a sad and poignant expression, and for a moment his gaze rested on the crucifix on the wall. I had noticed before that when the curé smiled you could always see it in his eyes too so that you knew all of him was smiling and that this was not a perfunctory and mechanical smile. Now he was not smiling. Looking at his strong face, seen in profile against the window, I thought that sometimes on an ancient coin you will see a head that has a certain quiet dignity, tinged with age, and this is how the curé looked then.

There was a long silence after the curé's story, and then he excused himself saying he would be back later that afternoon. When he had gone Jeanpaul sat in a pensive mood for some time. At last he asked me how I liked the curé and I told him I thought the curé was a fine man.

"Yes, he is," said Jeanpaul. "He is the kind of priest you would want at your side when your time to die has come." This was unexpected for I knew Jeanpaul was not a religious man. "The curé is certainly a man of deep faith," said Jeanpaul, "and he's a truly compassionate man. I'll tell you though, Bill, he probably would have made a fine officer."

I left the room to take Larue's place and I saw no Germans when I looked out the attic window. A few farmers were sitting at the café. The lunch and the talk had been fine but it seemed to me that the D/F truck still cast its shadow and we had not been able to let go of ourselves completely. I thought of Jeanpaul saying that the curé would probably have made a fine officer and I knew that, coming from him, this was a high compliment. I supposed that Jeanpaul held lawyers in rather low esteem, yet I knew that he accepted me, and even respected me, but of course that was because I was now an officer, though not a career soldier, and especially because I was a paratrooper and a volunteer. No doubt at some point in his life Jeanpaul, like most of us, had been seeking something, his selfhood or identity, or perhaps the ultimate. Whatever it was, the search had seemed to end when he entered the Military Academy at St. Cyr. But had it really ended there? He had made his commitment, but it was only in war that he could truly fulfill this commitment; only in combat could he meet the last great challenge. I thought of the French poet, Charles Péguy. Like me he was not a professional officer but an infantry lieutenant in the reserve. He was mobilized in 1914 and in the first bloody month of the First World War he led an assault when suddenly his platoon came under murderous fire and his platoon sergeant shouted, "Take cover, Lieutenant!" Péguy had refused, yelling back that a French officer leading an attack doesn't take cover. Those were his last words, for seconds later a bullet struck him in the forehead.

Such mad and hopeless acts of heroism, I thought, have tended to perpetuate themselves. This manner of dying, magnificent in its futility, became part of a long tradition at West Point, at V.M.I., at St. Cyr, at Sandhurst, inspiring men like Martel, and Jeanpaul, and Major Hartwell of the Guards. They felt they had to live up to these traditions, to test themselves against themselves, like the mountain climber, glassy-eyed and panting, forcing his way step by painful step through the last hundred yards to a summit that he has promised himself to reach. And the sticking point was that amateur officers like myself, officers only because of the Japanese bombers at Pearl Harbor, not inculcated with the creed of West Point and the other military academies, yet believing in those things, we also had to try. It is true that there were some who thought such valor was only stupid, and for them, the shrewd men, the important thing was not to die well but to avoid dying in any war. However, for those who believed, what was the difference whether they were professional soldiers, poets in uniform, or fighters from the Maquis? In the face of the enemy all became equal and each, alone with himself and struggling with his doubts and fears, would learn whether he could honor his commitment. And perhaps I myself would find out very soon, right here in the rectory. But this is a morbid thought, I told myself, and the stage here is not set for an inevitable tragedy as in a Greek drama.

My thoughts jerked back to the present as a German soldier came into the square. The farmers at the café were gone and he went there and sat down. I saw that he was very young and as he sat there, half-slumped in his chair, he seemed lonely and forlorn. Who was he, I wondered? And what sort of person was he? Did he and I have anything in common? What intertwining forces long in motion had brought us together, he sitting at the café and I hiding in the attic watching him? He sat there for a few minutes and then he left, walking slowly with a slight limp and with his head down.

A few minutes later another German came to the square, this one an officer. He stood hands clasped behind his back, looking first at the church and then at the rectory. I did not like the way he gazed at the rectory, and for a second I thought he could see me, although I was well back from the window. Was he making a reconnaissance before ordering his men to surround the rectory? But perhaps he was a newly arrived officer and was looking at the old church only as a tourist. He didn't move for some time and I was on the verge of going down to warn Jeanpaul when he turned and strolled off. I decided that he was only an officer-tourist, and the fear ebbed away slowly.

I went back to our room and told Jeanpaul that all was well. He was sitting on the bed, whistling to himself. Larue sat with his chair tilted back against the wall, scratching his head. After a while Jeanpaul said we still ought to have a lookout, just to play it safe, and told Larue to go back to the attic.

"*Merde,*" said Larue under his breath.

"What did you say?" asked Jeanpaul, speaking sharply.

"I said 'yes sir!' "

"Good."

"There are some big rats up there," Larue growled. "Just a little while ago I put my loaf of bread down and one of them . . ."

"Yes. And outside there are some big Germans," Jeanpaul snapped.

Larue scowled and ambled out of the bedroom.

The rest of the afternoon passed slowly as Jeanpaul and I climbed up there from time to time, both of us a little drowsy from our lunch and the wine, but still alert to every sound. It was about five o'clock when the curé came in again with another bottle and four small glasses. "Calvados," said the curé. I watched him as he poured out three glasses and I saw that he had a small makeshift French flag sewn on his right sleeve. I had noticed before that his cassock, while clean, was worn and frayed and several patches showed where it had been mended. But the little French flag had not been there at lunch. He saw me eyeing it. "You notice the little flag," he said. "Well, it's for Bastille Day. I had this sewn on a little while ago. Most of the villagers have done the same thing, and so far not a word out of the Germans."

We clicked glasses and said, "*Santé!*" and I took a hefty swallow and blinked. It was very strong, with the sweet yet sharp taste of fresh apples. I had never tasted Calvados before and I liked its warmth in my stomach. When I asked the curé how strong it was he said about 60 or 65 proof. This was hard to believe until I remembered that by French standards pure alcohol was 100 proof, so that this Calvados ran to about 120 or 130 proof by American standards.

The curé went on to tell us he had seen Raseur and Jaubert for a moment in the village and they would come after dark and take us to an abandoned farm about ten kilometers away. Jaubert thought he was being watched so he was going to be careful.

As I helped myself to more Calvados I felt more relaxed than at any time since Raseur had come pounding up the steps that morning. The curé kept looking at the flag on his sleeve and then he started to drum his fingers on the table as he hummed the tune of "*Madelon.*" He was watching Jeanpaul who sat there with a half-smile and after a few minutes the curé suggested that since this was Bastille Day we should sing a few songs, but of course not loudly. Jeanpaul, obviously surprised, replied that this was an excellent idea. So the curé closed the window and launched into "*Malbrouk s'en va t'en guerre,*" and Jeanpaul and I joined in, keeping our voices very low. Then we sang "*Sur la route de Louviers*" and for a minute Jeanpaul, although he was certainly not drunk, had that lopsided grin he wore on "Camerone Day" when we had all gotten gloriously high in the Peterborough pub. The curé was sitting erect and smiling broadly as he kept time with his right hand, still holding his glass. His hand was brown and strong like a peasant's, but surprisingly graceful as he waved it to the beat of the song. We sang other old French songs, but often I didn't know the words and then only the curé and Jeanpaul sang. I thought of Martel and how he would enjoy this, although these were gay songs and not the sad ones he sang so beautifully. I knew that in the Army the French were reticent about singing the "*Marseillaise,*" that to them it was not just like any song and that they considered it bad taste to sing their national anthem except on formal occasions. I hoped that now Jeanpaul and the curé would make an exception. They didn't, but I think the curé would have except for Jeanpaul. We sang some fine songs and it was, I thought, a most unusual celebration of July 14th.

When we finished singing we sat in silence for some time. The curé and Jeanpaul looked happy and contented. I thought that all during the day Jeanpaul, despite the pressure, had seemed more cheerful than he ever had at Milton Hall, even though most of the time his face still had that set and determined expression. I realized that he was happy because he was back in France and the danger was a challenge he needed. He's getting his wish, I thought.

"Well, anyway," the curé said at last, "life has not been boring around here for quite a while." He chuckled and added, "Especially since my three paratrooper friends dropped in for a little visit last night. Boredom can be a curse in a village like this."

While he was talking I was thinking of the conversation at lunch about duty and I remembered that General Lee had said that duty was the noblest word in the English language. I told the curé this and he said this was a fine sentiment, but he was puzzled about the name "Lee." It was vaguely familiar, but just who was General Lee, he wanted to know. Jeanpaul explained that I was a Southerner, and that General Lee, who had commanded the main Confederate Army, was the Marshal Foch of the Southerners, except that he had lost. He had been a fine soldier and a great man. It was clear that the curé was a little hazy about the Civil War. I told him a little about that war and how General Lee had not won at Gettysburg and that eventually he was forced to surrender at Appomattox. The curé said he was very interested in the United States, but there were many things about our country that he didn't know. So I talked about America, telling him things of which a country curé might not be aware. I told him how it took three days by train to travel from the Atlantic Coast to the Pacific Coast, and of the deep snows of Minnesota and the lazy waters of the Louisiana bayous. He wanted to learn of many things, of J. Pierpont Morgan and cowboys and Buffalo Bill, of the skyscrapers of New York and the deserts and canyons of the West. Like all Frenchmen he was interested in food so I told him about hot dogs and cornbread and ice cream cones, which you wouldn't find in France, but I said that nowhere in America could you sit down to a meal of rabbit stewed in cider and topped off with Calvados. He thought this was regrettable and I agreed with him. Then he asked if President Roosevelt was as great a man as Churchill and I said that I didn't think so but that I had met Englishmen who disagreed with me.

The curé got up to leave. "I must go down and hear confessions," he said. "Of course, my mind probably won't be on it, but I have to go if for no other reason than if I didn't show up people would wonder why. I must act as though everything were normal. My housekeeper will bring your supper but I won't be able to join you."

The curé stopped at the door and then came back into the room. "Sometimes when I hear confessions," he said, "I think of an incident about six months ago. It was late afternoon and a few men came to confession. That was unusual. Generally, you know, it's the women who go to confession, and especially the old, devout women. I gave them absolution and their penances, but I didn't give everyone the usual penance, you know what I mean, 'For your penance say five Hail Marys and five Our Fathers, or say the Rosary.' Sometimes I think this is a lazy way to give penance. We priests ought to do better than that, be more imaginative. So in some cases that day the penance I gave was to say a few prayers for all the people who were going to die that night, wherever they might be."

The curé walked to the window and stood with his back to us. "I didn't think any more of it until the next day when I learned that the Gestapo had raided a farmhouse the night before. They searched the barn and found some Sten guns hidden in the hay. So they took the farmer, stood him up against his barn, and shot him right in front of his wife and children." The curé turned from the window to face us and he said, slowly and in a low voice, "I have wondered ever since whether this farmer was one of the men who had gone to confession the night before. He might well have been. And if he was, why then of course when he said his penance he was praying for himself." The curé walked out of the room without saying another word.

Afterwards we sat without talking for some time and then Jeanpaul left to relieve Larue as a lookout. I thought of the curé and his story about confession. It was clear that for the curé the search had ended and that long ago he had found his own answers. Or had he? Were there times, I wondered, when he had his moments of doubt, periods of anguish, when he tried to reconcile God and evil? The war was here now, and with it a cause, but when the war was over he would once more have to endure a monotonous day-to-day life; he would have to live his faith, defending his ideals against the world, always fearing that those ideals might be eroded by the ceaseless, grinding pressure of reality. The curé would go on as before, trying to serve his God, a God who to him was not merely the conclusion of a syllogism. Since the war his obligations had widened to include not only his parishioners, or a cynical villager who had lost his faith, but a Resistance fighter like Raseur and now Allied paratroopers whose names he didn't even know. In fulfilling his new commitment he felt tormented because he saw that part of the price of destroying Hitler and his grisly gang was the murder of the blind beggar and the execution of the farmer. He knew that gory deeds such as these were multiplied a thousand times over throughout France, throughout all of occupied Europe.

And of course the curé might get caught. The Gestapo would torture him first to try to learn what he knew, and then they would probably shoot him or hang him. Even if the Germans didn't kill the curé, by the time they finished with him he would be a broken, twisted man much like some of the wounded veterans I had seen as a boy in the military hospitals of Paris, the sad-faced men who had exchanged both legs for a Croix de Guerre medal. But there would be no medals for the curé.

I was still thinking of him when Jeanpaul came down and Larue again took his turn as a lookout. Soon afterward the housekeeper brought our supper, two chickens sautéed in wine. I told her the rabbit stew had been delicious and she thanked me.

Jeanpaul finished supper and went up to the attic while Larue came down to eat. I watched Larue going to work on the chicken and breaking off big chunks of French bread. It was dark now and

Jeanpaul came back just as the curé walked into our room, once more in good spirits. "Everything looks fine," he said. "I have just talked to Raseur in the kitchen. He and Jaubert will be back in about an hour to move you out. And he'll have a guide to lead your other paratrooper friends from their hide-out. Raseur says that a German patrol was poking around this afternoon near the abandoned farm where he wants to take you. Nobody seems to know what they were looking for, but anyway they're gone now. It should be safe there, well anyway, much safer than here."

I told the curé that his prayers today had brought results.

"I hope you mean that," he said with a slight smile, "and that this is not a case of the guest making polite remarks to his host."

"I am quite serious," I said, knowing this was a half-lie. "My mother feels as you do about such things, and maybe some of this rubbed off on me."

"Your mother is French?"

"No, she is an American. My father was French."

"Ah, no doubt that accounts for the way you speak French. Practically no accent." There was a better reason but I didn't want to mention it.

"Of course I am not going to ask your names," said the curé. "I don't want to know any of your names. Much later, maybe, when this is all over."

"Father," I said, "I am an optimist, and . . ."

Jeanpaul interrupted. "We're all optimists. We have to be."

"Well, anyway," I said, "I think that somehow I'm going to come through all of this alive. And after the war I will come back to see you. I would like to do that very much."

"Yes, by all means," said the curé looking as if he didn't believe me at all. "Do you think you could?"

"Yes, I do."

Then Jeanpaul asked the curé if he had listened to the BBC tonight and remembered hearing the phrase about the wines of Anjou, because that was our identifying phrase and a guarantee of our authenticity. The curé laughed.

"Major," he said, "when you three walked in here last night with that arsenal you looked authentic, terribly authentic, believe me." He was still laughing. "You couldn't have looked more authentic if you had rolled up in an American tank."

Raseur and Jaubert came into the room. I did not get a good look at Jaubert the night before, and now I saw that he was a small, compact man with quick movements and sharp brown eyes. Like Raseur he carried a Sten gun, and a big leather-covered flask hung by a strap from his shoulder.

"That was a very close call with that D/F truck, Major," said Raseur. "A very close call. You came within seconds of . . ." and he made a slitting motion across his throat.

"I know that," said Jeanpaul.

Jaubert said that a German convoy would be coming through the village in a few minutes and even though we would be leaving by the back way we had better wait until the convoy had passed. We all went to the attic to watch for the convoy. In a few minutes we heard engines and two motorcycles came by with their lights out, the staccato throb of their exhausts reverberating in the dark and silent square. Then came the convoy, one horse-drawn wagon after another. They looked like the covered wagons of pioneer days. We could hear the horses' hoofs plodding on the cobble stones and the creak and groaning of the wheels and axles. A sudden shower had come up and the driving rain pattered down hard on the canvas tops. The drivers sat hunched against the downpour holding their reins. Occasionally someone barked out a gutteral command. Neither Raseur nor Jaubert knew where the convoy was headed nor what supplies it was carrying. But somewhere before daybreak, as a part of the mysterious and intricate pattern of army night movements, that convoy, barring ambushes, would reach its destination. And there would be no ambush in the region of Courcité.

It was a half hour before the last wagon passed. We went back to the room and sat down to wait a few minutes. After a while we got all of our gear together and went down to the kitchen. As we told the housekeeper goodbye I saw Casa, the fierce watchdog, asleep in the corner. We went out into the yard, the curé walking with us, and reached the stone wall in the back. The curé gravely shook hands with us, not saying anything, and walked back to the rectory. The others went over the wall and I was the last to go. Just before going over the wall I looked back. The rain had stopped and the half-moon I had seen the night before was out again. Against the background of the moon and the broken white clouds drifting across it I could see the spire of the church, pale gray as before in the soft moonlight, with the cross at the peak of the spire clearly outlined. Although we were going to a supposedly safer hideout I almost had the feeling that we were leaving a haven.

CHAPTER IX

Germans and Calvados Everywhere

After going over the wall we walked down narrow side streets until we came to a small field surrounded by thick hedges. Drouant's team and their guide were there waiting for us. Captain Truffington, André Drouant's English partner, told me that they had been undisturbed in their farm hideout except for one bad moment when two German officers came to requisition carts from the farmer. Raseur had assigned four young men from the Maquis to temporary duty with us and as we started for the abandoned farm the *Maquisards* carried most of our gear. Aside from my weapons, a canteen and a musette bag, all I carried was some of the parts for the radio. We moved across many small fields, through hedgerows, and then down a narrow dirt road with deep ruts. And now my ankle, which had given me no trouble when I jumped in, was bothering me as I stumbled over the bumpy path. Twice my ankle gave way and I sprawled on my face. Picking myself up, I thought the *Maquisards* must be forming a poor opinion of American paratroopers. But only Larue showed any concern and that was because of the radio parts I had with me. "Look out for the radio, Captain! Look out for the radio!" he whispered to me hoarsely. Several times we had to stop and crouch behind a hedgerow when German convoys passed on the adjoining highway. Once we took a break and Raseur passed around his big flask, full of hot coffee spiked with Calvados. We finally arrived at the farm situated on a low hill and surrounded by a grove of trees. Raseur said the nearest main road was over a kilometer away while the closest farm was even farther. Before leaving to go back to Courcité he also told us that a neighboring farmer would bring us food. As to contacts with Brittany, he was looking into this and would try to come back later that day to let us know.

When I turned on my flashlight for a quick look at the farmhouse we saw that it was half in ruins and in spots the roof had caved in. The main room was laced with cobwebs and a big hornet's nest hung in one corner. We decided to use our sleeping bags in the barn. But Larue, choosing to remain in the farmhouse, immediately started to install the radio, even though it was very dark and we were not scheduled to come on the air until noon. When Drouant's radio operator, Descartes, asked if he could help, his offer was curtly rejected. Larue assembled and mounted the radio very carefully, occasionally whispering to himself, like the priest of a primitive tribe setting up his altar for some mysterious nocturnal rites.

Just before dawn the farmer mentioned by Raseur brought us our breakfast. He was a robust, grizzled man in his late sixties who walked slowly, dragging one foot, and carried a bulging gunny sack slung over one shoulder. He doffed his cap as a polite French peasant would, saying his name was Maunay, and then unloaded his gunny sack containing cold chickens, a jar of butter, several loaves of bread, a thermos bottle of hot coffee, and two large crocks of rillettes, the minced pork paté which is a specialty of the region. Maunay explained that there were grandchildren in his house and he didn't want them to know what he was doing because children had a way of babbling. So he said he would bring us a gunny sack of food after dark when the kids were in bed, and again just before dawn. During the four days we had to spend at the farm "Papa" Maunay, as we called him, came punctually at eleven o'clock at night and then at five in the morning. The menu never varied except that at night he brought a big jug of cider while in the morning he carried the thermos bottle of coffee. "Papa" Maunay asked no questions, and his only comments were about the weather, which he invariably described as "hot for this time of year." We could tell that he was proud of what he was doing and that when the Germans had been driven out he would enjoy telling his story about the Allied paratroopers hidden at the deserted farm.

Late in the morning Raseur came back to our farm bringing a bicycle and civilian clothes. He told Jeanpaul that he had arranged a meeting with a Maquis leader in a village about twenty miles away and if Jeanpaul would go to meet him this man might possibly help with contacts in Brittany. Jeanpaul left after changing to an ill-fitting old blue suit. The baggy pants were much too large around the waist, but they were also too long so that they partly concealed his jump boots. When Jeanpaul came back late that afternoon he told us that the Maquis chief had no liaison with Brittany and that it would take at least ten days to establish one. Jeanpaul described a row he had in the village with a German soldier who wanted to take his bicycle away from him. Jeanpaul warned the German that if he didn't let go of the handlebars he'd get his face bashed in ("*Je te casserai la gueule*") and the German gave up. I was surprised that Jeanpaul, with no identity papers and wearing jump boots, would risk an argument with a German over a bicycle. Jeanpaul was wearing a dark blue French Army beret, much like the berets commonly worn in France. He had removed the paratrooper's insignia but I showed him that he had forgotten to cut out the label of the London shop where he had bought the beret. He shrugged his shoulders. "I wasn't going to walk back twenty miles," was all he said. The attempts to establish contacts with Brittany continued for three days. Jeanpaul made several bicycle trips, always with the same negative result. Once Truffington borrowed the bicycle and the civilian clothes but he had no better luck.

In the meantime we were using our radio to tell London of our predicament and to pass on information obtained from Raseur and his men on enemy troop movements, for example the alleged location of Rommel's temporary headquarters. We knew that our reports by themselves were of little value, but pieced together with many other fragmentary reports they might serve a purpose. We got an extremely long message from London one morning. At first Larue was receiving nothing at all, only feeble squeaks on the earphones. Larue began his loud litany of "*putain de putain*," and "*espèce de con*," when Jeanpaul walked over and saw that Larue had forgotten to plug in the aerial. Jeanpaul made a terse comment and Larue flushed as he adjusted his dials again. But even with the aerial connected, atmospheric conditions were so bad that time and again Larue had to ask for repeats of parts of the message. The hornets were active at the time and left their base in the ceiling to dive-bomb Larue relentlessly. He would yank off his earphones, swat at the hornets, then put his earphones on again, all the while going through his repertoire of blistering curses. He outdid himself that day. Because this lengthy message was badly garbled it took Larue and me over three hours to decode it and then we found that this dispatch consisted of detailed instructions on how to locate suitable D/Z's and how to give the exact location of such D/Z's in our area by reference to maps and compass bearings. Inasmuch as we had spent considerable time at Milton Hall learning to do just exactly that, this dispatch was not only superfluous, it was idiotic. The message had closed with the phrase, "Keep your chins up." When I showed Jeanpaul this London epistle, he cut loose for a good five minutes, swearing softly, quietly, intensely, with none of Larue's explosiveness but with what I thought was much more power.

"To the staff in London," said Jeanpaul when he had calmed down a little, "we're just colored pins on a war map. One pin is marked 'Team Gorin,' and the other is 'Team Gerbe.' These pins have to be moved to Brittany on the map so that everything will be neat and according to plan." He walked off, still glowering. "*Ah, vous savez*," Larue said to me afterward, "*si le commandant pouvait revenir à Londres maintenant, eh bien, il foutrait tout en l'air!*" The thought of Jeanpaul storming into London headquarters and leaving the place a shambles appealed to Larue, and to me.

There were some light moments during our stay at this farm.

On the second day Raseur came with a gendarme who was pushing a bicycle with a brown suitcase strapped to the handlebars. He told us that he was not a gendarme at all; he was in the Resistance and posing as a gendarme. He said that a week ago he had gone about among the Germans dressed as a monk. "Look at my head," he said, taking off his police cap, and he pointed to a round bald spot in his bushy hair. "It's my tonsure," he explained. "Since I was a monk I thought I had to have a tonsure." This gendarme-monk performance intrigued me, although as Jeanpaul drily observed later, "Very theatrical. But tonsure or not, he's not helping us get to Brittany." The gendarme looked thoughtfully at the rillettes and cold chicken we were having for lunch and then he removed his suitcase and put it down gently. When he opened it I saw that it contained nothing but bottles of wine. He selected three bottles of rosé, saying that while these should go well with the rillettes it was unfortunate that the wine couldn't be chilled. I asked him if he often travelled with a suitcase full of wine bottles, and he answered that he only did this at times, especially if he were going to a place where the wine cellar might be inadequate, "like right here," he added. After lunch I lit my pipe and offered him some tobacco and when he said that he had lost his pipe I gave him my other Dunhill, thinking that his tonsure was certainly worth a good English pipe.

No German patrols came near our farm while we were there. We did have an alert one night when one of the young Maquisard sentries, too much on the qui vive, fired a burst from his Sten gun at some suspicious shadows. The shadows turned out to be stray cows which he had fortunately missed. The next morning three German ME-109 fighters roared past, flying very low. They were headed for the front in the west and were of no concern to us. Despite the absence of Germans we took precautions, for example, in taking a bath. André Drouant and I had discovered a stream at the foot of a hill and several times we went there for a bath. While General Patton had supposedly said that a good combat soldier should have a strong, gamey smell, it seemed to me that this precept could be carried too far. So André and I took turns, one man washing in the creek while the other stood guard.

When I was naked in the stream and splashing around it did occur to me that having André on the bank was little protection—although it was better than nothing—and that if a German patrol stumbled on us it would be difficult for me to fight valiantly. We also used the creek to fill our canteens and whenever I did this the French officers were much amused because I always dropped two water purifying pills into my canteen, as we had been instructed to do. The French didn't bother with these pills, in fact they didn't have any with them. But I was doing it by the book and invariably when I took a swig from my canteen either Jeanpaul or Drouant would solicitously ask if I had remembered to drop in my two little pills. "*Ah, ce B-e-e-l, avec ses pillules,*" they would say, "*ça c'est vraiment marrant!*" (Ah, Bill and his pills, that's really hilarious.)

On our second day at the deserted farm Raseur brought us what we thought was an unusual piece of news. The past night two German fighters had strafed the D/Z used for our jump. Raseur explained that this was the German's way of letting the Resistance know that this field was "*grillé*," that is "burned out," thus forcing the Resistance to locate another suitable field, a difficult task in this area. We had not been told of this German technique at Milton Hall and it seemed to us that if the Germans suspected that a field was used for drops the logical thing would be to set up a patrol around the field and hope to trap the reception committee and the "bodies" with their matériel. But Raseur answered that while, of course, the Germans did that on occasion, a field which served as a D/Z so infrequently would tie up a German patrol for many fruitless nights. That's why they used the planes, and although there was only a remote chance of breaking up an operation set for that particular night, the main thing was to cancel that field for further drops.

It was on his last bicycle trip that, by sheer luck, Jeanpaul got in touch with a British agent operating as a civilian, and the Englishman arranged a meeting with the leader of a Maquis group in Brittany. The British agent, whose pseudonym was Raymond, came to see us. He had an ideal appearance for an agent, being a small, nondescript looking man who wore glasses. Raymond said he lived in a village about fifteen miles away, and that aside from radioing intelligence reports he had been able to set up only a few small night ambushes. "Toss a few grenades in the middle of a horse-drawn convoy," he told us, "and for a couple of minutes you have a jolly good show. Of course you can't stay to enjoy it. You have to bugger off bloody fast." We learned from Raymond that the leader of one of the Brittany Maquis was only temporarily in our area and that his *nom de guerre* was "Booboo." I thought this was an unfortunate choice of name even though it didn't have the same meaning in French as it did in the States. Raymond absolutely vouched for Booboo and told us that when France was overrun in 1940, Booboo, a French Communist, was a mechanic in a factory. He and a few other Communists had organized the first Resistance group in that sector of Brittany, and this group increased its activity after Germany attacked Russia. At first they had no weapons and no explosives, but with the help of a few druggists they made their own crude explosives and detonators. Later they stole weapons from the Germans and got dynamite from workers in a stone quarry. Booboo's Maquis was still operating in that part of Brittany, despite heavy casualties, whereas other Resistance groups had been wiped out.

Late that afternoon Booboo came to our farm. Booboo was a tall, thin, melancholy-looking man with a sleepy expression, but when I took a second glance I saw that his eyes were cold and watchful. After listening to Jeanpaul he suggested that Jeanpaul and Drouant leave early the next morning, in civilian clothes and on bicycles, travelling during the day and resting at night in a "safe house." The rest of us would leave after dark, walking at night and hiding in a "safe house" during the day. His guides would meet both parties at designated points along the route. We would have a rendezvous with Jeanpaul and Drouant at Le Ferré, a village about seventy miles west. Agreeing immediately, Jeanpaul told me to take command of the rest of our party when he and Drouant left. Raseur came to the farm when Booboo was still there and it was immediately evident that the two were not on good terms because Booboo was the chief of an F.T.P. Maquis (*Francs Tireurs Partisans*), a Communist-dominated band, while

Raseur was the leader of a non-Communist group. Raseur took Jeanpaul aside and said he had grave misgivings about the F.T.P. Jeanpaul answered that his orders were to get to Brittany, and while at some other time he might have enjoyed his bicycle excursions of the past few days, he had found that these *petits voyages*, as he called them, were a waste of time, let alone the risk. Raseur didn't insist and he agreed to bring civilian clothes for Drouant and said he would also try to get another bicycle. Bicycles were hard to get, he told us, because the Germans had commandeered many French bicycles and the owners of the few bicycles left needed them for their own use. As to our radio and extra gear, Raseur told Jeanpaul that the doctor in the Resistance could take them away in his car and cache them somewhere on the route to Brittany. Booboo, who had been waiting impatiently, came over to join the conversation. He admitted that the move he recommended would be dangerous for everyone, especially for Jeanpaul and Drouant who would travel during the day with no identity papers, but it was a risk worth taking. He said this as a man who, having taken many chances himself, saw no reason why we shouldn't do the same. He was right.

"Look, Major," he said to Jeanpaul. "Your chances are fifty-fifty at best. I don't know what those distinguished gentlemen in London told you, but the Gestapo hasn't been sitting idly on their *derrières*." His long face twisted in a sarcastic smile, almost a leer. "Now here you are, paratroopers fresh from the comforts of old England. You can stay holed up here, living off rillettes and cider, or you can stick your necks out, like the rest of us have for the past four years."

"You do what you said you'd do," said Jeanpaul, angry but keeping his voice even, "and we'll do what we have to do. We can take care of ourselves."

As we were standing around I was surprised to see two young girls pedalling up the road to the farm. "My couriers," said Booboo without further explanation. The girls were pretty, with pink cheeks and merry eyes, and they were laughing and chattering as they reported to Booboo. He called them aside, and as he talked to them their expressions changed and they became serious, nodding their heads as he gave them orders we couldn't hear. Apparently these instructions didn't suffice because he took a scrap of paper and a pencil from his pocket, scribbled a few words and handed the paper to one of the girls. She took it and nonchalantly stuffed the paper inside her bra, hitching her shoulders as she did so. It was the kind of thing you saw in the movies, and she knew she was on stage with all of us watching her. Since she had a fine figure I fully appreciated this bit of legerdemain. I remembered then that the French word for "bra" was "*soutien-gorge*," literally, "throat supporter," a sort of euphemism which had always struck me as not being characteristic of the French. The girls looked us over curiously, one whispered something to the other and they both laughed. Then they gave us a casual wave and took off on their bicycles, hair blowing in the wind, skirts billowing. I noticed they both had lovely legs.

Using our Michelin road maps, Booboo gave Jeanpaul and me explicit instructions on which roads to use, and he marked on the maps the exact spots where we would be met by his guides and escorted to "safe houses." He himself would meet Jeanpaul and Drouant at Fougerolles, on the way to Le Ferré. After giving us a curt "good luck" he left rapidly on his bicycle. When he was gone we sent a short radio message to London saying we were at last leaving for Brittany, thanks to the F.T.P., and that our radio would be cached so that we would be out of communication for an indefinite period. "Stand by," was the reply. In about ten minutes London came back on the air with a short dispatch: "All aspects of cooperation with F.T.P. must be carefully considered." Jeanpaul tore up the message without saying a word.

When Papa Maunay came with his gunny sack that night Jeanpaul told him we were leaving so would he please bring his bill for our food the next morning. Papa Maunay said he didn't want to charge us anything but Jeanpaul was firm so the next morning he handed Jeanpaul a neatly folded sheet of paper. It was his bill, obviously written with some effort, but very clear and fully itemized, with a ridiculously low total due. Jeanpaul paid him the exact amount, thanking him for all his trouble. And now Papa Maunay went beyond his usual comment on the weather and said he admired our weapons, particularly the paratrooper's carbines with their folding stocks. He added that he knew little of such weapons, they were so modern, and besides he had been in the artillery.

"You're an artillery man? You should have told me," said Jeanpaul, smiling broadly. "That's excellent." I could see that Jeanpaul was still thinking of Colonel Girard and the 88's.

"Yes, Major. In the last war I was at Verdun." He had drawn himself up straight and was looking Jeanpaul right in the eye. Jeanpaul was no longer smiling. "That's where I got this," he said, pointing to his bad leg.

There was a long moment of silence. Jeanpaul seemed to be looking off at something very far away, as if all that he had read and heard of the Battle of Verdun was now passing before his eyes: the constant crashing of the big shells, the shattered, muddy trenches, the battered earth soaking up the blood, and the cost of holding Verdun ("They shall not pass!"), three hundred thousand dead. Here was one of the survivors.

"You have been of great help to us, Monsieur Maunay," said Jeanpaul at last, speaking slowly, "and you have . . . you reminded me of what the French Army did in 1916." He shook hands solemnly with Papa Maunay and as the farmer limped away Jeanpaul's eyes followed him thoughtfully.

That morning Raseur brought an extra bicycle and an old suit for Drouant. Aside from the fact that the clothes fit very poorly, Jeanpaul and Drouant didn't look like ordinary civilians. Something about their walk, the way they held themselves, their manner of speaking, betrayed their military background. After casually shaking hands with us they left on their bicycles. I wondered what kind of cover story they had invented in case they were stopped for questioning, but no matter how plausible their cover story, unless they were interrogated by incredibly stupid Germans, it would be difficult to explain not having identity papers and wearing paratrooper's boots.

Shortly after dark an old car with a crumpled front fender came to the farm and out popped the doctor, a jolly, fat little man. Under Larue's supervision our radio was placed on the back seat.

Larue was most particular about how this should be done and he tried the radio in several different positions while the doctor stood there smiling and saying, *"Dépêchez vous! Dépêchez vous!"* But Larue was not to be hurried. It was as though he were the curator of an art gallery and this was a priceless statue that he was parting with reluctantly and which had to be transported with infinite care. Some of our extra gear was put on the floor of the car and then the doctor covered the radio and gear with a blanket and put his doctor's bag on top. It was not ideal camouflage, but this didn't worry the doctor who was very cheerful and seemed to look on this as a huge joke on the Germans, a feeling I didn't entirely share. The car was heavily loaded and as the doctor drove away slowly down the rough and narrow road we could hear the car bumping and scraping bottom. *"Ah cet imbécile!"* growled Larue, *"Il va me casser mon radio!"* (Ah, that imbecile! He's going to smash my radio!)

Then we burned our codes. If we were able to use our radio again we would have to resort to an auxiliary memorized code, a much more difficult procedure for coding and decoding. There was an oldfashioned open water well at the farm, the kind in which you lower a bucket on a rope, and we dumped our extra weapons and much of our ammunition into it. We wanted to travel light, and I carried only my carbine, pistol, canteen, and musette bag stuffed with emergency rations, a small first-aid kit, a flashlight, extra ammunition, and my Michelin maps.

As we set out we heard from far off the rumble of artillery. We didn't know it then but this was the heavy barrage preceding the breakout of the American forces at St. Lo. When we got near the main highway we had to stop because another long horse-drawn convoy, like the one we had seen from the curé's attic, was rolling by. I thought of what Raymond had said about the "jolly good show" you had if you tossed a few grenades at such a target. But we had no grenades, and while we could have opened up with our carbines, our objective was not to ambush this convoy but to reach Le Ferré.

We waited a few minutes after the last wagon had passed and then we set off. Our group consisted of Larue, Descartes, two of

Raseur's young *Maquisards* named Marcel and Louis, and Captain Truffington. I walked ahead, setting a fast pace. We moved on side roads part of the time and sometimes on main highways, following the route which Booboo had selected, hoping to keep clear of those highways most used by the Germans. Because of Allied air supremacy German convoys moved at night whenever possible, and to avoid having a convoy under air attack at daybreak before it reached its destination, they often stayed off the main highways which were under constant Allied surveillance. Several times that night when we heard German trucks coming down our road we scrambled through the hedgerows and into the fields. This was a gently rolling countryside with many small rectangular farms and little villages dominated by their church spires. Marching was easy, but after a few hours our little group was no longer walking in a tight single file as it should have been. Larue and Truffington straggled far back and I would have to wait for them to catch up. Evidently Larue was convinced that his primary role was only to operate the radio and not to walk hour after hour like an ordinary infantryman, and Truffington, an officer in the Royal Corps of Engineers, must have shared Larue's strong aversion to long-distance walking.

All went well and before daybreak we reached the crossroad marked on the map by Booboo. His guide was there and led us to a farmhouse not far away. The farmer shook hands in a perfunctory way, said "*Bonjour,*" and we followed him to his barn and hayloft. It was just beginning to get light and I could see the cows and chickens in the barn, and the packed dirt floor splattered with cow dung and chicken droppings. The hens were cackling while a few roosters strutted, flapped their wings, and crowed shrilly. Just outside the barn was a large pile of fresh manure giving off little wisps of vapor. The stench was very strong. The farmer said we would be safer up in the hayloft than in his house because occasionally Germans came to the house to get eggs or chickens.

"You will be all right here," he said, speaking in a low voice. "Of course it's a little noisy here now. And there is a little odor. But you won't mind that."

"No, of course not," I answered, not wanting to offend him. "I hadn't even noticed it."

The farmer brought breakfast to us in the hayloft and when we finished eating I watched Truffington loosening his boots and getting ready to catch up on his sleep. I knew Truffington was a capable officer, but I had never particularly liked him. Perhaps it was because of his dark-complexioned, delicate features, and his graceful, almost effiminate, gestures, but especially because of his precise manner of speaking. His diction was excellent, what I would have taken for an Oxford accent. He enunciated each word very clearly, sounding like an announcer on the B.B.C., and whenever he swore he rolled the words trippingly on his tongue like an actor enjoying his lines. Sometimes I thought he was a poseur, but I realized this was no doubt unfair. It's too bad I'm stuck with Truffington, I thought, instead of one of the British officers whom I liked, men like Major Whitley, Major Hartwell of the Guards, or the gay Major Tomlinson with his "piece of cake" view of combat missions. I also wished that Larue, who had fallen in love with his radio, were like Descartes. Descartes couldn't have been over twenty-one, and with his shy, boyish smile he reminded me of Martel. Except for those few minutes after we had jumped in and he had cursed the pilot, nothing seemed to bother him. I had confidence in Descartes.

As I found a comfortable spot in the hay I suddenly remembered Allan Seeger's poem, "A Rendezvous with Death," and even as I remembered it I thought again how strange it was that odd bits and scraps of poetry would sometimes pop into my mind at the most unlikely times, and these snatches of poetry were not passages I'd had to memorize in school but verses here and there which I had liked and which had stuck in my mind.

"Say, Truff," I said, "do you remember Allan Seeger's poem of World War I, you know, 'A Rendezvous with Death'?"

"Rather an odd question, that, old man," he said. "Why do you ask?"

"Well, there's a passage in it where Seeger says 'God knows t'were better to be deep, pillowed in silk and scented down, where love throbs out in blissful sleep, pulse nigh to pulse.' Remember that?"

"What an extraordinary thing to mention now, old man," he replied, looking at me curiously.

"Yes, I suppose so. I was just thinking that bedding down in this hay is a little different." Truffington was still staring at me. "You know, Seeger goes on to tell about his rendezvous with death, and how he intends to keep it. And he did." I was saying this because I knew it would annoy him. "Truff, do you think we have a rendezvous with death, and very soon?"

"What a macabre thought! What's the matter with you, anyway?"

"Nothing at all."

"Well, old man, instead of thinking about Allan Seeger and all that rot you ought to be doing something about getting us some bicycles. This walking is very tedious, very tedious. And much too slow, too." I knew it was the tedious part that bothered him rather than the slow part, but of course it was true we had only covered about fifteen miles and at that rate it would probably take five more night marches to reach our destination.

"Truff, we tried, you know that. Raseur couldn't get us any bicycles."

"Well, try again, old man. You're in command. Ask the farmer."

"Hell, Truff," I said, "this walking is not that tough. It's not like the Foreign Legion making a forced march across the desert."

"What! Such goddam stupid nonsense!" said Truffington, almost shouting.

"Not so loud, Truff, not so loud," I said.

Truff glowered, and he turned to Descartes, "You see what I mean, Descartes?" he said in a harsh whisper. "Here we are walking our bloody feet off, wasting valuable time, and Dreux has to bring up the frigging Foreign Legion!" Descartes sat with a mocking smile, not saying anything.

"All right, Truff," I said. "I'll try again. I'll ask the farmer. Good night, Truff, sweet dreams." Truff had turned his back and didn't answer me. I was tired and went right to sleep despite the constant cackling of the hens and the crowing of the roosters. I awoke when the farmer brought our lunch. He was talking in a low voice and trying to act casual as he brought out a bottle of Calvados. We had a few drinks after lunch, always clicking glasses and saying "*Santé*." The farmer kept looking at us but talked very little and kept his questions to himself. With Truffington standing by I asked the farmer about bicycles, and he replied that it would be impossible to get six bicycles. One, perhaps, and even that would not be easy.

"What the bloody hell is the matter with these god-damned farmers?" asked Truffington, walking away disgustedly.

"What did he say?" asked the farmer.

"The captain said that the war has caused severe dislocations, particularly in transportation," I replied.

"But yes, of course, didn't he know that?" said the farmer.

I asked Truffington if he wanted to try to get one bicycle and go to Brittany by himself, leaving us to catch up with him.

"I should say not!" he replied. "That would muck things up rather properly. What sort of chap do you think I am?" I thought I could answer that question because I was beginning to get tired of Truffington generally, and especially the way he always addressed me as "old man" rather than "Bill."

Another farmer walked in the barn, our farmer explaining that this was his brother who had the next farm. The second farmer took a bottle of Calvados from under his blouse, doing this with a sly and cunning look as though we were all joint conspirators. So we said "*Bonjour*," clicked glasses, said "*Santé*" again, and had a drink of his Calvados. The two farmers talked in a desultory way about their cows, one of which apparently had an infected udder, and meanwhile they darted sharp and inquisitive looks in our direction. The second farmer left looking very pleased with himself. Soon afterward a third farmer came in. Same performance: the knowing look, the bottle of Calvados, and we had another drink with him, and then still another. He was still there when a fourth farmer came in with his bottle. This one was stout and florid-faced and he looked a little drunk. The fourth farmer was more talkative and he carried a heavy walking stick which he flourished menacingly as he mumbled about the Boches.

"The Boches are done for," he said to me, brandishing his stick.

"Yes," I said, "the Boches are done for. *Ils sont foutus*."

"You are an American paratrooper, *hein?*"

"No. I am a captain on the Brazilian General Staff."

"Brazil?" he said, squinting his bleary eyes uncertainly and rubbing his chin.

"Yes. And that officer over there," I said, pointing to Truffington, "he is the legitimate son of the Commanding General of the Brazilian Army."

"Ah! That is very good." He peered at Truffington a moment and then nodded his head to show his understanding and approval. *"C'est épatant, ça! Vive le Brésil!"*

"Vive le Brésil!" I said, *"Vive la France!"*

Truffington called me over to a corner. "I should like a word with you, old man," he said.

"Sure."

"Well, you can see it for yourself, these bastards are queuing up to get at us with their Calvados bottles. Another half hour and I shall be tight. And then I should feel such an ass."

"Yes, of course."

"You must be getting tight yourself, old man. This bit about the Brazilian Army, well, come now. Too damn many farmers coming here. It's not safe."

Truffington was right. This cocktail hour was becoming a problem. The word about our being here was spreading from farm to farm. We had often been warned of such a danger at Milton Hall; people talked, they just couldn't help it. And the next thing you knew the Germans got the information. While we were drinking Calvados, round after round, I had heard at least three motorcycles going by, and also several trucks.

"Truff," I said, "here's the way I'm going to handle it. I'm going to turn my back when no one is watching and pour the stuff on the floor. It's dark in here. They won't notice."

"Seems a pity to do that, old man."

"It's the only way, Truff," I said. "We'll tell the others."

I didn't want to offend anyone by refusing a drink, but if the farmers were going to work on us in shifts that afternoon it was the only thing to do. I hated to waste good Calvados, yet here we were in a dangerous situation and this was hardly a good time to get loaded. It would be just great, I thought, if the Germans were tipped off, raided the barn and there I was, bleary-eyed and fumbling for my pistol. The cocktail hour went on and on and two more farmers came with their Calvados but it finally ended, and later we had our dinner in the barn.

We started out again after dark and it was the same as the previous night, except that the straggling was worse. Again there were a few German convoys but we always had time to get off the road and into the fields. Walking along a main road we came to a large stone bridge, and Marcel, one of our young Maquis escorts, told me that about a month ago our Air Corps had tried to bomb the bridge in a daylight raid but instead of hitting the bridge they had smashed a few houses nearly a mile away. His parents lived there and had escaped injury. Others had not been so lucky. Marcel sounded not so much bitter as surprised and disillusioned and he wanted to know how the bombers with their new Norden bombsights could have missed so badly. "With that bombsight," he told me, "they can drop an apple into a pickle barrel from 20,000 feet. I know because I heard that over the BBC news." I said that the Norden bombsight couldn't help much when there was heavy anti-aircraft fire or enemy fighters. "But that's just it," he said. "There weren't any anti-aircraft guns there, and no fighters at all." That's the trouble with the fly-boys, I thought, they've overdone the propaganda about the magical bombsight and in some of these raids, instead of blasting a railroad yard or a bridge, they flatten a row of houses. Afterwards the survivors in the smoking ruins could have a spirited discussion about the marvelous precision of the Norden bombsight.

"Sometimes the pilot or the bombardier make little mistakes," I told Marcel.

"That was hardly a little mistake," he said, and I realized that I had made a stupid remark.

"When I jumped into France," I said, hoping to placate him, "the pilot missed the D/Z and I landed half a mile away." But he showed little interest and I knew it would be a long time before he became a convert to the Air Corps doctrine of pinpoint bombing. The British had an excuse because they only bombed at night, at least earlier in the war, and the people in the occupied countries could understand how the bombers might miss the target.

After walking about fifteen miles we reached our rendezvous before daybreak and a guide was there. Again we were hidden in a barn that had an overpowering stench. The cocktail hour after lunch didn't last as long and only one other farmer came with his bottle of Calvados. Same story on bicycles: none available. We left that farmhouse after nightfall, our destination being a crossroad one kilometer east of Gorron. On this march Larue and Truffington fell even farther behind and once I had to stop and wait ten minutes while they caught up. I was getting irritated with their straggling.

"Look," I said to them. "We're not an army in retreat. We don't need a rear guard. For Christ's sake, let's get going so we can make Gorron."

"I say, old man," said Truffington, "you're setting a bit of a fast pace, you know. What we need are bicycles, as I trust I have made clear. We have money. Surely some of these farmers have a few bicycles they would sell."

"What are we supposed to do?" I asked him. "Go around knocking on farm doors, waving franc notes, and ask if they have bicycles to sell today?"

"Awfully funny, my dear fellow, awfully, awfully funny."

By now I was fed up. "Truff," I told him. "Do me a favor, will you?"

"Now what do you want?"

"Cut out this goddam 'old man' and 'my dear fellow' crap. Call me anything else, for Christ's sake, like 'Bill' for example."

He looked surprised and hurt. "All right, of course," he said. "You're in a frightful humor. Getting a bit edgy, aren't you?"

I didn't answer and we started off again. When we reached the rendezvous point outside Gorron it was still dark. No guide there. I checked my map again to make sure. We were at the right spot, no question about that. We sat in the ditch and waited. Certainly the guide would show up any minute now. Maybe, as Truffington said, I had set a faster pace than necessary and we had arrived early. I could now see the first faint streaks of dawn. We couldn't wait there more than ten minutes for by that time it would be getting light. Ahead of us about a hundred yards I could see farmhouses on both sides of the road. To the right and left of us there was nothing but open fields, hedges, and a few clumps of trees. There were no woods to hide in. Should we take a chance and try one of the farmhouses ahead? But suppose this was anything but a "safe house" and the farmer was unfriendly, or worse still, on the side of the Germans? After all, there were still a few Frenchmen who collaborated with the enemy. Or what if the farmer were friendly, but Germans were billeted there? For the first time behind the lines I had the lonely feeling of being completely isolated. I wasn't lost, but I felt lost.

We couldn't wait any longer so we clambered through the hedgerow and went to the far end of the field and sat behind another hedgerow. It was rapidly getting light now. I told Marcel, who wore civilian pants and an old French Army jacket, to shed the jacket, leave his pistol belt and Sten gun, and go back to the rendezvous point. Possibly the guide was late and would soon show up. After what seemed a long time Marcel came back and said there was still no sign of the guide. Marcel thought he should look around at some of the neighboring farmhouses, take a chance, pick one out, and ask the farmer for food and shelter. After talking this over with Descartes I sent Marcel out again. By now I was hungry and I ate a concentrated chocolate bar from my emergency rations. It was very hard, so that I could only bite off a little piece at a time and it had a bitter and disagreeable taste. Larue was sitting with one boot off, looking morose. He asked me to come over, and after stripping off his sock he showed me a large, ugly blister on his heel. "Captain, look," he said in a reproachful tone. I looked and said, "*Courage, mon brave*," and walked off quickly before he could reply. When I glanced back he was holding his boot and sock in one hand and his face was red with anger.

Marcel came back with good news. He had found a farmer who

would hide us in his barn, and by going there the back way along the hedgerows we stood little chance of being seen. When we got to the barn the farmer stood at the entrance. He was smiling broadly. This was an unexpected honor, he told us, and he was sure we would be safe in his hayloft. The Germans had never come to his farm for any reason. As he talked I watched him carefully, wondering if he could be trusted, and I quickly decided that we could depend on him. Besides, I had little choice. I was not like a tourist arriving at a resort and checking all the hotels until he finds the one with just the right view of the ocean.

Later that afternoon I asked again about bicycles and got the same answer. But then the farmer paused and said, "Perhaps I could get you a car. I'm not sure, but I have a friend who has kept his old car hidden away for four years. Maybe he would sell it."

Truffington jumped up and Larue hobbled over. "That's it! A car!" said Truffington excitedly, and he added, "Bill, we simply must get that car!" I was glad to see he had dropped the "old man." Truffington went on, "Larue is lame now, and a few more of these god-damned forced marches of yours and none of us will be fit. And that includes you."

I was frowning. "How is that bad ankle of yours, by the way?" asked Truffington.

"It's perfectly all right," I said. "Sorry to disappoint you."

"Now, I don't mean to be critical," Truffington said, "you're doing what you think is right, marching up and down these bloody roads, but here's our chance, old man. Oops, sorry, forgot about this peculiar aversion of yours. We've already had one balls-up, no guide this morning." He had a sarcastic smile I didn't like. "I assume you would like to get to Le Ferré before the end of the war, and if so I should judge the car is our only hope."

Larue was repeating, "*Bien sûr, bien sûr, bien sûr,*" and then, pointing his finger at me, he slowly and gravely said, "*Qui risque rien n'a rien,*" as though this proverb about nothing ventured nothing gained was an irrefutable argument in favor of our buying the car.

I was wondering about our chances if we tried to get to Le Ferré by automobile. Certainly not as good as if we walked, but we couldn't be sure we would make it by walking either. As Truffington had said, something had gone wrong that morning. Moreover, it was true that, despite our walking steadily at a good pace, with no stops for a breather, we were making slow time because the period of darkness in mid-summer was so short. And if I said no I would probably have a near mutiny on my hands.

"All right, Truff," I said. "Go see this bird and if the car looks all right tell him we'll buy it."

Truffington wasted no time. He changed to an old suit borrowed from the farmer and they both set off to see about the car. The farmer came back saying Truffington was still checking over the automobile. Then he called me aside to say he had a message for me. That morning after we arrived he had seen an Allied agent, an Englishman he thought, who was hiding in another farmhouse. The agent had almost been cornered by the Gestapo in a neighboring village a few days before. The farmer asked if I didn't want to see the agent and maybe we could work together.

"No, no!" I said, "I don't want him coming here. Let him stay where he is. He's in less trouble than we are, he's not in uniform. I've got my own problems."

The farmer seemed to find my attitude strange and no doubt felt that the parable of the Good Samaritan should definitely apply behind the lines.

"He's not wounded, is he?" I asked.

"No. He's just stranded and needs help."

"It's very important," I insisted, "very important that he stay put. I can't help him."

The farmer left for his fields and as I lay down in the hay I saw Larue sitting with his naked foot stretched out, contemplating his blisters. But he seemed much happier and obviously the prospect of travelling by car had done much for his morale.

CHAPTER X

Dialogue with a German

I had just dozed off when I was awakened by Truffington shaking me. He was beaming. "It's all laid on," he said. "That farmer has an old Citroën touring car, seems in fairly good condition, tires are O.K. and he has two big tins of petrol. He'll sell the car to us for ten thousand francs."

"Did you run the engine?" I asked him.

"Well no, actually I didn't. The battery is dead, but he thinks he can get another one somewhere. And he says the distributor needs a bit of tinkering with."

I didn't like this explanation. The price didn't bother me for it was then only the equivalent of three hundred dollars and we had much more than that.

"What the farmer will do," Truffington went on, "is drive the car after dark to a field about a mile from here. We're to meet him there, hand the old boy his ten thousand francs, and off we go to Brittany." Truffington made it sound very simple.

"Well, thanks a lot, Truff," I said. "I hope it all works out."

We rested in the barn until dinner time when the farmer came to ask us if we would do him the honor of joining his family for dinner. "It will be perfectly safe in the house," he told us, "just our family and they won't say anything on the outside." I was dubious but again I didn't want to hurt his feelings so we went to the farmhouse. I was not prepared for what I found. The farmer's whole clan must have come from adjoining farms, and they were gathered in the one big room. At least twenty-five persons were sitting at a long table, including several children and a few old people. All eyes were on us as we took our places, keeping our carbines slung over our shoulders and our pistol belts strapped on. Looking around I saw that this was the only room in the house and it evidently served as kitchen, dining room, living room and bedroom. Big old-fashioned beds were set in alcoves with heavy dark blue curtains. There was a huge fireplace and hanging over the burning logs was a great black kettle in which a pot-au-feu was simmering, giving off an aroma far superior to the pungent smell of the barn.

As we sat down to eat the kids kept staring at us, scooping their forks into the stew without looking at their plates. After we were served our farmer poured wine all around. A very old man with a leathery face and watery eyes sat at the head of the table. He held up his glass for a toast, his hand trembling a little, and in a clear but feeble voice he said, "*A la victoire!*" We all said, "*A la victoire!*" and drank. It was *vin ordinaire*, very *ordinaire*. "*C'était bien, ça, grand-père,*" remarked one of the women. The old man seemed not to hear her and said there was too much salt in the pot-au-feu. Several times during dinner he proposed the same toast, the woman would say, "*C'était bien, ça, grand-père*" and he would say again that there was too much salt in the stew, this peculiar ritual being repeated as though on cue and with no one smiling.

The people talked little, mostly about the weather, and there were long periods of silence when all you could hear was the munching of food and the scraping of knives and forks against the plates. When the people did speak to us it was only to ask if we didn't want more wine or more stew, but once the farmer next to me turned and politely said I looked a little fatigued. When I answered, "*Oh, un petit peu,*" Larue, his mouth full of bread and stew, burst into a loud laugh and then stopped and blushed when everyone looked at him. While the children had their eyes fixed on us constantly the others only stole glances at us from time to time. Those looks were eloquent. The people were curious about us, of course, but there was more than curiosity in those glances. Being polite, these people did not want to ask questions. As the French generally are, these farmers and their families were reserved, and also probably shy in our presence, but I could read in their faces what they felt and could not adequately express. It was too soon for an outpouring of joy—that would come with liberation—and now their eyes told us only how proud they were to have us sharing their dinner. More than that, there was a deep and silent expression of sympathy and understanding. I had the odd feeling that to these people in their conquered land we and our weapons were the long awaited sign, the first flash of light in the darkness that had enveloped them for four years. And I realized that the farmers who had come to the barn with their Calvados bottles were moved by the same feelings. Putting those feelings in the right words, nicely phrased, as they would want to do it, was beyond them, so instead they brought their Calvados, made from the apples in their orchards, as an offering of gifts in lieu of words. They wanted to make a courtesy call and pay their tribute to us.

I remember particularly a little white-haired woman sitting across from me. She wore a black dress, perhaps in mourning. With her kind face and her pensive expression, she reminded me of my mother as I had known her in Paris during World War I. I sensed that I too reminded her of someone. She looked at me steadily from time to time, but she never spoke except once when I passed a loaf of bread to her and then she smiled and murmured, "*Merci, Capitaine.*" I was surprised that she recognized insignia of rank and I stumbled over my words as I replied, "*Il n'y a pas de quoi, madame.*" In her eyes I saw sadness and compassion. She seemed to be saying to me, "During my life I have seen many young soldiers such as you. Like you, they were very sure of themselves. Or perhaps some of them just pretended to be. Many of them never came back, but I do not want to speak of this to you." That dinner had a quiet and touching simplicity and great dignity too.

During the meal I heard the rhythmic clattering of many hob-nailed boots as troops marched past the farmhouse. It sounded like at least a company of infantry, and I got up to peer out the window but the trees screened the road and I couldn't see anything. I knew those Germans were no danger for us and that if the enemy had somehow been tipped off they wouldn't come marching down the road. Still it was a reminder, and here we were violating security precautions by having dinner with many people of the neighborhood. Well, we're getting away tonight, I thought, and you just can't do everything by the book.

As I walked back to the table, hitching my carbine around on my shoulder, I saw one little boy watching me intently, and to have fun with him I took out my forty-five, removed the clip, jerked the slide back and forth several times and snapped the trigger. He was goggle-eyed.

"*Maman, Maman!*" he cried, "*Regarde le gros pistolet!*"

"Shh, shh," his mother said, tapping him reprovingly on the hand, "*Un petit garçon bien élevé ne parle pas à table,*" (A polite little boy doesn't speak at the dinner table.)

When we finished dinner one of the men called me aside and told me he thought he knew why no guide had met us that morning. "Why?" I asked, a little uneasy that he knew anything about the guide.

"The Gestapo raided Fougerolles late yesterday," he said. "That's a village not far from here."

"I know where Fougerolles is," I said. I also knew that Jeanpaul, Drouant and Booboo had agreed to meet in Fougerolles.

"What happened?" I asked.

"Usual thing. They threw a cordon around the village, sealed it off. Took about six men into custody."

"Who? Do you know who they were?"

"No, I'm not sure. I hear they didn't get the men they were looking for. I don't know. But maybe that's why your guide didn't get here."

"Thanks for telling me," I said, more disturbed than I let on.

Our farmer was getting out the Calvados, but after one drink we were able to excuse ourselves to go back to the barn. The old man who had proposed the toasts, "*A la victoire!*" was at the door and I stopped to tell him I had appreciated his toast, using the singular. He thanked me and then he looked at me fixedly with his pale blue eyes.

"Tonight when I say my prayers," he said, "I will say some for you and those other paratroopers."

"Thank you," I said. "We will need them."

"Everyone needs them," he replied. "The *Bon Dieu* understands." I wasn't at all sure that the *Bon Dieu* understood quite so well, and I wondered if *le Bon Dieu* was fully aware of the problem of Truffington's car and the dead battery and the distributor which needed adjusting.

When I reached the barn Truffington was changing back into civilian clothes. "What's up?" I asked.

"I'm going back for another look at the Citroën," he said. "Maybe I can help the old boy get it in proper working order, tinker with it a bit, you know. Clean the plugs and the distributor." I could see that for Truffington the car had top priority. When I told him about the raid at Fougerolles and warned him to be careful he frowned a moment.

"I say, that's a shocker!" But in a few seconds he was smiling again. "Well, must be off. Be back shortly, ta-ta," he said, and he left taking Marcel and Louis with him.

Larue, Descartes, and I stretched out on the straw to wait. It was not dark yet, but soon after Truffington got back it probably would be and we could start for the field where the farmer would have the car. As I lay there I thought of some of the other Jeds. Where were they now, Farley, Cambray and Martel? They must have jumped in by this time. Were they hiding as I was in a barn reeking of cow dung, or were they in a sparsely populated area, one with hills and large forests and suitable for guerrilla warfare? I imagined Farley out in the hills, stripped to the waist, leading a Maquis group in calisthenics and then taking them on a ten-mile cross-country run. I knew this was impossible, that the tough Maquisards would never put up with Farley's physical fitness obsession, however forceful Farley might be. Still it was an amusing picture. As to Cambray he would be intently studying his map, measuring distances, and making exact time-kilometer calculations. And Martel might have loosened up enough with a Maquis band to sing a few French-Canadian folk songs, doing it with that gentle, half-sad smile.

As I lay there day-dreaming our farmer came into the barn. "This agent I told you about," he said to me. "He's here."

I jumped up. "Where?" I asked, grabbing for my pistol. "*Nom de Dieu!* I told you not to bring him here!"

"I'm very sorry," he said, looking embarrassed. "He's right outside now. You see, well, he told me it would be all right if he came and he was sure you would approve."

"Just a minute," I said, trying to keep my temper. I went over to Larue and Descartes and told them the farmer had brought the agent, the one he had told us about earlier. "He may not be an agent at all," I said. "Maybe he's a Gestapo man trying to trap us and some of the others around here. He may think we have a radio and he'll trick us into using it. This might tie in with that Gestapo raid at Fougerolles."

"What are you going to do?" asked Descartes.

"I'm going to bring him in here and grill him. You and Larue stand by the door, and if he makes a break to get out, grab him. Don't let him get away. Shoot him if you have to."

"Don't worry, Captain, I'll strangle him," said Larue, holding out his big, hairy hands.

"Tell him to come in," I said to our farmer.

The man who entered was thin and stoop-shouldered and wore a shabby brown suit. He must have been about my age but he was almost bald and looked much older. As far as I could tell he was unarmed, but I kept watching his hands and I had him covered with my pistol. He seemed amused when I called Descartes over to search him. He had no weapons, only a pocket knife. I motioned him to a corner and he sat down on a bundle of straw and looked at me. He had shrewd grey eyes.

"Good evening, Captain," he said nonchalantly, with an ironic smile. "You don't take any chances, do you? My name is Alfred. Well, let's say my name is Alfred anyway."

"All right," I said. "Let's say your name is Alfred." I didn't like his manner.

"You have a radio, don't you, Captain?"

"No."

He looked thoughtful. "Pity," he said. "I have some messages

I should like to send straight away. Rather urgent, you know." I didn't say anything. "But you have a car, don't you?"

"What makes you think so?"

"The farmer told me you were getting one. I should like to join your party."

"What's the matter," I said. "Are you getting lonesome behind the lines?"

"This is hardly a time to be facetious, Captain."

"You're godamned right it isn't. I'm going to ask you some questions, Alfred, and I want straight answers. Now I warn you, don't try to go for the door, because if you do, Alfred, you'll get plugged."

"I must say I find your manner rather offensive, Captain."

"You'll probably find it much more offensive very shortly. Tell me your story, Alfred."

He told me he had been dropped in civilian clothes about forty miles south of Gorron. Two nights ago the Gestapo raided his village, and he barely managed to get out in time, abandoning his radio and leaving his papers behind in the rush. As he told it, this was a plausible enough story. I asked him if he knew this area well and he replied that he knew the region south of here and towards the Loire. I questioned him about details of his training, his favorite pubs in London, what sort of code he used, the names and ranks of any British officers he had met. He had all the answers; so would a Gestapo officer. Falling back on my lawyer's training I kept boring in on him as in the cross-examination of a tricky witness. I tried to trip him up with sudden questions, changing from one subject to another. At last I caught him. He told me he had made only four practice jumps because he had broken his ankle on his last jump. Five minutes later I reverted to his ankle and he said he had sprained it.

Seizing on this, I said, "A few minutes ago you said you broke your ankle. Now you tell me it was a sprain." I thought I detected a flicker of fear in his eyes. "You don't have your story straight, do you, Alfred?"

"Captain, what happened is that I broke a small bone in my ankle and I sprained it too."

This answer, quietly given, seemed credible. But it was also the kind of quick thinking to be expected from a clever and resourceful member of the Gestapo. We had been repeatedly warned in England of the amazing success of the Gestapo in infiltrating the Maquis. Resistance leaders far more experienced than I had been badly fooled and had paid the price. Then there was the raid at Fougerolles. Was this tied in with it? Did someone at Fougerolles talk under torture? If Alfred were from the Gestapo he would think we had a radio and so the ruse he had in mind was to get us to use our radio and code. He probably thought I lied when I said we didn't have a radio. At any rate, he would try to infiltrate our group and, through us, trap the Maquis leaders of the area. That would be Alfred's bold plan. It had been carried out with devastating results, particularly in Holland.

As I continued my cross-examination of Alfred I saw that he was gradually losing his aplomb. Although it was cool in the barn he was perspiring and wiping his forehead. And then I noticed that I too was perspiring. Alfred, whether or not an Allied agent, knew what was running through my mind and what might happen to him if I didn't believe his story. If I decided that he was a Gestapo man we would not simply tie him up and gag him. Eventually the Germans would find him, our farmer would be shot, and an alert would go out for us. The only thing to do, as our British instructors had told us in a matter-of-fact way, was "to kill the bugger, and be quick about it. Then get rid of the body." Kill him? How? If he made a break for the door we could shoot him. Nothing hard about that. But supposing he didn't try to escape? How do you kill a man in cold blood? I had never really considered that. The curé's story about the blind beggar came back to me. Should I approach Larue and ask him in a whisper to choke Alfred to death? No, this was my responsibility and if I decided Alfred was lying I would have to be the executioner. It would be best to strangle him or slit his throat. Then there would be no sound of a shot and afterward we would drag his body away and dump it somewhere. I couldn't do that, I said to myself; I ought to, but I just couldn't. Had he looked like a vicious brute, one who had tortured many Frenchmen, then I could have done it, but he didn't look the part. No, but it's stupid to assume that all members of the Gestapo have evil faces, and it was true that "there was no art to find the mind's construction in the face." What I would do was tell him to turn around, that he had thirty seconds to make his peace with the Lord—this was the important thing—and then shoot him in the back of the head. If he made a break for it I could shoot him with no compunction, or Descartes and Larue would get him.

But suppose he was really an Allied agent and I killed him? Then I would be court-martialed, when I returned to England, and my defense would be that I made an error in judgment, under pressure. I would probably be exonerated and get a reprimand. But for the rest of my days I would have to live with Alfred's ghost, like Macbeth with Banquo's. That's just the trouble, I told myself, you're not sufficiently cold-blooded. Some men wouldn't be bothered at all; to them it would be just one of those things that happens in a dirty kind of war. And anyway, I might not get back to England and there was no point in looking so far ahead.

I kept looking at Alfred and he spoke up, "Captain, for God's sake, man! You don't think I'm working for the Germans, do you?" His breezy manner was long gone.

"You don't have any credentials," I said, knowing this was a weak rejoinder because as an agent he would only have false identity papers.

"Holy God, Captain!" he said, his voice getting shrill. "I told you why. You know this business. You don't expect me to carry a letter from General Eisenhower in my pocket?"

I didn't reply and for several minutes we stared at one another. Thinking it all over I finally concluded that his story was true. Perhaps I'm wrong, I thought, and I'm being taken in, but if I am he's a hell of a good actor. That's just fine, I said to myself, if I let him go and we're captured then when I'm lined up in front of a firing squad I can console myself with the thought that the Gestapo has marvelous actors. I put my pistol back in its holster.

"I'm stranded, Captain," Alfred said at last. "All I ask is that you let me join you."

Larue had come over to listen to our conversation. "Captain, let him join us," he said, "he can help us."

"Stay out of this, Larue," I said, speaking sharply. "I'll make the decision."

"No you won't. Not alone. We're all in this together and I . . ."

"Larue, I told you I would make the decision. Stay out of this. That's an order." I hoped my voice carried authority.

I faced Larue who stood with his feet apart and his powerful shoulders hunched forward. I noticed that unconsciously my right hand was closed tightly on my pistol holster. Christ, I thought, maybe Truffington was right and I am getting edgy. I had not expected this from Larue, and now here it was—a show-down between us. No one was here to back me up. Descartes hadn't said anything and obviously, as a French second lieutenant, he didn't want to get involved. Larue and I glared at each other. Then his eyes dropped and, turning away, he muttered, "All right."

"All right, what, Larue?" I said, determined to press my advantage.

"All right, Captain," he said sullenly.

I faced Alfred again. "Alfred," I said, "I believe your story. You had me wondering though. I hope to Christ I'm right."

Alfred took a deep breath and his body sagged. He smiled weakly. "God, Captain!" he said. "You gave me a rough time."

"Sorry. I had to."

"Then I can come with you?"

"No. You'd be in the way."

"I don't understand why, Captain."

I explained that we did have a car, but I had three more men in my party and we would have to squeeze six men into the car. Furthermore, he didn't know the area where we were going so he couldn't help us. He had no weapons. He would be a burden.

Alfred stood up. "I'm sorry that's your decision, Captain," he said. "If you get in trouble later on I hope you get more help than I got from you."

"Now wait a minute!" I said, getting mad. "Our mission is the only thing that counts. You sure as hell know that. When we jumped in, if one of our men broke his leg we were to do what we could for him right there and then leave him. And you godamned well know that's how it is!"

"Yes, I suppose so, but . . ."

"But, hell!" I said. "If I have to leave a buddy with a broken leg I can damn well leave you. Shift for yourself. Hide out. You don't have it as tough as we do."

He smiled briefly. "I don't know about that, Captain. But maybe in your position I'd do the same thing. And then again, maybe not."

He held out his hand. "Well, cheerio. And good luck."

"Good luck to you too," I said, shaking hands, and he walked slowly out of the barn.

Soon afterward Truffington came back with Marcel and Louis and I told him about Alfred. "I hope you did the right thing," said Truffington after mulling it over. "Pity I wasn't here. I could have tripped him up better than you. I'd have asked questions about his life in England that wouldn't occur to you."

"Of course. I know that. But you weren't here so I did the best I could."

"The chap may well turn out to be a bloody Jerry after all. Educated at Oxford before the war, and all that."

"I don't think so, Truff. Anyway, it's done now. What about the Citroën?"

"All properly laid on. Stop worrying. I know a bit about motors and I fiddled with it."

"What about the battery?" I wanted to know.

"He's getting it. Probably got it right after I left."

"Truff, how can you fiddle with an engine, adjust the distributor and all that crap, with a dead battery and the engine not running?"

"Oh, for Christ's sake, man! Stop always looking at the dark side. Bloody pessimist, you are. Look at it this way: if the car is in the field when we get there, why then the engine is running, isn't it? The old boy could never push that car over a mile just to pick up ten thousand francs. Rather elementary, what? This won't be bitched up, I promise you."

"I guess that's right, Truff."

Truffington changed back into his uniform. It was dusk but I decided to take a chance and leave now for the field rather than wait for total darkness. I was still thinking of Alfred and the possibility that I was wrong and if so the sooner we left the better. Our farmer was wearing a blue suit, Marcel and Louis had old khaki French Army jackets and black trousers, and with us wearing our camouflaged paratrooper's jackets I didn't think we could be spotted from any distance if we moved carefully. When we had left the farm outside Courcité we had dumped our helmets into the open well. The helmets were a hindrance at night, and now we wore the Army wool caps with their half visors. Before leaving I told the others that if we had to disperse for any reason I would later give a whistle call, two shorts and one long, as a signal to join me again. We followed Truffington across fields and along hedgerows. The twilight had turned to night and I was glad to see that the sky was overcast and there was no moon. We were walking along a country road when we came to a gap in the hedgerow along the road. Truffington led us through this gap and into a small field. Off in one corner I thought I could see what looked like a car with a man standing alongside. The man came forward to meet us and Truffington said in a low voice, "*Bon soir, monsieur,*" with what I thought was needless formality.

Truffington turned to me. "Now, you see, Bill, here's our 'Rolls.' We hop aboard and we're off. Get out your map."

I looked at the old black touring car. I had forgotten how small a Citroën touring car was. It would be a tight squeeze for the six of us. The farmer had camouflaged the car with branches along the sides, on the top and even over the hood. This was a good idea which I hadn't thought of. The Germans camouflaged all of their Army vehicles so they would certainly do the same thing with cars requisitioned from civilians. I tried the right front door. It was stuck.

"How's the battery?" I asked the farmer.

He shrugged his shoulders. "The battery is not like new, that must be admitted. We'll have to push the car to get it started. My brothers gave me a push so I could drive here. The motor ran well, though not perfectly. Monsieur here," he said, pointing to Truffington, "made a few adjustments to the motor."

"That's fine," I said, without enthusiasm. I took off my money belt and counted out ten thousand francs and handed the money to him.

"Thank you very much," I said.

"But no, it is I who thanks you," he replied, tipping his cap.

"If I am not indiscreet," he said, "may I ask where you are going?"

I hesitated. But tonight I would have no guide to tell me the best route to avoid Germans and I needed whatever tips this farmer and our farmer could give us.

"To Le Ferré," I said, "or as near to it as we can get." I got out my flashlight and shielding it with my hand I studied my Michelin roadmap. This was flat country with many villages, and the road network going west was a criss-cross of main highways and secondary roads. What I didn't know was where it would be best to detour around a particular village, or when to stay on the highway instead of using side roads. I saw that, as the crow flies, Le Ferré was about twenty-five miles away, but we would be making wide detours and would have to cover about fifty miles. The two farmers were looking at the map over my shoulder.

"If I may be permitted to say so," said our farmer, "you must by all means avoid Fougères. It would be dangerous to go through Fougères. Also do not go through Louvigné."

"I think you're right about Fougères," said the other farmer, "but I beg to disagree about Louvigné. If you detour around Louvigné that puts you on Route Nationale 799, and it is well known that the Germans use that highway at night constantly."

"I must repeat my warning," said our farmer. "Evidently my friend does not have the latest information. It would be folly to go through Louvigné. I strongly advise against it."

I could see that this polite discussion could go on a long time and I was getting impatient. "We will make a decision later," I told them.

"Descartes," I said, "do you know how to drive this Citroën?"

"Yes, sir. I've often driven a Citroën like this."

"Good. You drive and I'll sit next to you and do the navigating." I was trying to hurry things up. "Let's get going, *Allons! Vite! Vite!*"

We pushed the car out of the field through the gap in the hedgerow and into the road. Descartes got behind the wheel and I climbed over the stuck front door and sat next to him. With our weapons and musette bags it was a close fit. Larue sat alone in the back seat while the others pushed the car to get it started. I had my flashlight out and I was bending down holding the map below the dashboard and studying it again.

It happened then, so quickly and without any warning, that I was taken completely by surprise. A German troop truck with its lights out shot around the bend just ahead of us, slammed on its brakes to keep from hitting us, and as it stopped about ten feet away a German jumped off the running board and was on top of us, standing next to me with his *Schmeisser* submachine gun poking at my chest. Deep inside of me everything stopped. "Good Christ Almighty," I thought, "this is it, this is how it ends." I had let go my flashlight and map but I knew I couldn't reach for my forty-five. He'd plug me before I could get it out. "*Was ist los? Was ist das?*" he growled. I didn't move. He trained his gun on Larue on the back seat. Again he asked "*Was ist los? Was ist das?*" and then added something else. Not a sound out of Larue. I could see that the men pushing the car, evidently hearing the Germans at the last second, must have scrambled to safety in the fields. And now three more Germans, each with his submachine gun, were standing next to our car. Yet now even in those few seconds since the Germans had come around that curve, the first shock, like a hard punch to the pit of my stomach, was wearing off ever so slightly. The instinct born of our training was reminding me: never freeze, do something, it may be the wrong thing, but do it. Yes, but do what? I can't reach for my pistol. Desperately I struggled to take command of myself. I could guess that the German had been asking, "What is this? What's going on?" And then I knew what I had to do. I had to answer him. Stall, gain time, try to bluff him. Go for my pistol if I got half a chance. I looked straight at him, seeing a hard, square face with the lips twisted by a jagged scar. He was a big man and looked very tough. Speaking in English, I said to him, "O.K., take it easy, take it easy. Everything is all right." I tried to keep my voice calm, knowing that I had never tried so hard for anything in all my life. The German looked perplexed. "*Was ist los?*" he asked again, but now the tone of his voice was different. Keep it up, keep it up, I told myself. Maybe you've got him a little confused. "I told you to take it easy. Take it easy," I said to him, "everything is fine. Just take it easy." He stared at me and shook his head. But he didn't move and his gun was still on me.

I could feel that now the scales were not so completely loaded in his favor. He's puzzled, I thought, that's it, he's not sure of what's going on. "Your truck is in our way. Get it off to the side, you dumb bastard," I said firmly, attempting to make it sound like an order. Shaking his head again, he turned away and he and the other three Germans started to walk back to their truck. They were talking among themselves. In that second I lurched out over the stuck door, through the camouflage branches, and jerked out my pistol, all in one desperate convulsive movement. The four Germans stood by their vehicle. Off in the dark I could see six or seven others who had climbed down from their truck to join them. They were milling around and the big German was telling them something. Descartes was out of the car, and so was Larue. But Larue was standing in the middle of the road holding his hands high in surrender. I cursed him inwardly. I backed off a few steps to use our car as cover and I raised my pistol to fire. An impulse kept me from squeezing the trigger. The Germans are baffled, I thought, and if I start firing we may be able to shoot our way out. But they outnumber us and they have a lot more fire-power in those automatic submachine guns than we have in our carbines and pistols. And if there's a gun battle, even if we get away the alarm is given and we'll be hunted. Our best chance was to take advantage of their confusion, get off the road and into the field. We would have to do this without hurrying, casually, as though our strolling off was a perfectly normal thing. I whispered to Larue, "Put your hands down. Follow me." I motioned to Descartes. We turned away and walked towards the opening in the hedgerow. It was only about twenty-five yards away. But those were long yards and I fought an urge to run. Any second I expected to hear the Germans shouting for us to halt. Or they might fire without warning. I had to take that gamble. Stepping away with my back to them, I was ready to whirl and shoot. Aim low, I reminded myself, there's a tendency to fire high at night. Squeeze off two quick shots, then another two. We reached the gap and then ran down the field about a hundred yards and crouched by a hedgerow. Good Christ, I thought, we got away! The bluff worked! Now if they came after us we could run and shoot, run and shoot, especially run. As I knelt down on one knee I could feel my heart pounding hard. The reaction set in and my mouth was very dry. I took a long swig out of my canteen. My hand was steady, and I felt good about that.

We remained crouched next to the hedgerow, breathing hard. I heard German voices from the road then I heard them driving off. After a few minutes I went back to the road and I saw they had pushed our car off to the side so they could pass. I rejoined Descartes and Larue and tried to give the signal to join me, but it was a weak and thin whistle. So Descartes put two fingers to his lips and blew twice, two short blasts, and then one long. In the stillness it sounded to me like the whistle of a steam locomotive. There was no response and after waiting a while I asked Descartes to try again, but with less volume. The two farmers and Marcel came to us. The farmers shook hands with us and they kept whispering, "*Ah, Bon Dieu de Bon Dieu! Oh, là, là!*" Descartes whistled again several times, but after a good fifteen minutes there was still no sign of Truffington and Louis. Evidently they must have thought we were either prisoners or had already been shot so they had headed back for our farm hide-out. I decided we couldn't wait for them any longer. The Germans might have second thoughts and be back any minute.

Our farmer came to me and said, "Pardon me, but there is one thing to consider."

"What's that?" I asked. I was in no mood for these low-voiced discussions. I wanted to get away.

"If you go ahead on this road you pass through Columbiers, that's about a kilometer from here. Yesterday a battalion of SS stopped off in Columbiers and they're there now."

"We'll go the other way, then, detour around Columbiers."

"That presents a problem. You see, down this road in the opposite direction from Columbiers, the Germans have set up a barrage, a check point. They stop all traffic and check the driver's papers."

The farmer who had sold us the car joined in. "Yes," he said, "the check point is a definite problem for you."

"Can't we turn off this road somewhere before Columbiers or the check point?" I asked.

"Ah, no, unfortunately not," said the second farmer. "You have to go either through Columbiers or past the check point."

"If that's so, how did you get your car here?"

"Oh, I came by way of a little road, no more than a track really, and it ends at my farm."

This bad news was unexpected. "Why didn't you tell me that before, when we first started out? Nobody said a word about this."

"You were in a great hurry," the second farmer replied. "You kept saying '*Allons! Allons!*' and '*Vite! Vite*' and I suppose we forgot."

I called Descartes to talk this over. In all probability there would be sentries in Columbiers. They might challenge us, and being trapped in a village street, with the houses built right up to the sidewalk like a solid wall, was not like being caught on a country road. Even if we knocked off one or two sentries we certainly couldn't fight our way out of a village taken over by an SS battalion. We could go the other way and perhaps break past the check point, but then the alarm would be given.

"About this check point," I asked our farmer. "How do the Germans work it? Do they just flag you down or do they have a cart or a barrier of some kind across the road?"

The two farmers looked at each other. "I am not sure," said our farmer. "I am not sure either," said the other one. "I do not think they bar the road during the day, but perhaps at night they do. I have heard that the Germans do that at night elsewhere."

I decided that going through Columbiers was probably the lesser risk. At the check point all vehicles were flagged down, or worse, had to stop because of a barrier, but in Columbiers the sentries would probably not ordinarily halt a car. We would have to take the chance that the sentries would assume we were Germans travelling in a requisitioned French car. The camouflage branches would add to the deception. Since the Maquis had been inactive in this sector, the Germans would not expect a car full of *Maquisards* to go through Columbiers. The last thing the sentries would suspect was that we were Allied officers driving through the village.

"What would you do?" I asked the two farmers. "Try Columbiers or try the check point?"

"Ah, indeed that is the question," said our farmer, waving his hands in the air.

"Yes, that is undoubtedly the question," said the second farmer.

"I know that's the question," I said, getting impatient again and not wanting another debate, "but what do you think?"

"If I were in your place," said our farmer, "I would go through Columbiers. That presents less risk." He had spoken slowly and deliberately.

"There I find I am in complete accord," said the second farmer. "I would choose Columbiers."

"That settles it. We'll try Columbiers. Let's go."

"I think you have made the right decision," said our farmer, and the other farmer added, "There is no doubt. And you will have no trouble going through Columbiers." He said this with the splendid assurance of a man seeing a casual acquaintance off on a perilous journey. They both said "Good luck," and insisted on shaking hands once more.

With Descartes at the wheel we shoved the car and as it got up a little speed and Descartes let out the clutch the engine started, coughed and sputtered, and then ran again. Descartes stopped the car and raced the engine a few minutes. I climbed over next to him while Larue and Marcel got in the back. We drove away slowly, the engine missing a little. As we came near Columbiers we heard at a distance the fine, full-throated singing of German soldiers and the noise of their singing grew louder as we entered the village. I recognized the tune. They were singing "*Lili Marlene.*"

Then we saw the first pair of sentries ahead, one on either side of the street, with their rifles slung over their shoulders. The engine had begun to sputter badly. Descartes was jerking the hand choke, pumping the accelerator furiously, and cursing softly. I was looking straight ahead but out of the corner of my eye I could see the sentries idly turning their heads as they watched us pass. The engine continued to cough and miss. I knew that if the car stopped we were done for. The sentries would approach the car unsuspectingly, just to see if they could give a hand. It would do no good for me then to say "O.K." and "Take it easy." The Germans wouldn't make the same mistake twice. Only once could you be as lucky as we had been. Like Descartes I was urging the car forward by whispering "Son of a bitch! Son of a bitch!" Then the engine was running well again, and we passed another pair of sentries, and then a third pair. We were getting to the end of the village street and once more the engine was sputtering and backfiring. Another pair of sentries was ahead, one of them standing in the middle of the narrow street. As we bore down on him he shifted the sling of his rifle from one shoulder to the other and sauntered out of our way. Like the other sentries, he turned his head to look at us and I saw him yawn.

We were out of Columbiers and Descartes and I turned to each other, smiling tightly and not saying anything. In the back seat Marcel sat quietly, but Larue chuckled and mumbled something to me. I ignored him, for at this point I wanted no more of Larue. First there was the showdown between us and later when we were trapped he had stood in the road with his hands up. The Germans couldn't have noticed him, I realized, otherwise we wouldn't be riding away in the night. I was beginning to relax a little and as I tried to stretch out in the cramped front seat I found that I had been gripping my map so hard it had crumpled and I had to smooth it out.

We were rolling down a straight stretch when Descartes spotted a convoy headed in our direction. There was no side road on which to turn off. Descartes' hands tightened on the wheel and as he stepped on the accelerator the car gathered a little more speed, the engine not sputtering but running well, and we passed a long line of trucks loaded with troops. A few minutes later the engine coughed and died as we were climbing a slight rise. Pushing and grunting and cursing we shoved the Citroën to the top and with the car coasting down on the other side of the grade Descartes let out the clutch and the engine sputtered and started up again. Descartes didn't want to force the engine, so after that we chugged along with the speedometer needle flickering near the fifty kilometer-per-hour mark, and from time to time I checked my map to direct Descartes, doing this by guess, trying to avoid the larger villages, yet never knowing whether this was safe. We passed three more convoys, the engine always running steadily then, but dying out several times later when going up a slope. One such time we had to struggle a good ten minutes, pushing the car foot by foot to the top of a steep hill, but there were no Germans around and so far Truffington's "Rolls" had only stopped when we had the road to ourselves. We were now only a short distance from Fougères and I kept staring ahead for the road forking off to the right before the village. Suddenly as we came around a bend we saw a convoy stopped on our side of the highway. Someone in the road was flagging us down with his flashlight. "*Merde!*" said Descartes, and he stomped on the accelerator. We were getting very close when at the last minute I saw the fork to the right. "*A droite! A droite!*" I said, trying not to shout, and yanking at Descartes' sleeve. He gave the wheel a sharp twist and we shot off the main highway. When I looked back the man with the flashlight was running back to the rear truck. We went around a bend and I lost sight of the convoy.

The road we had taken soon turned into a bumpy, twisting track and we entered a forest. It was pitch dark in the woods and finally I had to get out in front and lead Descartes with my flashlight. When this didn't work he had to turn on his lights and we jolted along for a good distance before emerging on a better road. We approached a small village that I couldn't recognize on my map so I told Descartes to stop while I went ahead to reconnoiter. I was nearing the village square when I heard a rumble and I flattened myself against a wall. The rumble grew louder, and a tank entered the square and headed up a street to my left. It was followed by another and then still another until about twenty-five Tiger tanks had gone by. They were dark, ugly monsters, the throbbing of their engines reverberating in the square, the treads clattering on the cobblestones, and the long gun barrels poking forward. When I was sure there was no more traffic I went back to the car and we started out again.

Dawn came but we kept driving until we reached a point close to Le Ferré. Leaving the car in the road we hid in a small clump of trees while Marcel went to look for a "safe house." He was back in an hour, and as at Gorron he had found a farmer who would hide us. So again we were in a barn reeking of cow dung and full of cackling hens. A taciturn old farmer brought us breakfast and said nothing except "*Bonjour*" and "*il va pleuvoir, aujourd'hui, je pense.*" When I asked if there were any Germans around he grunted "*non*" and shook his head. He's certainly undemonstrative, I thought, but I believe he can be trusted. He came back a little later and said he knew the Resistance leader here, a Colonel Taureau, and if I wished he would send for the Colonel to come here. I told him I would very much like to meet Colonel Taureau. I stretched out in a corner and closed my eyes, feeling dead tired, much more so than on the preceding nights when we had made long forced marches.

Descartes sat chewing on a piece of straw. "Captain," he said, "I'll never understand it. I mean how you talked your way out back there at Gorron."

"*C'était la chance de la route*—the luck of the road," I said, and he laughed. For a second I could see myself again scrambling out over the stuck door, and I knew that the adrenalin must have really been pumping through my system and that never before had I gotten out of an automobile so fast nor would I ever again.

"One thing though, Captain," said Descartes. "Why did you answer him in English?"

I didn't feel like talking about our night ride. It was as though I had suffered through a long nightmare and if I could get back to sleep I might forget it. We could talk about it later, but now sleep was what I wanted and the line about "sleep which knits up the ravelled sleeve of care" drifted through my mind.

"Why, Captain?" Descartes persisted.

"Look, Descartes," I said, "I didn't really have much time to think it over, did I? I had to say something. I can't speak German. If I spoke French, he would recognize the language, even if he didn't understand. Then he'd think we were in the Resistance. So I spoke English."

"Well, I don't know," Descartes said, shaking his head. "I guess he's never heard any English. That must be it. One thing though, it certainly confused him."

"Yes, apparently so."

"But Captain," he said, grinning, "you didn't have to call him a dumb bastard."

"That slipped out."

"If somebody told me that story, I'd never believe it," he said.

"No. But we have each other as witnesses." I was thinking like a lawyer who is pleased to have reliable witnesses to back up his client's unlikely story.

"Luck was a goddess for us tonight," I said to him in English, "and she was also a dirty bitch." I translated this for him and he smiled.

"What do you suppose happened to Captain Truffington and Louis?" he asked.

"Went back to the farm, I guess. *Sauve qui peut*—every man for himself." I said. "You know, Descartes, the car almost stopped cold in Columbiers when we were passing the sentries. I thought you were going to jerk that choke button out of the dashboard. With the extra weight of Truffington and Louis the engine probably would have conked out. And then we wouldn't be here."

"When something like that happens I can't help thinking about fate, don't you?"

"No, not right now. Right now I'm wondering what happened to Jeanpaul and Drouant. And I would like to get some sleep, even just a little sleep. God, Descartes, aren't you tired?"

"Yes sir, I guess so. It's just that I keep thinking about Gorron."

I dozed off and woke up with a jerk. The farmer was standing over me. "Colonel Taureau will be here any minute," he said.

"Good. Thank you very much," I said and stood up to wait for the colonel.

CHAPTER XI

The Maquis Leader

Assuming that Colonel Taureau was a former Army officer I was surprised to see a man in his middle twenties saunter into the barn. He was holding a Sten gun loosely in one hand, muzzle down, and an automatic pistol was stuck in his belt. Taureau was a small, slender man with a gentle and pensive expression. Without his weapons he would have looked like a teacher from a small-town *lycée*, and I wondered how a man of such meek appearance had become the leader of a tough F.T.P. Maquis. He must have guessed what was running through my mind for he smiled faintly.

"*Bonjour*," he said. "My name is Taureau."

"*Bonjour*," I said, shaking hands. "I'm Captain Dreux of the American Army."

"Can I help you, *mon Capitaine?*" he asked, speaking softly as if he wanted to show kindness to tired wayfarers who needed his assistance.

"I certainly hope so, Taureau," I said. I had realized immediately that he was a Maquis "colonel" and I wanted to make it clear at once that I had the rank and that he didn't. But I knew now that this wouldn't be necessary for he had introduced himself only as Taureau and had addressed me as "*mon Capitaine*," so I was sure he understood how things stood between us.

I asked Taureau if he knew Booboo and when he said, "Of course, he's the chief for this region," I told him that Booboo had planned our move from Courcité but that we had run into trouble at Gorron.

"You're the American who was with Major Jeanpaul and Captain Drouant?"

"Yes. What's happened to them? Where are they?"

"They're fine. They're at a farm about five kilometers away. I'll let them know you're here."

For the first time since our guide had failed to show at Gorron I began to feel that our mission was on the track again.

"I see you have two French lieutenants with you," said Taureau, "and a kid from the Maquis. But wasn't there an English captain in your party?"

"Yes. But never mind about him. He missed the bus at Gorron," I replied.

"*Ah, çà alors! Quelle blague!*" said Larue, laughing loudly. Taureau turned to look at Larue, frowning slightly, as if he thought this was an impolite interruption of our conversation.

When I asked Taureau if there were many Germans in this area he replied that up until yesterday the Germans were everywhere but with the Americans pushing west out of Normandy most of the enemy, including the SS and other crack units, had gone north to Dinan and St. Malo and the bunkers and pillboxes along the coast. The heavy fighting would be there. "What's left around here," he added, "are scattered pockets, mostly service troops. It won't be hard to mop them up. Some will fight, many will surrender."

"What about the Gestapo?" I wanted to know.

"Ah, you're concerned about the Gestapo?" He smiled a little and I could see that he must have been amused to hear this question from a paratrooper who had just jumped in.

"Certainly. We heard they made a lot of raids in this part of Brittany lately."

"The Gestapo has pulled out too. Please do not disturb yourself about them."

"The question of whether or not I'm disturbed is really not the point," I answered coldly. "The point is that London had had no contact with this area for over three months. That's why . . ."

"Maybe they didn't want any contact with us," Taureau said. "Perhaps London does not like the F.T.P. because we have Communists. As to whether or not the F.T.P. likes London, I will express no opinion."

"How successful was the Gestapo?" I inquired so as to change the subject, and then realized too late that this was the wrong thing to ask.

His jaw clenched as he stared at me for a moment before answering. "They had a great deal of success, to use your word," he said finally. "They got the leaders, most of them anyway. That wrecks a Resistance network. But only for a while, only for a while." He stood there with his head down, rubbing one foot back and forth across the dirt floor. "About six months ago they got my brother," he said, raising his head. His wide blue eyes had an intense and penetrating look which I found somewhat disconcerting. "My brother was afraid he might talk under torture. He was able to commit suicide." Taureau paused a moment. "He did it with a piece of broken glass."

He had said this quietly, without bitterness, and I could tell that to him the important thing was not that his brother was dead but that his brother had done what was right, using a piece of broken glass. And in saying this Taureau had made me feel small. I was beginning to think that I had done well in escaping the Germans at Gorron, and now I was imagining Taureau's brother in a filthy jail cell fumbling to slash his wrists. Here I was in the uniform of a paratrooper captain, with my jump wings and the Special Forces shoulder patch, and I had a new folding stock carbine and a forty-five, but Taureau and his brother and the others had lived in the shadows while I was drinking beer in the officers' mess at Milton Hall. And long before that too.

"My brother was the leader here," Taureau said in a flat voice. "Now I am."

"How many men in your Maquis?"

"Right now about thirty. Of course there are other units besides mine."

"What about other groups, besides the F.T.P." I asked.

"Captain," he said with a fleeting smile, "evidently your briefing was not quite complete, maybe a little fact here and there left out." He snapped his fingers. "Things which London thought of no importance. For example—and to answer your question, Captain—there aren't any other groups. Just the F.T.P. We're the Resistance here."

He shifted the pistol in his belt and brushed his hair back from his forehead. "Stay right here," he added. "There should be no trouble. I'll go look up the major and the captain." Taureau walked towards the door then he stopped and turned back. "You know, Captain," he said. "Those friends of yours have really done a lot in the last few days. Met all of our leaders. Covered a lot of ground. I was with them most of the time." He was smiling again. "What got me," he added, "is that there they were with no papers, pedalling around on their bicycles as though they were on an inspection tour and the Germans were our own troops. Those two, well *ce sont vraiment des chics types*."

"Very true," I said. "They're fine officers."

He shot me a quick look. "Yes, oh yes. Excellent officers. Too bad there weren't more like them in 1940."

Here it is, I thought, the party line. He's anti-Army, and probably anti-deGaulle, and giving me a wholesale condemnation of the French Officer Corps.

"There were great strategic mistakes in 1940," I said. "General Gamelin and the French staff made catastrophic errors. And that is something over which combat officers have no control. Bravery is of no use then."

"Yes, of course," Taureau admitted. "There were also strategic errors before the Battle of the Marne in World War I. But if you'll remember, the French won that battle, Captain."

"All right. Maybe we'll have a chance to discuss it later." I looked at my watch. "But right now I'd appreciate it if you would go tell Major Jeanpaul that we're here."

"*Bien, mon Capitaine.*" He walked to the door and suddenly his face lost its gentle and thoughtful expression, as though he had taken off a mask, and his eyes grew hard as he peered towards the road, his Sten gun at the ready on his hip, and his finger on the trigger guard. Then he slipped out and was gone.

As he left Larue looked at him suspiciously. "He reminds me of a little librarian I knew before the war," he said. "He went around dusting books with one of those old-fashioned feather dusters." And Larue, rising on his toes, went through the motions of flicking dust from a row of books high on a shelf. "*Merde alors*," he said contemptuously.

Since Larue had the physique of an orang-outang, as Jeanpaul had once remarked, he thought of himself as being tough, really tough, *un vrai dur* as the French would say, and anyone who reminded him of a harmless little librarian could not possibly have this quality. But I saw Taureau differently; he was a man possessed by a cause. The death of his brother, savage Gestapo reprisals, Maquis attacks turning into bloody failures, none of these things would break him. The Germans would have to kill Taureau to stop him. As a guerrilla fighter he would march alone, if need be, to the sound of his own drums. But what was his cause, I wondered, France, or the Communist Party, or both? Perhaps it was truly neither, and he had simply given his pledge to some shining ideals of his own, a poet who carried a Sten gun. This doesn't matter, I told myself, I am in no way concerned with his ideology.

A few hours later Jeanpaul and Drouant came to our barn during a hard, drenching rain. Their clothes were soaked, their boots caked with mud, and they were unshaven. A little bedraggled dog trotted in after them and sniffed around. The breast pocket of Jeanpaul's jacket was torn and the flap dangled. I had a passing thought of how foolish he would look now wearing all his medals.

"*Bonjour, B-e-e-l*," they both said, shaking hands. "*Comment ça va?*"

"*Bonjour*," I replied. "Fine, thank you." It seemed to me that their greeting was strangely casual, as though we had just run into each other in Piccadilly Circus while on a weekend leave in London.

Jeanpaul had taken off his coat and was wringing it out. "What's this about Truffington?" he asked. "Where is he? I didn't quite understand your message about Truffington missing the bus."

I started to tell about our night ride. He had stopped wringing his coat and with his dark eyes boring into me I felt self-conscious telling him this unusual tale.

Descartes interrupted to pick up the story. "*Ah, çà mon Commandant!* You should have been there!" Descartes was grinning broadly and then imitating the German poking his carbine at me, he growled, "*Was ist los?*" Starting to chuckle he said, "That's when Captain Dreux started making speeches in English. Ho, ho, ho!" Descartes was laughing so hard he couldn't talk.

"Ho, ho, ho," I said, angry with Descartes because now this seemed like a big joke to him. "It didn't seem funny then, did it? And I wasn't making speeches. And you sat there at the wheel like a goddam idiot."

"Well, no, Captain," said Descartes. "Of course it wasn't funny then. *Ah çà, non!* But now . . ." and he laughed again and then mimicking me with his strong French accent, "Get your truck out of the way, you dumb bastard. Ho, ho, ho!"

"That's enough, Descartes," Jeanpaul said. "Go ahead, Bill."

I told him the whole story. When I finished Jeanpaul kept looking at me. Finally he said, "*Eh bien, B-e-e-l, je vous félicite. Oui, vraiment je vous félicite. Beaucoup de sang-froid.*"

Since I knew that Jeanpaul didn't hand out compliments lightly, this pleased me but it also embarrassed me and I mumbled, "Thank you," feeling like a schoolboy who has been praised by the principal in front of the class.

"Truffington must be all right," Jeanpaul went on. "He probably headed back for your hide-out. At top speed, too. He's very athletic. Remember how he used to run the obstacle course?"

"That was an extraordinary escape, Bill," said Drouant. "One thing is certain: if you had shown the slightest sign of fear with that German on top of you, none of you would be here."

I remembered how when we got away and crouched in the field my heart was pounding and my mouth felt terribly dry, but I didn't want to admit this to Drouant. And then I thought this was silly; Drouant knew how I felt. Even a combat veteran like himself would have been shaken by that encounter.

"Of course," Jeanpaul said, looking thoughtful, "you told me it was very dark. And remember there are foreign units in the German Army." He smiled. "Maybe they took you for Rumanians."

"*Mon Commandant,*" said Larue loudly, "the Germans thought this was an ambush. That's why we got away. No doubt about it." Larue had given this explanation with an air of authority which contrasted oddly with his behavior the night before when he had stood helplessly in the road with his hands up.

Jeanpaul looked at Larue as if he were an unusually stupid recruit. "For your information, Larue," he said, "that is not the way the Germans would react to an ambush."

"There's something else, Bill," Jeanpaul said. "Do you know the greatest weakness of the German Army?"

"No," I said. "I think maybe it's a little too early for me to tell." I was wondering what he was driving at.

"They're too methodical. No flexibility. They have detailed orders for everything. You ought to see their Field Manuals. Page after page on how to dig a slit trench. But when they're confronted with the unexpected, they don't know what to do. That's a big weakness. They can be outwitted."

"Absolutely," said Drouant as though this were something on which it was impossible for intelligent minds to differ.

"Oh, for God's sake!" I said. "This is ridiculous. We didn't outwit them at all. Not in the way you mean. We were lucky, just plain lucky. Wouldn't happen once in a thousand times."

Jeanpaul and Drouant only shrugged their shoulders. But now I could see what was running through Jeanpaul's mind. It gave him great satisfaction to think that the Germans had been tricked. For one of the immutable principles in French military thinking ever since the glory days of Napoleon—and even long before that—was that the French, being more intelligent than other peoples, naturally excelled in the art of war, an undertaking calling for *l'esprit clair.* This was particularly true when the foes were Germans because Teutonic races were slow-witted—they had *l'esprit lourd.* It seemed to me that this cherished belief was now of questionable validity, considering the Blitzkrieg of 1940 when Rommel and other German generals had shown rather conclusively that they were several lessons ahead of the French in strategy and tactics. World War I could be rated a stand-off. And I remembered other

French military delusions, such as the myth in August of 1914 that French *élan* and bayonet charges would prevail over German machine guns. That view had to be revised slightly after enough French corpses had piled up on German barbed wire.

When I asked about the raid at Fougerolles they said they had both been there and that the Gestapo had missed nabbing them by seconds. Shortly after Jeanpaul and Drouant reached Fougerolles someone talked and the Gestapo learned that there were two strangers in the village. Unaware of this, Jeanpaul and Drouant waited there to meet a Resistance leader.

"We had just sat down at a table outside a little café," said Jeanpaul, "when the waiter came over immediately. And I thought he was in an awful hurry to get our order. The waiter leaned over to wipe the table, not looking at us. Then, talking very fast, he told us that the Germans were throwing a cordon around the village and we only had a few seconds. He said that maybe someone was watching the café right now and that we should go inside and the *patron* would take care of us."

"Any Germans around then?" I asked.

"No, not that we could see. Nobody in uniform, anyway. So André and I went inside the café. There was the *patron*, a big, fat man, very excited. He rushed us down a long corridor and out into the yard. It was an enclosed yard. He pointed to the back wall and jabbered, 'Over the wall! Hurry up!' and ran back inside. Just then we heard what sounded like a staff car roaring up to the café. Heard some shouting, too. So over the wall we went and we were in the fields. We took off fast across the fields."

"Who's that American buddy of yours," asked Drouant. "You know, the guy who thinks he's a champion runner?"

"Farley," I said. "Bob Farley."

"Yes, that's the man. *Drôle de type*. Well, we would have beaten him easily that time."

"That was a close call, all right," said Jeanpaul. "I hope nothing happened to the café owner."

Jeanpaul was frowning. "What got me," he said, "is there we were, a couple of French officers dressed like tramps and having to run away from the Germans with our tails between our legs. It was humiliating."

"Fougerolles was a very risky place," I said. "You knew that."

"What were Drouant and I supposed to do?" asked Jeanpaul in a cutting tone. "Hang around that deserted farm back at Courcité until your General Patton got there? And keep getting 'chins up' messages from London?"

Before I could say anything our farmer came in the barn followed by a squat man with a bullet-shaped head and hard, squinty eyes. He's built like a fireplug, I said to myself. The man carried a German rifle and his coat pockets bulged with ammunition clips. Jeanpaul introduced us, saying the man's name was Bourret and that he had a Maquis group not far from here. Bourret looked at me curiously and gave me a gruff "*Bonjour.*" Jeanpaul then asked him how things were going.

"*Quelle putain de guerre!*" he grunted.

"What's the matter?"

"Everything. The weather stinks. Everything stinks. This barn stinks. And that imbecile Taureau gave me the wrong directions so I slopped all over the fields before I found you. Do you know what that dreamer is talking about now?" Bourret snorted. "The future of Europe! Such crap! My Maquis is not a discussion group. And the Gestapo? And the SS? Do you think they are debating societies? My men are after blood, Major!" and Bourret, glaring at Jeanpaul, spit on the dirt floor.

"Ah, yes, of course. Killing Germans," said Jeanpaul in an even tone. "That is precisely what we are going to discuss."

Our farmer had gone out and now came back with a bottle of Calvados and some glasses. "*Du Calva,*" he said, "*ça vous fera tous du bien.*"

Bourret grabbed the bottle and a glass and without saying a word he downed three big slugs. "Here, do you want some?" he asked Jeanpaul, handing him the bottle and wiping his mouth with his sleeve.

"Thank you," said Jeanpaul. "If you're sure you've finished with it."

We all had a drink. Our farmer apologized for not asking us into his house—it would be quite safe, he said, but he had three sick children.

"I'm very sorry to hear that," said Jeanpaul. "Don't worry about us." He looked around the dilapidated barn with its cows and chickens. "This is absolutely ideal as a command post. Temporary command post."

Sitting on a bundle of straw Jeanpaul pulled out his Michelin map and studied it. Still looking at his map he said, "Bourret, we have to plan some patrols. So I want you and Taureau and the others to report to me here at eight o'clock tonight." He checked his watch. "No, better make it eight-thirty. Get the message to them."

Bourret spit again. "Not enough time," he growled. "Can't make it before nine-thirty at the very earliest."

Jeanpaul looked up. "Perhaps you didn't understand me," he said without raising his voice. "I fixed eight-thirty as the time."

Bourret's face flushed and his ugly features twisted into a scowl as he glared at Jeanpaul. He's not going to take this, I thought. Jeanpaul was looking at him steadily. Finally Bourret drew himself erect as if standing at attention. "*Bien, mon Commandant,*" he muttered, and he stomped out.

"Rather hard on Bourret, weren't you?" I said to Jeanpaul.

"Had to be. I'm in charge here, and Bourret had damned well better get used to it."

"Suppose he had just told you to go to hell?"

Jeanpaul laughed. "Then I might have borrowed your forty-five to support my authority."

I guess he would have at that, I thought. With Jeanpaul still scrutinizing his map, I turned to Drouant and told him of meeting Taureau and my impression of the man. Drouant said that Taureau's exploits in the Resistance had so enraged the Germans that they had threatened to shoot hostages. "A very unusual man," he added. "In civilian life he's an *archiviste-paléographe*. Graduated first in his class at the *École des Chartes*." The way Drouant had said this showed the typical French respect for a man of letters. "You sized him up right," Drouant went on. "A hard-core party man. But gripped by his ideals. Totally committed. *L'homme en-*

gagé. The kind who keeps shooting his arrows into the sun."

"I think André and I know the tactical situation," Jeanpaul said to me. "It has changed a lot since our briefing. The American spearheads are here and here," he added, pointing to his map. "South of us and east of us. They are driving for Combourg, no doubt. Now what we have to do is coordinate the efforts of the Maquis groups here. Go after the Germans with patrols. Harass them, cut them off, keep pressing. We'll start tomorrow. Then push on to Combourg. After that we'll see. But the Americans are going to overrun us very quickly at the rate they're going." And looking at me with a wry grin, Jeanpaul said, "Bill, it looks like you jumped into France to be a reception committee for American tanks."

"That's great," I said bitterly. "Just great. That's why you and I got 'married.'"

"Well, that's the way it is. Look at Larue. He wanted to be a radio operator. Now he doesn't even have a radio. You wanted to blow bridges. You won't. Any bridges that get blown now, will be blown by the Germans."

Marcel had gone out to see about our car. He came back and reported it was gone. Descartes and I swore. We had become attached to that coughing, sputtering old Citroën.

The others climbed up in the hayloft and as I joined them I noticed that Jeanpaul was gone. He was back in a short time and stretched out next to me, lying on his back and staring at the rafters. When I asked him where he had been he replied that he had gone to visit the farmer's sick children. "They remind me of my kids," he said. "Especially the little girl. I have one about the same age. She's my favorite, I guess."

Although I knew that Jeanpaul had a family this was the first time he had mentioned them. And now I saw that his face no longer had that firm look with the mouth clamped shut, but bore a wistful expression I had never seen before.

"Where is your family?" I asked.

"In Morocco, in Marrakesch," he said. "I haven't seen them in a long time."

He lay there for several minutes, his eyes still fixed on the beams above us. "I think I'll ask for leave after this mission," he said finally. "You know, Bill, thinking about the war and all, sometimes you wonder, you really wonder."

"Wonder? Wonder about what?"

He looked towards me for a long time. "Nothing."

This is no time to be talking that way, I thought. What's happened to him? I've never seen him like this before, and if something is beginning to drain the will out of him, we're in trouble.

"God, what a dreary day!" he said. "Listen to that rain pelting down on this old roof. It's a mournful sound, isn't it?" He sighed and rubbed his eyes. "I guess I must be tired. No rest last night," he said, smiling a little. "Maybe a little sleep will fix me up."

I lay there a long time, listening to the rain, and then I dozed off. When I woke up Jeanpaul had climbed down from the hayloft and was walking up and down. Looking at his watch he growled, "Taureau and the others are late."

"How do you feel?" I asked.

"Fine. Why?"

"I mean, did you get enough rest? Are you all right?"

"Of course," he snapped, squaring his shoulders and giving me a sharp look. He's the hell-for-leather officer again, I thought and whatever was troubling him he's rammed it out of his mind.

About nine o'clock Taureau and Bourret came to our barn. It was still raining hard and they stamped their feet and muttered about the weather as they took off their raincoats. A few minutes later four other Maquis chiefs walked in. They were young, burly, tough-looking men.

"Sorry to be late, *mon Commandant*," said Taureau in his soft voice, "but we have some little presents for you. Bring them in, Bourret."

Bourret stepped out and returned holding three German battle helmets by their chin straps. He laid these in a row, said, "*un petit moment*," went out again and came back carrying a German MG42 light machine gun with its ammunition belt. He put the gun by the helmets and stood back. "*Voilà!*" he said. He smiled broadly, showing some broken front teeth. Only a few hours ago

Bourret had been surly and snarling, but now he appeared very pleased with himself and in a fine humor.

Jeanpaul, looking perplexed, hadn't said anything. The men were grinning slyly, nudging each other and watching Jeanpaul closely. "For me?" asked Jeanpaul.

"Of course," said Taureau. "We persuaded a few Germans to lend us the gun. And then we thought of you. A French major, unarmed. That's very dangerous. So we want to give it to you, compliments of the F.T.P."

Jeanpaul had recovered from his surprise and he laughed. "*C'est bien, ça, les gars,*" he said. "Say, Bourret, try on a helmet. Let's see how you look."

When Bourret put on one of the helmets it was far too big and came down over his eyes. We all laughed and Bourret joined in.

"It won't do, Bourret," said Jeanpaul, shaking his head. "Even a dumb Breton can't look like a German."

The men guffawed and one of them slapped Bourret on the back. Apparently the men at first had not been sure of how Jeanpaul would react, but now that he joked about the "presents" everything was fine. I realized that these tough, proud, independent leaders wanted to show Jeanpaul what the F.T.P. Maquis could do and had been doing for nearly four years, without the help of French officers or anyone else. And yet from the way they looked at him I sensed that in the short time he had known them he had earned their respect. And Jeanpaul had accomplished this without his paratrooper's uniform and his rows of decoration ribbons. He had done something even better: he had won their friendship.

Bourret was using his dirty handkerchief to wipe the gun barrel and clean the sights. Kneeling next to the gun, Taureau said, "Now we ought to instruct the American," and turning to me he added, "If you'll step over here please, Captain, I'll show you how to load and fire. First you . . . "

"Never mind, Taureau," I said angrily and not liking the ironic tone of his voice. "I know all about German machine guns."

"Captain Dreux learned about German machine guns during our training," Jeanpaul explained. "And when we fired it on the range he was a real marksman. He's an expert, the best shot in the outfit."

Taureau and the others looked at me with narrowed eyes and I could see they were impressed. What Jeanpaul had said was not right; I was not the best shot in the Jeds, although it was true that we had been taught German machine guns and we had fired them. But I was glad that Jeanpaul had given me the status of an expert machine gunner. For I needed the confidence of the F.T.P. chiefs and I would be off to a bad start if they looked on me as a dilettante in guerrilla warfare.

Drouant got out the Calvados bottle and Taureau immediately proposed a toast, "To the American paratrooper, our new machine-gunner!" The men drank, smiling in a good-natured way, and I saw that the toast was not meant as a gibe.

Jeanpaul then asked the leaders for the last-minute details on enemy movements in their areas. Much of the information was conflicting. "There are two 88's just this side of Combourg, of that I am positive," said one. "Hah! I am equally sure this is false," said another, "for I myself saw the Germans pull those guns back this morning." The first man shrugged his shoulders. "You are demonstrating your customary enormous stupidity," he answered. "And stupidity is a serious handicap in the Maquis. Or anywhere else, for that matter." These disagreements between some of the leaders were expressed with much shouting and many "*merdes;*" while Taureau stood off to one side, working the bolt back and forth on his Sten gun in an absent-minded way.

Jeanpaul was listening impatiently to these contradictory reports, "*Mais c'est un bordel!*" he exclaimed. This vulgar slang, sometimes used by the French to describe utter confusion, had always intrigued me since, for all I knew, perhaps a good many bordellos were run with marvelous efficiency.

"*Assez! Assez!*" said Jeanpaul curtly. "*Quels foutus renseignements!* Enough of that. I've made my plans. Now for the patrols. They will start tomorrow morning at six o'clock sharp." He looked at the Maquis chiefs gathered around him. "I repeat, at six o'clock." No one said anything. Pointing to the map Jeanpaul gave precise orders to each patrol leader, speaking in a low intense voice, the words sharp and crisp, looking each man in the eye and jabbing his finger at him. The men were listening closely and their eyes never left Jeanpaul. Bourret, who was nodding his head in agreement, started to cough and apologized at once.

When Jeanpaul finished the men hurried out, except Taureau who called me aside. He told me he had obtained Jeanpaul's permission, and would I be willing to lead a Maquis patrol tomorrow? I said I would like this very much. Taureau cautioned me that these would be new recruits, some fifteen or twenty of them, and they were inexperienced. "They've never been on a patrol," he said. "Have you been in combat, Captain? Ever been shot at?"

"No," I admitted, annoyed that he would bring this up, "but I've had a hell of a lot of training." I shifted my pistol belt and patted my holster.

"Ah yes, of course."

"And so if I were you," I said, "I would worry about other things, lots of other things, before I worried about my taking out a patrol."

Taureau didn't answer and he looked at me pensively for a moment. "In a way this is an advantage," he continued, "not having been shot at, I mean. If you have been shot at enough you tend to become too cautious. These kids will be reckless. So it will be up to you to command them properly."

"I can handle it all right," I said.

"I think you can, Captain," he replied with his gentle smile. "Good luck to you. Good hunting."

After Taureau left I helped myself to a tumbler of Calvados which I downed in a few gulps the way these Bretons with the leather stomachs did. After a while I started to hum the tune of "*Les Quatre-Vingts Chasseurs*," a bawdy, merry old French song which I had heard in the officers' mess at Milton Hall. This lusty barracks ballad tells of a beautiful *marquise* who had invited eighty hunters to her chateau for a weekend of hunting. Each guest, when reaching the chateau, was astonished to learn that he was only one of many. The afternoon hunt was most successful, and it was followed by a soirée of feasting and drinking, all terminating in a night devoted to *l'amour*. During that memorable evening each hunter, in some way or other, found his way to the bed of the *marquise*. The last verse tells of the birth some nine months later of "a joyous bastard" as the song describes him, and when he became curious about his parentage he was told that he was the child of the *marquise* and the son of eighty hunters.

Tomorrow, I thought, I too will be a hunter. Admittedly it was unlikely that I would end up in the bed of a lovely *marquise*, but I would certainly return with a few prisoners (after all, hadn't I just heard that the Germans were on the run?) and best of all with a captured machine gun which I would present to Taureau and Bourret with appropriate remarks. Bumping into the Germans at Gorron—and many other things too—had left nasty memories. It was high time that the roles be reversed and that I become the hunter instead of the hunted. And so as I lay down in the hayloft for the night I sang the first verse of "*Les Quatre-Vingts Chasseurs*," not loudly but with a gusto perhaps derived in part from the Calvados. Jeanpaul and Drouant were amused. They applauded my singing—although they said I was slightly off-key —but they pointed out that it was quite late and if I waited until some other time to sing the rest of the verses they would have no objections. I drifted off to sleep with high hopes for the morrow.

CHAPTER XII

"C'est magnifique, mais ce n'est pas la guerre"

Early the next morning Jeanpaul and Drouant left on their bicycles to make a reconnaissance in the direction of Combourg. The other Maquis patrols had already gone when Taureau's recruits reported to me in our barn. There weren't fifteen or twenty of them, as I had been told, but only eight boys the oldest of whom couldn't have been over eighteen. The kids seemed very eager and they were chattering excitedly but they stopped when they saw me and came to attention, doing this clumsily and gripping their weapons self-consciously. I told them to stand at ease and tried to hide my surprise. Holy God, I thought, these are Boy Scouts and I am the Scoutmaster and we will all go for a nice hike in the fields and then sit around a fire and toast weenies. Three of the boys carried Sten guns, two had German rifles, one had a shotgun, and another was armed with an old rusty revolver which he held as though it were a trophy. The youngest-looking one, a lad of about fifteen, carried an ancient French rifle of the kind used in World War I, or quite probably even before that. When he saw me looking at his rifle he said in a matter-of-fact way that he would get a submachine gun from the first German we killed. I told him that I was appointing him my personal aide and that he should stick close to me, and he smiled happily.

The boys kept staring at me. It's my uniform that really impresses them, I told myself, that and the carbine, the commando knife and the big forty-five. They see me as a veteran of the American campaigns in Africa and Sicily, and I'm stuck with the role they've created for me, the tough, battle-hardened, quick-shooting paratrooper captain who has dropped out of the skies to lead them. So I gave them a rousing little talk about our mission on this patrol, making it all ring like the Spartan's appeal "to come back with your shield or on it." They cheered and then suddenly stopped because they realized that disciplined veterans did not usually yell like that when addressed by their officers. I knew that this spirited, wild-eyed response was not due to what I had said; it was really not because of the lines spoken by the actor but because the actor was dressed perfectly for his part.

I told them we would move out in single file, with myself in the lead, and that they should watch my hand signals. Using my map to show our route I gave my orders, trying to do this in a quiet, sure way like Jeanpaul with the Maquis chiefs. "Now listen carefully," I said as I finished, "this is a strict order: you fire only on my command." Nothing I had told them was as important as that one order which, I hoped, would keep trigger-happy kids from blazing away wildly in all directions and probably hitting each other. I warned the boys with the Sten guns that this was sometimes an unreliable weapon which had a disagreeable way of going off accidentally, and whenever this happened it was disconcerting, at the very least, to anyone in the vicinity. As I spoke I noticed that one of the kids held his Sten gun carelessly on his hip, pointing straight at me. I stepped forward and shoved the gun barrel down. He mumbled, "Sorry, *mon Capitaine,*" and blushed, looking down at his feet.

"What's your name?" I asked.

"Yves Pépinreau, sir."

He was a short, sturdy boy with a pug nose, tousled red hair and sharp blue eyes, and he seemed to be the oldest one in the group. From the way the others watched him I sensed that they looked on him as their leader.

"We call him Pépin le Bref," chirped one of the boys. "Well, really just plain Pépin."

"Pépin le Bref? Very good," I said, trying to remember where I had heard the name. "But don't point your gun that way, Pépin. You know better than that. That's how people get shot. The wrong people. Very bad." I smiled at him. "Especially if it's an officer."

And now I recalled that I had heard the name of Pépin le Bref during my early school days in Paris. Pépin le Bref was one of the first kings of the Franks, the father of Charlemagne, and he had defeated German tribes who were gentle in their ways like the present German tribes. Our history teacher then was a seedy-looking man with a pasty complexion and I had a vague memory of his telling us about the exploits of Pépin le Bref and then adding that Pépin's wife was called Bertha of the Big Foot—that name had stuck with me—which, he had said, might account for Pépin's being off to the wars so much of the time.

I asked Pépin if any other recruits were due to report to me this morning and when he said a few others might show up I decided to wait a little while. But my mind was made up that if the other boys were even younger, children really, I would have to send them home with a pat on the back. This group was young enough. "Taureau's Tots," I thought, or maybe I should call them "Dreux's Dragoons." As we waited I got out my map and questioned Pépin. He squatted by me on his haunches, carefully holding his Sten gun with the barrel pointed straight up. Were there any Germans billeted in any of the farms along our route? Not now, he said. Had he seen any Germans in this area in the last few days? Only a few. The boy with the old revolver broke in to disagree with Pépin. He said that yesterday he had watched the Germans—at least a squad—setting up machine gun emplacements on both sides of the country road that crossed our route. "Right at the Le Manchec farm," he continued. "If you don't believe me, ask old lady Le Manchec." Several of the boys nodded in agreement, but since "old lady Le Manchec" was not now part of our group it would be difficult at present to check this out with her. Pépin called the revolver boy "*un petit imbécile*," and stood up to announce that he and the captain were having a serious conference and that he wanted no more interruptions. The others walked away muttering and it all reminded me of last night when the Maquis chiefs had argued violently with each other.

This also brought back memories of an afternoon at Milton Hall when a British colonel who had served several months with the guerrilla forces in Yugoslavia came to give us a lecture. He was a tall, thin man with an expressionless face and thick drooping mustaches. He had seemed very bored. Speaking in a droning voice he had mentioned several times the difficulty of getting hard, precise, confirmed information. "Frightfully difficult, you know," he had murmured. "Everything gets terribly botched up. So you have to use your own judgment, or better still, go out and make your own reconnaissance." He had stared out the window a moment. "One peasant will tell you positively there's an SS battalion camped exactly three miles up the road. Along comes another bugger—just as sure, mind you—and he'll tell you that the battalion left yesterday. So what the hell can you do?" said the colonel raising his voice.

Farley, who had been dozing during the lecture, came to, and seeing the colonel watching him, thought that the question had been directed to him. Always the man of action, Farley immediately had blurted out, "Throw a grenade, sir." The rest of us had chortled, and a pained expression had come across the colonel's face. "Oh Christ," he had said quietly, shaking his head. "Good Christ. I'm wasting my bloody time here. Now the rest of you, if you have any questions—and not you, Captain," he had said, pointing to Farley, "see me after tea. Righto." And he had ambled out of the room.

Pépin and I knelt down again by my map and he pointed to the location of the farm where he lived. What about his father, I wanted to know, was he in the Resistance and what did he think of Pépin's joining the Maquis? His father had been killed in the war, Pépin replied, his mother had died soon afterward and now he lived with his grandmother. I asked him how old he was and he told me he was seventeen. He then began to tell me things about himself and now he was speaking freely the way he might to an older friend whom he liked and trusted. As we talked and looked at each other I knew Pépin and I would hit it off.

Pépin said he remembered very clearly the first Germans he had seen. They had come to his grandmother's farm when this army had overrun Brittany in 1940. They were big, rough-looking men in gray-green uniforms who talked loudly in poor French and wanted to get some chickens and eggs. His grandmother wouldn't answer them so they had shoved her aside to go to the chicken coop and this had frightened Pépin. Trying to back away from the soldiers he had tripped on a chair and sprawled over backwards and the Germans had roared with laughter. "I'll never forget the way they laughed," he said, tight-lipped and his eyes full of hatred. It was easy for me to understand that there was something symbolic for him in that incident: it represented the shame he felt not only for himself but for all of France where the heavy-booted Nazi conquerors were then swaggering.

Pépin looked away for a moment and then turned to me with his frank and open gaze. "I know what's on your mind," he said. "You don't think we're old enough to fight. But we're better than you think. Don't worry, Captain, we won't let you down."

"Sure, I know that. I'm counting on all of you," I said, knowing that perhaps I could count on their courage but that the bravery of a boy with a World War I rifle might not be enough.

No other recruits came and we were getting ready to leave when a scrawny priest with a cadaverous face and a threadbare cassock rushed up on his bicycle and said that he wanted to go on patrol with us for he could be of great help. "I'm Father Melançon," he added, as though no further explanation was necessary.

"Good morning, Father," I said, wondering who he was and why he was here. He seemed most determined. Could it be that here was a truly zealous priest who wanted to accompany us as a sort of chaplain? No, that was too ridiculous. "You can help us, Father? Uh-huh," I said without showing lively interest. "And just what did you have in mind?"

"Well, you see I was a prisoner of war for nearly four years. Only released recently. I speak good German. Now when we spot some of them, or maybe we think they're hiding nearby, I'll holler out in German to come and surrender to an American paratrooper major, meaning you of course. It's bound to work. And let me tell you," he said, shaking a long, bony finger in my face, "after those years in a prison camp I want to get back at the Boches!"

I stared at him in disbelief. "Father," I said, "in the first place I'm not a major, only a captain, and in . . ."

"I know that," he interrupted. "I can tell your rank. But I know the German mentality. They don't want to surrender to the Maquis. That's understandable. It would be humiliating, and besides they're afraid of how the Maquis would treat prisoners. But they will surrender to an American officer, and the higher the rank the easier it is for them to surrender, especially for their officers. Less of a disgrace."

"That's an interesting psychological approach, Father," I said. "But if I'm to be promoted I'd like to be a brigadier general."

"No, no! Wouldn't do at all." He was very serious. "The Germans wouldn't believe a general would be here like that. But a paratrooper major, yes."

I couldn't help smiling and this made him angry. "Perhaps you were trying to be humorous, Captain," he said in a harsh tone.

"Yes. Weak joke. But you know, Father, some of these Germans may not want to surrender at all. So by going out and yelling like that you would be giving them a target. And not just you, but these kids as well." He was scowling. "And myself, too," I added drily.

"Bah!" he snorted, obviously regretting that he had run into a timorous paratrooper. "The Germans here are *kaput*. Most of the ones who might give you trouble are gone."

God Almighty, I thought, if I let him come along I'll be going on my first patrol with eight Boy Scouts and one crazy priest. It was true that at Milton Hall we had often been warned to expect the unexpected, but surely our instructors couldn't possibly have had anything like this in mind. And if a squad of Germans, the hard-nosed kind with the fast firing "burp" guns, heard the priest and came storming after us the result could well be a massacre of the innocents, plus one paratrooper captain. Still his idea might work at the right time. What the hell, I said to myself, it's worth a try.

I told him he could come with us and he expressed his thanks, doing this in a deep, resonant voice which must have sounded fine from the pulpit.

"But there's one condition," I said. "You're not to spout any German until I give you the O.K."

He just stood there eyeing me.

"Did you hear me, Father?"

"Yes."

"Good. Just so we understand each other. In your church you're in charge. Here I give the orders."

"Very well, then," he said biting off the words, "but I must protest against this abuse of your authority."

A hell of an overbearing and dogmatic man, I thought. Maybe the Breton priests were like the Irish clergy—after all they were both Celts—or like some of the priests of Irish descent in the States who were convinced that at all times God spoke through them, no matter what the occasion. I saw the kids grinning and I was getting mad.

"Look, Father," I said in a sharp voice. "There's nothing personal in this at all. I'm not anti-clerical. I'm just anti-getting our tails shot off because of some ah, ah . . ." I was trying to think of the French word for "quixotic" but I couldn't remember it. "Because of some crazy priest," I finished, feeling this was perhaps showing too much disrespect for the Roman collar.

He glowered and turning his back on me he walked back to his bicycle.

We set out down a country lane in single file with myself in the lead and the priest pushing his bicycle and walking last as a sort of sullen rear guard. After all those days of hiding out it felt strange to be moving cross-country in broad daylight, but although I didn't know what to expect I felt very sure of myself as I scanned ahead and occasionally peered through the bushes into the fields. The hard rain last night had left the hedgerow leaves green and glistening under the bright sun, and the earth was wet and soft so that we walked without noise. It was very quiet and I could hear none of the sounds to which I had grown accustomed, the roar of German motorcycles, the growling of their truck engines as they shifted gears to climb a rise, and the steady, rhythmic boot-pounding of marching troops. I checked my carbine and the click-click of the bolt sounded very loud. I could see no one in the fields or in the first farmyard we passed, and grazing cows were the only signs of life. Shortly after we started two of the boys scurried through an opening in the hedge and started trotting across the field toward a farmhouse. I whistled them back and said that the next one who did that without any order from me would be sent home, and the next one too, and if I ended up alone on this patrol that is how it would be. They looked flustered and said, "Yes, Captain," while Pépin stared at them sternly.

The stillness was oppressive and menacing and I began to feel uneasy. When we came to the top of a wooded knoll I held up my hand for a stop. I wanted to check my map and be sure of my bearings, and especially I wanted to talk to Pépin. I called him over.

"It sure is quiet," I said. "Where are the farmers? Can't see anyone. Isn't that unusual?"

"They're mostly older men around here, and women and kids," he said. I wondered about that for a moment until I remembered that many of the younger men had been casualties of the 1940 campaign and were either dead or prisoners, others had been deported to the forced labor camps in Germany, while still others had joined the Maquis, so that there were few young men in this area of France. "The people are going to stay inside these next few days," Pépin continued.

"Why? Why now?"

"They've been listening to the BBC news and they think the Americans will get here any time and the shooting will start. Or there will be fighting between the Maquis and the Boches. So it's safer to be inside."

Looking round at the other boys I saw that they had taken up positions around the knoll as though we were a large infantry unit setting up a perimeter defense. And as I watched them I knew that there was a bond between us, and that for the first time I was feeling the elation of leading men into combat, the power and pride of command. It's really ridiculous to feel that way, I thought; after all I was not commanding an infantry company or even a platoon. I had only eight kids, still they were my men who looked up to me and depended on me, and they might have to pay dearly for any of my mistakes. They were so young, much too young to die, or have a leg or an arm shattered by a machine gun burst, but then of course everyone, except the very old, and infirm, was always too young to die.

It was true that there were really nine men in my command, if I included the priest. But I didn't count him or worry about him. He was on his own as far as I was concerned. The Church had all these special purpose saints that few people had ever heard of, such as Saint Blaise for tonsilitis, and there must be a Saint Something or Other, whose special assignment was protecting daft priests on unusual ventures. Just then Father Melançon came up to me and said he was taking the liberty of pointing out to the Captain ("*Si le Capitaine me permet . . .*") that we hadn't flushed out any Germans yet and now was an opportune time for him to use his skill in German and his persuasive powers. Without saying so he conveyed the impression that I had been obtuse in waiting so long. I wanted to tell him to go to hell but with an effort I restrained myself and, thanking him courteously, I said, "I'm sorry, but not yet, Father." He rolled his eyes upward as though imploring Heaven to grant him patience and went back to his bicycle.

Starting out again we eventually came to a sharp bend in the lane at a point I guessed was several hundred yards away from the Le Manchec farm. I told Pépin that I was going to make a reconnaissance, leaving him in charge, and if I didn't return in an hour, or if he heard firing, he was to take our group back at once to our farm headquarters. This was an order I was afraid he wouldn't obey. I wanted to detour and approach the Le Manchec farm from the back so I left the lane and went into the field. There was a path there but I cut around it to stay close to the concealment of the hedgerow and to avoid open stretches as much as possible. I walked cautiously, pausing often to look and listen, but I saw nothing and heard nothing except the twittering of the birds now and then. Once I stepped on a fallen branch and it broke with a loud, sharp snap and I felt myself grow tense and my hands tightened on my carbine with my finger curled rigidly around the trigger. I went ahead a short distance and then looking through a clump of bushes I saw the farmhouse very clearly about fifty yards off to the side. Its white stones reflected the glare of the sun and a haycart with its upturned shafts cast a sharp, angular shadow on the wall. In the farmyard chickens pecked away at the ground. I decided to make a dash for it and I ran through the yard, the chickens cackling and flapping, and I knocked on the door. There was no answer and I pounded again. The door opened half-way very slowly and I saw a small and frail old lady with white hair who was clutching a black shawl around her shoulders. Her sharp eyes peered at me suspiciously from her wrinkled and weather-beaten face. Obviously she did not recognize the American uniform.

"*Américain,*" I said. "*Je suis Américain.*"

"*Eh?*" she said, holding a hand to her ear and still squinting at me.

"*Américain, Américain,*" I said very loudly.

Her face suddenly lit up with a broad, crinkled smile.

"*Ah, un Américain!*" she exclaimed in a quavering voice and she threw up her hands. "*Les Américains sont ici! Dieu merci!*" She made the sign of the cross and motioned me inside, her eyes wide with surprise.

"Any Boches around here?" I asked.

"Eh? Eh? Speak louder if you please. *Ah les Américains! C'est la Sainte Vierge elle même qui vous envoie ici! Ah, oui!*"

I didn't think that now was the time to dwell on the role of the Blessed Virgin in all this. "*Les Boches,*" I repeated, almost shouting. "Have you seen any Boches around here?"

She kept staring at me. "Boches? Here? No, no. Not now. Day before yesterday, yes, not now."

I told her to think carefully, that this was very important, and she again answered that she hadn't seen any Germans.

"This is the Le Manchec farm, isn't it?" I asked.

"Of course," she said, looking annoyed.

"Yes, well, ah . . . it's a fine farm," I replied, nodding my head. She opened the door to look out and wanted to know where the other Americans were. I had to admit that right now I was the only American and that the others would come later.

"Later?" she asked, looking anxious. "When? How many? Are you a pilot who's been shot down? You're not going to try to fight the Boches by yourself?"

"I'm with the Maquis," I said. "But don't worry. The Americans are coming. Lots of them."

She thought about that for a moment. "*Ah, Bon Dieu!*" she groaned, and her face clouded up. "That means there will be shooting around here, and then what will happen to me, to my poor little farm, I have . . ."

"There will be no fighting here," I assured her, and I quoted Father Melançon, "The Germans are *kaput*."

She shrugged her shoulders, giving me a curious look, and after a moment she said it would give her the greatest pleasure if I would have a glass of her cider or some Calvados. I told her that I was very sorry but I didn't have the time. She seemed so disappointed that I changed my mind and told her I would love a glass of cider. She shuffled over to the cupboard and got out a big tumbler and a bottle of cider. When she poured the drink her hand shook badly and the cider spilled over. She apologized. "*Oh, là, là. Je m'excuse! Je m'excuse!*" She urged me to please be seated and I took a chair where I could watch the door and also look out the window. Glancing at the mantel I noticed a faded photograph of a bearded soldier posing self-consciously in his World War I uniform. The picture was set in its frame against a wide black mat with a Croix de Guerre medal pinned on one side and a Médaille Militaire on the other side.

"My husband," she told me. She looked at the picture for several seconds. "*Mort pour la France en 1914,*" she said in a quiet voice, using the ceremonial phrase rather than "he was killed in the War," or "He's dead." She stopped there and said nothing about his medals. I thought her silence was eloquent.

We didn't talk for a few minutes as I sipped my cider. "Do you live here alone?" I asked finally.

"Yes. My son was killed in an accident before the War. After that my daughter-in-law and their two children lived with me." She sat there, still clutching her shawl and looking off into space, and then, speaking hesitantly, she told me that in 1940 her daughter-in-law and the two children tried to escape to the south of France when the Germans advanced into Brittany. Along with other refugees they had been caught out in the open by German planes strafing the road, and all three were killed. I could imagine the scene, the German fighters roaring in at tree-top level, machine guns blazing, then banking steeply to return and strafe the broken screaming column of refugees again and again. And all this had been done for the glory of the Third Reich which, Hitler had sworn, was to last for a thousand years. A sudden feeling of rage swept over me and I said under my breath, "Oh, God, how I'd like to get those bastards!"

I put down my glass and thanked her, saying it was the best cider I'd ever tasted and she smiled and nodded her head. I was ready to leave but she wanted to talk some more. Would I be back? Yes, I lied. And then would I bring other Americans? It would be my pleasure. She said she would offer them some of her good cider too, and Calvados, and would American soldiers like Calvados? Beyond any doubt, I replied emphatically. She said that the young men in the Maquis were wonderful, so brave, but there were so few of them and so many Germans and the Maquis could not drive the Boches out of Brittany all by themselves, now could they? No, I really didn't think they could. And now, with a cunning gleam in her eye, she told me that she had been helping the Maquis by hiding weapons for them and that there were rifles hidden under the hay in that cart in the farmyard. Thinking of the old World War I rifle carried by one of my kids it didn't seem to me that the Le Manchec arsenal was a real threat to the Germans. Yet if the Gestapo or the SS would find the cache she would not get off with a mild rebuke, and it would have been so easy for her to do nothing. I said goodbye and walked out.

When I got back to my group I said all was clear at the Le Manchec farm and Pépin, turning angrily to the boy with the old revolver, hissed, "*Crétin! Petit imbécile!*" The boy flushed but he didn't say anything and I gave him a pat on the back and said, "Let's go."

We kept moving cross-country, down lanes, through fields and patches of woods, along narrow side roads, and still the countryside appeared deserted. At last I decided to go back to our farm headquarters, and when we were about half-way back I realized that we would not find any Germans. Either they were all gone, or they were staying well hidden rather than have a skirmish with my kids. But there was one more thing to try and, smiling to myself, I thought: now I am a strategist, a master strategist, one who knows exactly the right moment to throw his reserve into action, and the priest was my reserve. I would now unleash Father Melançon in one bold and brilliant stroke. We were on a side road at the top of an incline when I called him to join me. He came to me looking stern and forbidding, like one of those figures in an El Greco painting. I started to tell him that now was a good time for him to try his German but he didn't let me finish, and jumping on his bicycle, he darted ahead madly. His cassock was flapping in the breeze and I noticed for the first time that he had no trousers and that instead he wore what looked like long black stockings extending well above his knees. His skinny legs were pumping furiously up and down. I found this quaint priestly garb somewhat surprising; it reminded me of our days in the Highlands up at Arisaig when we had wondered just what, if anything, the Scots did wear under their kilts. We had never wanted to ask them this rather delicate question, and even Bob Farley, who always knew everything about everything, admitted that he wasn't sure.

When Father Melançon reached the bottom of the grade he leaped off his bicycle and ran to the side of the road where there was an opening in the hedge. Cupping his hands he shouted in German across the field. Nothing happened. He tried once more, and then a third time, but the only result was that some birds took fright and flew off. On our way back this wild charge by Father Melançon was repeated many times without success. After Father Melançon had made a few of these sorties one of the Maquis kids looked over at me, tapped his forehead and shook his head a few times. Eventually Father Melançon began to get hoarse and he looked tired and discouraged, but he never gave up. Once we did see a peasant digging in his field, the first farmer we had seen, and when he caught sight of us and heard the loud German yells he dropped his spade and ran back to his farmhouse as fast as he could. It was all like watching an old slapstick movie. I remembered the comment of the French general who was an observer at Balaklava when the Light Brigade had made its charge: "*C'est magnifique, mais ce n'est pas la guerre.*" This wasn't magnificent, and it wasn't war either.

When I got back to our farm I learned that one of the Maquis patrols had ambushed and gunned down a lone German cyclist and had carried the badly wounded soldier to the barn. A Maquis fighter in the farmyard told me that the German was an older man, a Luftwaffe sergeant who undoubtedly belonged to a ground crew. Walking into the barn I saw him lying there on the straw, breathing heavily, and his grimy, sweaty face was gray and showed his fear. He had been shot through the guts and someone had applied a crude bandage made out of a frayed towel. Blood oozed through the towel, staining the straw a dark red. He must have recognized my uniform for I thought I saw a flicker of relief in his eyes. Bourret and a few others stood off by the door talking in low voices and occasionally glancing over their shoulders at the German.

Father Melançon burst into the barn then and shoving the men roughly out of his way he got down on one knee by the wounded man and spoke to him softly in German. I had always thought of German as a harsh and guttural language but now, hearing the priest, it was a soothing sound much as though he were crooning. A thin stream of saliva trickled from a corner of the man's mouth and the priest used his handkerchief to wipe the German's face, doing this very gently with a caressing motion. I decided that I had to change my opinion of Father Melançon. Without saying a word to me Father Melançon snatched the canteen from my belt and held it to the man's lips. Giving a drink to a man shot through the stomach was the wrong thing to do, but here it didn't make any difference because the German couldn't swallow, although he tried with a weak, sucking noise. There was no mistaking the German's expression now; it reflected both relief and gratitude. The priest stood up and in a sharp tone asked Bourret if anyone had sent for a doctor. Bourret wouldn't look at Father Melançon. Keeping his head down he mumbled that this had been done. "But you know how long that will take," Bourret said. "And by the time a doctor gets here, well . . ." He shrugged his shoulders, still looking at the ground.

Father Melançon started to say something but then Taureau walked in, and after one quick look he immediately took off his jacket which he folded and eased under the German's head. Taureau attempted to adjust the bandage, his fingers working with a light, sure touch, but the blood kept seeping through the towel and dribbling down to the straw. The German tried to say something to Father Melançon bending over him, his lips forming words which couldn't be heard.

In the pocket of my jump jacket was a compact emergency medical kit with a tiny syrette of morphine and I wondered whether I should give him a shot but then I decided it would be wasted and I had best save the morphine in case I might need it later on. Staring at the wounded man I realized he knew he was dying, and probably most of the pain was gone now. His breathing was getting shallower and his eyes had a glazed and far-off look as though he were gazing dimly at something a great distance away. The priest and Taureau were still kneeling by the dying man when I left the barn.

I went outside the farmyard and sat in the sun with my back to the stone wall and my legs stretched out. I still had a little tobacco left and I lit my pipe. I was thinking of how the shooting of the German had brought me no satisfaction. It would have if I could have imagined him as a brutish Storm Trooper, smashing his victim's face with his rifle butt, or if he had been one of the Luftwaffe pilots who had strafed the Le Manchec family back in 1940. And had he and I been shooting at each other then I could feel it was he or I, and I had won and that was the way of war. How disappointing the morning patrol had been, I thought. As I sat there puffing my pipe, a 1940 newsreel flashed vividly in my mind.

It had been filmed during the German invasion of Norway and showed three British destroyers steaming in the twilight towards the German-held port of Narvik. The newsreel commentator reported that the flotilla commander had just heard by radio from the Admiralty in London that the German batteries at Narvik were much stronger than at first believed and caution was recommended. The commander on the lead destroyer was in communication with the other two warships by blinker light, and he had not hesitated a moment, his light blinking rapidly to flash his defiant response to the warning: "Am going into action." This morning I too had gone into action but there had been nothing dramatic and heroic, and it had all ended with my standing over a frightened enemy bandaged with a blood-soaked towel, a man who would soon be a corpse.

After a while Taureau came and sat beside me. "He's dead," he said quietly. "Never had a chance."

I just kept smoking, looking out at the blue sky and drifting clouds and the rolling fields in their neat checkered patterns.

"Perhaps you think he was murdered," Taureau said.

"No," I said. But I wasn't too sure about my answer, although I could understand that up until a day or so ago it had been impossible for the Maquis to take prisoners, and that after four years it was hard for them to abandon all at once the rule of kill or be killed.

We sat there for some time not saying anything. "That Father Melançon, I know him very well. He's one of the very few good ones," said Taureau finally, looking pensive.

I didn't want to let that go by so I told him about the curé in Courcité.

"That's interesting," he said. "Well, apparently he's also one of the few. But I'm talking of the Church, the Church in France as a whole. The Church anywhere, as far as that goes." He had spoken calmly, in that soft voice of his, with what seemed almost a note of regret.

"Look, Taureau," I said quietly, "I don't give a damn what you think about the Church."

Taureau looked up at me with a kindly expression. "I shouldn't have said that to you," he said. "You're a *croyant* then, a believer?"

I stood up and looked back at him, not saying anything.

"I'm sorry if I've offended you," he said. "Please accept my apologies."

His courtesy irritated me and I walked away without answering. Entering the farmyard I saw Jeanpaul and Drouant who had just returned with a Maquis patrol which had taken six prisoners now being held at another farm. From what Jeanpaul had seen that morning, and from the scattered reports received from some of the Maquis leaders, he decided that we should head for Combourg, a small town about seven miles to the west, south of the Brittany coast and the German's so-called "Atlantic Wall."

We started out that afternoon, Taureau and some of the others having left earlier to meet us there. Jeanpaul saw no need for us to move cross-country so we set out down the main highway to Combourg, Jeanpaul and Drouant leading the way and pushing their bicycles. We hadn't gone far when we were suddenly overrun by the American forces. First we heard the rumble of approaching tanks and Jeanpaul, glancing at me with a sardonic smile, said I would soon be able to greet my compatriots. The rumble grew louder and then, coming around a bend back of us, we saw the lead tank with the big white star insignia. It was followed by at least a dozen other tanks roaring by at full speed, their treads churning up the dust, the tank commanders standing in the open turrets, wearing goggles and staring straight ahead. Then came several jeeps, the motorized artillery, and a long line of trucks loaded with troops. Not a shot was fired; this could have been maneuvers back in the States.

Truck after truck rolled by as we trudged down the shoulder of the road half choked by the swirling dust and the exhaust fumes. A hot sun was beating down and I could feel my shirt sticking to my back and the sweat running down my face and stinging my eyes. It was a long convoy and as the snarl of each passing truck faded I would hear the roar of the next truck, all in a steady, ceaseless pulsation and crescendo of deafening sound. There was the American Army in all its might and power rolling irresistibly toward Combourg, and then our little band plodding along. I thought the contrast was ignominious. I didn't see the American breakthrough as a great victory but only as the end of our mission. As is true for most soldiers, the war was a very personal thing which centered around me. I had thought long about the war, trained hard for it in Scotland and at Milton Hall, but somehow the staff in London had miscalculated so that the American armor was reaching our zone of operation at the same time we were. When we had been alerted at Milton Hall we had high hopes for our mission, and afterwards we had the briefing by Colonel Girard and were told about the bridges to be blown and the 88's to be captured. But now I was just a paratrooper captain, with the winged Special Forces shoulder patch, who had been reduced to insignificance by all the big, lumbering Sherman tanks.

Finally the convoy passed and then we could see Combourg with its castle overlooking the town. By the time we reached Combourg the combat troops had already passed through on their way to the coast and the supply trucks were arriving. In the town people were in a frenzy, jostling and pushing in the streets, and American and French flags were hung everywhere. We arrived by way of a deserted side street and only a few people paid any attention to us; we came in like dirty, tired stragglers tagging along after the armored columns. The Military Police were already in the town square directing traffic and surrounded by yelling women and children. The M.P.'s were tall, good-looking young men in natty uniforms with sharp creases in their trousers, and they wore glossy helmets with the big "M.P." letters and brightly shined jump boots. It was the boots that I particularly resented. Like all paratroopers I had a strong feeling that boots were something you earned by jumping, and not by directing traffic or raiding a pub full of brawling GI's.

Taureau had told Jeanpaul that we could use the City Hall as our headquarters but when we got there everyone had gone out to welcome the Americans. We did find that a room had been set aside for us. It was a dingy back room whose single window looked out on a small courtyard cluttered with garbage cans. The room had a stale smell, the floor was dirty and littered with trash, and flies were buzzing around. Except for one battered chair the furniture had been removed and stained and lumpy straw mattresses had been brought in.

Jeanpaul sat in the chair, staring moodily at the floor. The rest of us sat on the edge of our mattresses and no one spoke. Larue, whittling on a stick, was humming to himself. After a while Jeanpaul called out, "Larue!" and when Larue looked up Jeanpaul made a quick, closing motion with his thumb and fingers and Larue stopped humming. From time to time I could hear the shrill whistles of the M.P.'s and the rumble of more tanks and trucks going through the town. Finally Jeanpaul got up and stood with his back to us, gazing out the window. Then, speaking deliberately and enunciating each word clearly, he recited the phrase given us in our briefing as the radio signal which London would send to order us into full-scale action: "*Le chapeau de Napoléon est-il toujours à Perros-Guirrec?*" He paused and turning to us, his face impassive, he added "*Merde!*"

CHAPTER XIII

Orders from a General

We spent the next day in Combourg doing very little. Jeanpaul was morose and taciturn, answering my questions with a blunt "yes" or "no" and sometimes only grunting. But he had spoken to the mayor and he must have made it extremely clear that our dingy back room was not suitable for a French major and his party. We were soon moved to a much larger front room with a big desk and comfortable chairs. Cots and blankets were brought in. Some other official, a little man with an important air, bustled in and put a bottle of Calvados and glasses on the desk.

"*Voilà, monsieur,*" he said to Jeanpaul with a little flourish.

"*Commandant,*" Jeanpaul corrected him curtly.

"Ah-ah, I beg your pardon!" the man stammered. "It's just that, just . . . I forgot. Well, I hope this, ah-ah, takes care of everything."

"*Bien. Sortez,*" said Jeanpaul. The man left hurriedly.

During the morning the word had spread gradually through the town that a few French parachutists were quartered in the City Hall, and small delegations, mostly women, came to pay their respects and satisfy their curiosity. Since Larue and Descartes were in French uniforms they became instant heroes and replaced the M.P.'s as the liberators of Combourg. Surrounded by the younger women Larue and Descartes were enjoying their popularity, especially Larue who strutted down the corridor like a general of one of Mussolini's conquering legions. Jeanpaul and Drouant were ignored, no doubt because in their torn and dirty clothes they were taken for refugees from the battlefields of Normandy. A buxom lady with a monumental flowered hat and a frozen smile cooed sympathetically to Jeanpaul about the cruel hardships he must have endured as a fugitive from the horrors of war. Bowing slightly, Jeanpaul gravely thanked her, "Madam is very understanding and most kind." She turned to me to say that President Roosevelt was such a fine man, and I told her it made me very happy to hear her say this.

"Oh, but you speak such good French," she simpered.

"So do you, Madam," I replied.

Her stiff smile disappeared and after giving me a suspicious look she joined the circle of chattering women around Larue and Descartes.

That afternoon as I sat outside on the City Hall steps a jeep pulled up and stopped in front of me. The driver was a sleepy-faced American sergeant and next to him was a British major with a closely cropped mustache. The major sat erect and looked very dignified.

"I say, Captain," the major told me. "You must be one of the chaps I'm looking for. You're a Jed aren't you?" He had spoken in a precise way, with his lips barely moving.

"Yes sir. I'm Captain Dreux."

"Just as I thought. Good." He took a little black notebook out of his pocket and checked something.

"I'm Major Rockbrooke of the staff at London headquarters," he said, "and my mission is to locate you paratrooper chaps after you've been overrun. Glad to see you came through all right. Congratulations."

"Yes sir, thank you." I was glad to see him because I had a few things I badly wanted to tell a staff officer from London.

"Located you immediately," said Major Rockbrooke. "We have a way of finding things out, don't we, Sergeant?"

"Yes sir," said the sergeant, and he yawned.

I leaned close to the major, and keeping a straight face, I whispered, "My wife Nancy is a Kappa."

He drew back, looking startled. "I beg your pardon?"

"That's my identification phrase, sir."

"Oh yes. Quite so. Very good. Not actually necessary under the circumstances, though, Captain."

"Yes sir. But I wanted to follow the proper procedure. It's been on my mind. You know how it is, sir. Maybe I'm overly conscientious."

He looked at me solemnly for a moment. "I see." He reached for a cigarette. "Where are the others?"

I told him we were all here except Captain Truffington, and I explained why he was missing.

"I'm sure Truffington is all right," he said. "Must make a note of that though." Out came his notebook again. The major then informed me that London had been quite concerned because they had received no messages from us for some time. "In fact," he continued, "Colonel Burton-Smith was a bit put out, I'm afraid. He was not getting the intelligence reports he needed, you know."

"We had to cache our radio," I said, trying to hold my temper. "We told London that in our last message."

"Ah, yes. Well now, that was a pity, wasn't it? Cuts off communications completely, doesn't it?" He sounded reproachful.

"Oh, it does, Major, old boy. You're so goddamned right!"

He turned his pale blue eyes on me. "I remind you that you are addressing a superior officer and . . . "

"Bullshit, Major!" I growled. "We've had a hell of a time! London had this mission all screwed up! We get here and it's all over."

He raised his eyebrows. "Bit upset, aren't you?" Major Rockbrooke went on in a soothing tone. "Quite understandable, I dare say. You chaps stay put here. I'll radio your location to London and we'll have you back there in no time. O.K.? Cheerio. Carry on."

I jerked my middle finger up stiffly and held it in front of his face. "Up, Major," I said quietly.

He flushed. "Drive on, Sergeant," he said. The sergeant was trying to hide a grin as they drove off. I wondered if Major Rockbrooke would report me for insulting a superior officer. That might cause trouble, but this encounter had been most satisfying.

The next day Jeanpaul suggested we buy another used car so

Descartes and I bought a Matford touring car, the French Ford of the late thirties. It was in fair condition except for the tires. The owner said we could get new tires from a black market operator named Béchard. Giving us his opinion of Mr. Béchard at some length, he concluded by saying, "*Béchard, c'est un cochon.*" There are few French epithets stronger than *cochon* and these he had already used.

I replied that no *cochon* would get my money and that I would simply requisition the tires by giving Mr. Béchard a fictitious voucher for four new tires and telling him to present it to the nearest American supply depot. The reaction of a hard-boiled supply sergeant when shown this paper, I said, would not be favorable. Descartes stood up saying, "This is what the sergeant will do. *Allez! Foutez le camp!*" and grinning he swung a swift kick. The imitation of the supply sergeant booting Mr. Béchard out on his ear made the Frenchman guffaw and he said this called for Calvados. So there was another cocktail hour like those we had while hiding in barns on our way from Courcité with the important difference that if I heard any troops marching by they would be American infantry. We drank a toast to the unknown supply sergeant, to each other, to the Matford, the liberation of Combourg, and finally to General Eisenhower.

Next we went to see Mr. Béchard. I anticipated finding an obese, repulsive man with squinty eyes set in a porcine face. But Mr. Béchard was a gray-haired man of distinguished appearance who looked like a bank president and greeted us with great courtesy. I informed Mr. Béchard that we needed four tires and I scribbled a voucher on a piece of paper which I shoved under his nose, warning him that I didn't have time to argue with him. Mr. Béchard shrugged his shoulders, went to get the tires and helped us put them on. When he had finished he carefully wiped his hands and taking the voucher from me he opened the car door for us as though showing his respect for esteemed customers.

I took the wheel and we drove off. The Matford ran well, probably, as I told Descartes, because Truffington had not tinkered with the carburetor and distributor. Then a splendid idea came to me. We would drive to the little village near Fougerolles where I believed Booboo had cached our radio and the rucksacks containing our extra clothes. No doubt this village had been liberated by now and we could recover our things. While the radio no longer mattered to me I had been wearing the same uniform for nearly two weeks and the smell was getting strong. We rolled along heading east, enjoying not only the countryside but the certainty that there would be no "*Was ist los?*" interruptions on this happy, carefree journey. We had been driving for some time when I noticed troops deploying in the fields and guns being moved into position. At the same time we heard sporadic small-arms fire and I wondered if we were getting close to the front lines which might not be as far east as I had thought. Rounding a bend below a rise in the road we suddenly came upon a few American tanks, hull down just below the crest of the ridge. As we passed the tanks a turret popped open and a soldier shouted and waved frantically. We slowed down and just as we reached the top of the rise we ran into a burst of machine gun fire, the bullets ripping through the hedgerows and slashing through the canvas top of our car. I yanked the wheel and desperately spun the car around and as we headed back down the hill the gunner in the open turret yelled, "Tried to flag you down, wise guy. Them woods are full of Krauts!"

Through all this Descartes hadn't flinched but when we reached the bottom of the hill he asked if I wanted him to drive and he seemed a little disappointed when I said no.

I found a battalion headquarters and told the commanding officer that I wanted to go to Fougerolles and would like to know how long it would be before his men got there.

"You do, eh? Why the hell do you want to go to Fougerolles?" asked the lieutenant colonel.

"Because there are some things of mine there, sir."

He leaned back against a tree and studied me. "Some things of yours? Well now, that's a very interesting story, Captain. Particularly considering that the Germans have been there since 1940, and before that the French, and before them the Gauls, I believe."

"Yes sir. But I was in that area not long ago."

"You were? That's even more interesting." He turned to a young lieutenant standing by. "Hey, Walton! Come over here.

Listen to this. The captain here says he's been in Fougerolles. Real tourist." The lieutenant colonel's eyes grew hard and cold. "Let me see your AGO identification card," he said in a menacing tone.

While getting out my AGO card I remembered my "passport" signed by General Koenig in London. Certainly this passport had never been intended for such a contingency but this would no doubt be my only chance to use it and I wanted to see what effect it would have on a front-line commander. I handed over the card and passport and the lieutenant colonel's eyes widened as he carefully read the English version and turned the paper over to look at the French version. Then he glanced at my AGO card. His manner had changed completely and he smiled broadly.

"I'll be goddamned! Behind-the-lines stuff, eh?" He took off his helmet and scratched his head. "Hell, Captain, why didn't you say so?"

The lieutenant colonel questioned me about the Fougerolles region, but I couldn't give him any up-to-date information and all I could say was that when I was near there I had the feeling that the entire German army was there. He left to inspect his outposts, telling Lieutenant Walton to "give the captain the picture." I learned from the lieutenant that the Germans had launched a heavy counter-attack at Mortain, extending to this sector, and that American forces were on the defensive here and would not resume their advance towards Fougerolles for at least forty-eight hours.

There was no point in our waiting that long so we headed back to Combourg and on the way almost collided with a dilapidated touring car which careened around a curve and slammed to a stop as we pulled off to the side. The car had the letters "F.F.I." daubed on its sides and was flying a small French flag. Packed in the vehicle were Resistance fighters armed with old rifles and wearing crudely made F.F.I. armbands. The men piled out followed by a squat, young woman wearing the same kind of armband. She had a big bosom, brawny arms, and a hairy upper lip. The woman carried a Sten gun and looked very tough. They all started talking at once and told us they were hunting Germans. Descartes said that since there were no Germans around here they were wasting their time. The squat woman gave him a contemptuous look. "He doesn't know what he's talking about," she snorted. "*Merde! Allons!*" They clambered back in their car and roared away.

"What a broad!" said Descartes, as we rode off. "She'd scare hell out of the SS."

Further along the road we saw several more decrepit cars flying French flags, with the same F.F.I. insignia, and all were loaded with *Maquisards*. At times we passed small groups of young men and women wearing the armbands and as we went by they would brandish their weapons and yell excitedly. The women appeared more ferocious than the men and seemed to be urging them on. It seemed as if these roving bands were everywhere and that this little corner of Brittany had suddenly sprung to arms. The scene was like something out of the French Revolution when angry peasants armed with clubs and pitchforks were roaming the countryside and hunting the King's soldiers. I thought that these women might be descendants of the *tricoteuses*, those Parisian women in tattered dresses who sat stolidly near the guillotine and knitted as they watched the tumbril bring the next load of victims and then screamed and cheered when the prisoners' heads were sliced off and held up to the mob. Seeing these F.F.I. groups I wondered how Taureau and Bourret and the other F.T.P. leaders would react to this wild resurrection of the rival F.F.I. forces. Perhaps unfairly I thought of these F.F.I.'s as warriors who march proudly on the field of battle only after the enemy has been routed. There was a wild, riotous carnival atmosphere about this Maquis eruption and I knew that Jeanpaul and Drouant with their strict concept of discipline would take a poor view of these frenzied demonstrations by exuberant, tardy heroes.

Then there was the matter of the collaborators. I was sure the F.F.I. would handle them much more roughly than German prisoners. They were like vigilantes, it seemed to me, or a self-appointed posse of the Old West gunning for cattle rustlers. If a suspected collaborator were caught he would be presumed guilty, but of course if afterward he turned out to be innocent he would have the satisfaction (if still alive) of showing his scars and protesting the injustice of it all. If the suspect was actually guilty of collaborating, I would feel little sympathy for him, despite my legal training and my staunch belief in "due process of law." Justice might have a bandage across her eyes, as depicted in painting, but Justice could peek just a little and tip the scales.

In Combourg I dropped Descartes off at a café and returned to our room at the City Hall. There I was surprised to find Truffington who had apparently caught up with us after Gorron had been liberated by American tanks and infantry. Truffington still had his breezy manner and he greeted me effusively.

"Bill, old man! By God, am I glad to see you!"

"Hello, Truff," I said.

"Thought sure you were a goner there at Gorron."

"So did I, Truff. For a few minutes anyway."

"Heard later you got away, but how did you do it, old man? Things looked damned sticky to me."

I told Truffington how we had escaped and had then driven past the sentries in Columbiers.

Truffington let out a low whistle. "Whew! I say! Taking a real chance weren't you, going through Columbiers with an SS battalion there. I'd have crashed through that check point instead. Odds of getting through were better." He had a small cut on his chin, probably a razor nick, and he kept picking at the scab and dabbing it with his handkerchief.

I reminded him that we had successfully gone through Columbiers, and this, I thought, was a fact of some significance which possibly he shouldn't overlook if he was going to make a thorough critique of my actions that night.

"Oh, quite right, old boy. It worked, as you say. Bloody lucky, you were. Did you know the Jerries came back soon afterwards?"

"No, I didn't know that."

"Well they did. One of the farmers told me about it. Seems a truck full of Jerries came back and without getting out they just sprayed the hedgerows all around for a few minutes. And off they went. Scared hell out of the farmer."

After Gorron, I had thought of what I would say to Truffington if I ever saw him again. But now I realized that instead of resenting Truffington I was amused, and his "old man" and "old boy" no longer annoyed me.

"Where did you go when we became separated?" I asked, feeling that phrasing the question in this manner showed great restraint.

"Back to our farm hide-out. Of course I was bloody well sure the lot of you were dead or prisoners, and I was the only one left. Gave me a nasty shock."

"Sure. That kind of thing can be upsetting."

"The next day I got busy and made some contacts with the Maquis there. Not at all easy. Ran into a gendarme in the Resistance and told him what had to be done. He was a terribly keen chap. Big help to me. So when the Yanks got there we were ready and I was in the thick of it. We knocked the Jerries about a bit, I can tell you. You missed a good show, old man." He made it sound almost as though I had abandoned him and he and the American Army had to batter their way into Gorron on their own.

"Sorry to have missed that, Truff."

"Couldn't be helped."

"No."

"Don't feel badly about it," he said with a pleasant smile and giving me a pat on the back.

"The English captain waxed wroth at Gorron," I said in a sonorous voice, "and he smote the mighty Teutons across their pates."

He scowled. "I suppose that's meant to be frightfully funny. At times I really wonder about you. Not quite right in the head."

"*Je salue le Capitaine Truffington,*" I said, "*le grand et puissant Chef du Maquis de Gorron.*"

"Silly bugger," he muttered and stomped out.

Early the next morning an American corporal came to our headquarters and said that he had been sent here by General Haggerty, commanding the Infantry Division north of Combourg, and that the General wanted me to report to him immediately. Since Jeanpaul was absent I asked Drouant to come with me and we climbed in the back of the corporal's jeep and drove off. When we were about five miles out of Combourg we headed out on a highway where the combat engineers had already erected a big roadside marker: "Caution—This road under artillery fire." Off in the distance we could hear the crash of guns. The corporal, hunched over the wheel, must have been dodging imaginary shells for he drove very fast, skidding wildly around turns and bouncing over pot holes and bumps while Drouant and I were hanging on tightly.

We reached division headquarters in an abandoned villa and were taken to the dining room which had been converted into an operations room with maps tacked on the walls. A Major General sat at the big dining room table cluttered with more maps and papers. The General stood up and took off his steel-rimmed glasses and tossed them on the table. He was a tall, lean man with thin lips and a square chin, and his eyes were sharp and penetrating. I noticed that his face looked drawn and tired.

"You're with the Maquis, Captain?" He spoke in a drawl and pronounced "Maquis" as though it were "Mackay."

"Yes sir. Parachuted in some time ago to work with the Resistance."

"Good. I'm General Haggerty. Just learned that there were a few Special Forces officers in Combourg." He was eyeing Drouant who was standing at attention in his dirty, rumpled suit.

"Who's that man with you?" General Haggerty asked.

"This is Captain Drouant of the French Army. He jumped in with me."

Drouant gave him one of those sharp French salutes, the palm facing out.

"Captain Drouant had to hide his uniform and change into civilian clothes," I explained.

General Haggerty casually returned Drouant's salute. "*Je parle français très mauvais,*" he said, looking at Drouant and smiling a little.

Drouant in his halting English politely said he was sure the General spoke much better French than Drouant did English.

"*Non, non. Très mauvais. Pas bon,*" the General chuckled.

"Come over here, Captain," he said, "and I'll show you why I need your help." The General put his arm around me and led me to one of the wall maps. I thought back to the time when I had been a GI in basic training at Camp Wheeler and after that an Officer Candidate at the Fort Benning Infantry School. In those days of K.P. duty and all the rest of it a kind word from a sergeant was a cherished reward. Now a Major General had his arm around me and was asking for my help.

The wall map showed the region from Combourg to the port of St. Malo, and the jagged coastline with its many coves and bays. The overlay covering the wall map had red arrows and blue arrows and markers designating the position of American units and the enemy forces.

"We have to get to St. Malo," said the General. "And we have an armored division helping us there and there." He stabbed at the map with his pencil.

"Yes sir."

"We're having a hell of a time though," General Haggerty drawled. "Intelligence reports from Corps headquarters indicated only about two thousand Germans, front line troops that is, in this entire area." The General had put his glasses on again and he was peering at his map and tapping the rim of his glasses with his pencil. "Trouble is G-2 was wrong," he went on. "We've already taken twice that many prisoners and we're nowhere near where we should be." He slapped his hand down hard on the table and stared at me.

"The Krauts are fighting like hell," General Haggerty continued. "We've lost too many tanks already. Some of our patrols got bloody noses. Had to pull back. You see our positions there. You know that area well?"

"Yes sir. We know it from our maps."

"From your maps, Captain?" he said, dragging out the words. "Hell, I know it that way too." He was frowning.

"Yes sir. But we have men in our Maquis who live there and they . . ."

"All right then. That's more like it. Now I'll tell you what I'm afraid of. It's our flanks. They're exposed as we push on to St. Malo. You see where I mean?" Again he punched the map with his pencil.

"Yes sir."

"That coast is crammed with bunkers and pillboxes, and they extend inland too. Too many Krauts there. They can come out of those strong points, drive into our flanks, cut communications, raise hell."

"Yes sir."

"'How many men do you have in those Maquis of yours?" asked the General.

I took a wild guess. "About two hundred and fifty, maybe more," I said.

"Good. Now I want those Maquis forces to take over that whole stretch between our right flank and the sea. Here." He took his pencil and slashed a broad red line below the coast. "Send out patrols, starting tomorrow. Keep the Krauts off balance, and off our backs. Got it?"

"Yes sir. But we'll have to organize those Maquis groups first. Get them coordinated. We just got here and the situation is kind of confused, and . . ."

"What the hell, Captain! That's your job, isn't it? When you jumped into France that wasn't supposed to be a dry run, was it?" His drawl now had a hard, flat tang.

"No sir, General. It's only that . . ."

"Captain, one simple question. Can you do it? Yes or no?"

"Yes sir," I said emphatically. "We can do it."

"*Certainement, mon Général*. Of course," Drouant chimed in. "We do this with pleasure." He smiled and the General smiled back at him.

"Fine!" said General Haggerty. "You paratroopers are supposed to be such tough hombres, here's your chance." He put his arm around me again. "Now son," he said kindly, "this will really be a big help to us. But I want aggressive patrols. Puttering around won't do. None of this snooping and pooping."

"Yes sir, I understand. But sir, if the General will permit me..."

"Now what?" he asked sharply.

"About weapons and supplies, sir. I think maybe we'll need some." I was thinking of Pépin and some of the other boys with their World War I rifles.

"No problem, Captain. Go see Colonel Robertson right now. Two doors down the corridor. Tell him I said to give you what you need. O.K. That's all, Captain."

We saluted and left to see Colonel Robertson.

Colonel Robertson was a barrel-chested man with a bulldog face and a crew cut. He listened with a frown as I started to tell him what we wanted, and then held up his hand to cut me off. "The Maquis?" he said in a scornful tone. "What kind of crap are you trying to hand me anyhow?" He grabbed his phone and asked for General Haggerty. "General? Colonel Robertson, sir. Some damned fool captain just barged in here and he says you told him . . ."

I saw Colonel Robertson's face flush as he listened. He became rigid, as though coming to attention while still sitting down. "Yes sir, General," he answered quickly. "Yes sir . . . I see . . . no sir, I mean yes sir . . . right away, General." He banged down the phone and glowered at us. "All right, what do you want for your Maquis?" he asked in a rasping voice.

I told him we could use captured German rifles, submachine guns, light machine guns, ammunition, and we would like some M-1 rifles and carbines if possible.

"And mortars," added Drouant, accenting the word improperly.

"More tars? What the hell do you mean?" he snapped.

"He means mortars, sir," I said.

"No. Positively not. No mortars. No M-1's or carbines either. The rest of it I can let you have, but why the hell we should do that for these Frogs is . . ." His voice trailed off. Out of the corner of my eye I could see Drouant's face grow hard but he didn't say anything.

The colonel got out a pack of Camels and offered me one, but not to Drouant. I declined.

We arranged with Colonel Robertson to have these supplies brought by truck to Combourg and to a village designated by Drouant. When we came out of the colonel's office we found our jeep and driver waiting. "Move over, Corporal," I said. "I'll drive."

"Ah Bill!" exclaimed Drouant, as we rode off. "I could have hugged that General Haggerty."

"I'm glad you didn't try," I said drily. But I was as elated as Drouant and the feeling of frustration was gone. While we might not blow any bridges, or ambush any convoys, nevertheless fighting the Germans in any way at all was certainly better than returning to London only to report that we had been escorted into Combourg by Sherman tanks and that the town was safely in the hands of the M.P.'s. Mission accomplished.

On arriving at the City Hall in Combourg Drouant leaped out of the jeep and ran up the steps of the City Hall to find Jeanpaul. When I came in the room I was surprised to see that Jeanpaul was in uniform again, but Drouant was so intent on telling Jeanpaul about General Haggerty that he didn't notice it. Drouant was talking very rapidly, pounding his fist into his palm, and as Jeanpaul listened his somber expression vanished and he broke out into his broad, crooked grin. He patted me on the back as though I, as an American, was responsible for General Haggerty's decision. Bourret was in the room and Jeanpaul told him to get Taureau at once. Bourret bulled his way past Larue at the door and shot down the steps. "*Bon type, ce Bourret,*" said Jeanpaul. "*Il a le feu au derrière maintenant.*"

Only then did Drouant take in Jeanpaul's uniform, and Jeanpaul said that our rucksacks had been brought here only a short time ago by some of Booboo's men who in some unexplained manner had gone through or around the German lines. They had informed Jeanpaul that, unfortunately, our radio was lost. "I don't believe it," Jeanpaul told us. "But then what can the F.T.P. do with our radio? Why do they want it?" Jeanpaul looked thoughtful while Larue, separated probably forever from his true love, exploded into a string of resounding obscenities.

As we waited for Taureau and Bourret we discussed how to carry out General Haggerty's orders. In planning any military operation a commander may be unsure about the enemy's strength, but at least he knows his own strength. We knew neither, for although Taureau, Bourret and the other F.T.P. leaders could tell us how many men they could furnish and what weapons, we knew nothing about these F.F.I. groups which had been sprouting up everywhere. How many men did they have? What weapons? Who were their leaders? Could the F.F.I. be organized into efficient combat units? What about cooperation between the F.T.P. and the F.F.I.? The best we could do for the time being was to study our maps and decide tentatively on objectives and patrol routes, what key points such as crossroads should be taken and held, what roads should be sealed off to prevent German penetrations, and at what points the German defenses might be probed.

When Taureau came in with Bourret, Jeanpaul told them what General Haggerty wanted.

"I expected this," said Taureau laconically. He looked Jeanpaul straight in the eye. "The F.T.P. will be ready," he said.

Jeanpaul mentioned the F.F.I. and Taureau, smiling derisively, said the F.F.I. had best be assigned to the least important sectors, and even then Jeanpaul would probably have to call on the F.T.P. to reenforce the F.F.I.

"I saw some of the F.F.I. groups," I said to Taureau. "Of course, they're not well organized yet, but they sure looked eager and enthusiastic."

"Oh yes. Very enthusiastic," he said. "With the Americans here it's not too difficult to be enthusiastic, is it?" His voice had a cutting and bitter tone. "You might ask them where they were a year ago, or a week ago, for that matter."

I didn't say anything, and Jeanpaul went back to his maps and showed Taureau and Bourret the proposed routes for the F.T.P. patrols and the assigned objectives. Taureau and Jeanpaul reviewed the plan at some length, but Bourret showed little interest in these discussions of tactics, his sole contribution consisting of occasional grunts. However when it came to the problem of distributing the weapons and supplies being sent by the Americans, Bourret loudly insisted that his Maquis group was entitled to priority, especially for the light machine guns. "And you know it!" Bourret said angrily, pointing his finger at Taureau.

"Oh, undoubtedly," replied Taureau. "And the other leaders, they will say the same thing, won't they? Now as for me," he continued in a calm, detached manner, "I'm ready to take on the Germans with only what we have now."

"*Putain de putain!*" shouted Bourret. "And so am I!"

"I knew you were," replied Taureau smoothly. "The weapons, the blankets, the rations, all so generously furnished by our American allies, these will be apportioned among our groups according to needs and the situation." He turned to me with a half smile. "And Captain Dreux will see to that, isn't that so, Captain?"

"I'm not a supply officer," I said coldly.

"No, no. In the Maquis we have no supply officers, chiefly because we've had no supplies, or so little."

Bourret was laughing now. "What I look forward to is going after the Boches with those big American tanks in support."

"I don't think it will be quite like that," said Jeanpaul.

"Probably not," said Bourret, "but Taureau says every man should have his dream. Very well. Right now that's my dream."

There was a commotion at the door just then and a girl carrying a rifle and wearing an F.F.I. armband marched into the room followed by a young Luftwaffe pilot who limped in with one boot off. Unlike the squat woman of the day before this girl was extremely pretty with flushed cheeks and red lips and a tight blouse that revealed the outline of her breasts. She gave Jeanpaul what was intended as a military salute, and the pilot, after a quick glance around the room, ignored everyone except Jeanpaul, whom he saluted. Jeanpaul returned the pilot's salute and nodded at the girl who then said that the pilot had bailed out when his plane was shot down, he had twisted his ankle in landing, and he had been captured shortly afterward by the F.F.I.

"*Voilà notre prisonnier,*" she said proudly.

"*Bien, mademoiselle,*" replied Jeanpaul as though such incidents were routine.

Jeanpaul interrogated the prisoner in French and broken German but the pilot refused to answer questions. He insisted on being placed in custody of the Americans, and demanded that this be done at once. Since the German was not in a very good position to be giving orders his arrogance irked Jeanpaul, but he reluctantly told the girl to turn the prisoner over to one of the M.P.'s, and the girl marched out with the pilot hobbling after her, his eyes fixed straight ahead.

Jeanpaul had finished his briefing and we walked out to the head of the steps overlooking the town square. About fifty young F.F.I. men were gathered there, as well as a few girls, and they all had rifles and the armbands. When they saw Jeanpaul they started shouting and waved their weapons over their heads. Jeanpaul, his face hard and stern, looked out at the crowd and the yelling stopped. He began to talk to them then, standing very erect, with his hands on his hips. France deserved more from them than cheers, he told them, and more than wild rides up and down roads and streets. Now the honor and pride of the Resistance was at stake. Suddenly he pointed to me and said that I was an American paratrooper who had jumped in with him and that all Frenchmen, whoever they were and wherever they might be, should be willing to offer to France that which I was prepared to give to the Allied cause. This embarrassed me and I walked off to one side. I saw that everyone in the square stood very quietly, many of them looking at the ground. "The Germans are still fighting hard north of here," Jeanpaul continued, "and it is you, you and not only the Americans, who must liberate this corner of Brittany. I expect every member of the F.F.I. in the Combourg area to report to me here tomorrow morning. As a major in the French Army I tell you that this is your duty and that you as Frenchmen cannot do less."

He was through now but he still stood there facing them. There had been something about Jeanpaul, the way he had kept himself under control as he spoke in his firm, quiet way, a sense that within himself he had a power stronger than his listeners, so that as he finished the F.F.I. all raised their heads to look directly at him and they came to attention spontaneously. After a long period of silence a man stepped forward and addressed Jeanpaul, "Major, I don't know you and I've never seen you before. But I speak for all of us when I say that I respect you. What you said had to be said. We'll be here tomorrow." He stepped back and the crowd quietly dispersed.

Taureau went to Jeanpaul and without saying a word he shook hands with him and then he walked over to me. "The major mentioned honor," he said. "Now when the Resistance first started and everything looked hopeless, I would remind myself of what Francis I had said after losing a battle, '*Tout est perdu hors l'honneur.*'"

I thought this was an apt quote but I didn't say anything.

"I will say this for Major Jeanpaul," Taureau went on, "he understands the irresistible power of a cause." Taureau's eyes seemed to be looking through me and beyond me. "Because he does, because he himself believes, men will listen to him. And they will follow him. You just saw it, didn't you?"

"Yes."

"And without such an ideal, all those German 88's, and your Sherman tanks too, they're not worth much."

Taureau turned away and walked rapidly down the steps.

CHAPTER XIV

It Did Not Take Him Long to Die

The official report covering our operations during the next few weeks states that the Maquis groups in our sector took more than fourteen hundred prisoners and destroyed over one hundred trucks. As so often with Army reports this statement is misleading. Many of the prisoners must have been service troops, and most of the trucks were probably destroyed by American artillery or even by our Air Corps. The pilots and bombardiers did not always miss the target, particularly if there was no flak. In two or three sentences the report also mentions the action at a place called La Bastille and in closing says, "The patrol withdrew." These are my words for this is how I concluded my terse official account of what happened that day. But this statement, while true, is only relatively true, like the World War I communique that all was quiet on the Western Front.

The Resistance Forces under our command included the Communist dominated *Francs-Tireurs-Partisans* and the *Forces Francaises de l'Intérieur*, and one or two units were mixed. These groups were named after the villages where the men lived. Thus we had the St. Pierre de Plesguens group, the St. Domineuc group, the unit from Louvigné du Désert and about six other bands. These were lusty young men, many of them in their late teens, whose blood and bones were of the soil of Brittany and, while they certainly had no wish for a glorious death, they did feel that the shame and agony of France in 1940 must be avenged and that this was more important than staying alive. It may be that some of them had heard Jeanpaul speak at Combourg, or his words had reached them. They were careful not to show this sentiment and they bantered a lot, insulting each other in a good-natured way, so as to make it seem that fighting Germans was a game one should joke about.

Since these men thought of themselves as soldiers they wanted to dress the part and an armband was not enough. They had strange attires. Some of them wore old French Army tunics while a few others had managed to get American combat jackets, and what they had never fit properly. There were a few French helmets and one or two men wore American battle helmets of which they were very proud. Most of the young men carried their Sten guns or rifles nonchalantly, like a swashbuckling cavalier with his hand loosely on the hilt of the rapier at his belt. We also had some older men, sturdy, taciturn peasants who occasionally muttered about "*ces sacrés gosses*," "those damned kids." But whether old or young they had traits in common; they lacked discipline, they were stubborn and highly individualistic and, except for a few of them, they were green as gourds when it came to infantry fighting. Maquis chiefs such as Taureau and Bourret were skilled in the hit-and-run night raid, slitting a sentry's throat and then setting fire to an army dump, but they knew little of infantry tactics and daytime operations. All of the men had a quality on which Frenchmen like to pride themselves; they were very *débrouillard*, a word difficult to translate, which denotes resourcefulness and an ability to improvise. For example, one of my kids had figured out that his ancient French helmet would be cooler if he drilled a few holes in it. This also gave him the appearance of one who has miraculously survived a murderous fusillade.

In addition we had about a dozen Algerian and Senegalese soldiers who had served with the French Army in 1940 because their homelands were French colonies at that time. They had been taken prisoners during the blitzkrieg in France and after several years of captivity had escaped and joined the Maquis. Jeanpaul had remarked to me that the Senegalese and Algerians made good infantry although sometimes they were a bit shaky under very heavy artillery fire. He had told me this with a straight face, knowing very well that I had never been under artillery fire, unless you counted my boyhood days in Paris when Big Bertha was shelling the city. Jeanpaul had added that while the Algerians and Senegalese spoke French they—or perhaps it was only the Algerians—always said "*tu*" to their officers instead of "*vous*" but they did this with everyone because there was no equivalent of "*vous*" in their native tongue and I was not to take this as a sign of disrespect. "They're good soldiers," Jeanpaul had concluded, "but they have to be properly led."

The Maquis men firmly believed that killing Germans was what mattered and that no set tactics were necessary for that. Our operations were rather freewheeling and seldom followed the rules of the Infantry School Manuals at Fort Benning where every tactical problem had a neat answer, the "School solution" as it was called. The instructors there presented these solutions as something immutable, much like the answers in a catechism. But those manuals were certainly not written by an officer who had led guerrilla bands, especially one made up of Maquis kids and Algerians and Senegalese. When taking out a patrol I always walked at the head of the column because I wanted to see for myself what lay ahead. This was not the way patrolling was taught at Fort Benning, or at Milton Hall either. The rule of tactics was that every patrol should have a "point man" ahead. This put the leader in a better position to control his squad, but this precept was also based on the supposition that the patrol leader, either an officer or a N.C.O., was much more valuable than the enlisted men and therefore should not expose himself needlessly. The point man, of course, was expendable. This theory may be sound generally, but it does not have the wholehearted approval of everyone who has served as the point man.

Sometimes patrols deviated temporarily from their assigned missions, for example by calling at a farm whose owner was suspected of collaboration. We tried our best to prevent these side ventures. Once a kid in my patrol suggested to me that we make a detour so as to avoid a dangerous crossroad. One of his friends called me aside and after winking at me he explained that the other kid had proposed this detour because his girl lived in a farm there and he wanted to impress her as being a warrior. The friend described the girl vividly, using his hands in flowing gestures to depict her figure, rolling his eyes and letting out a low whistle. I thought this Gallic, "*pour l'amour*" whim should be respected, and maybe I wanted to see the girl myself. Since the detour would not take us much out of our way I changed our route but unfortunately the girl was not there.

It was probably the anti-personnel mines which I dreaded most. For the protection of their own troops the methodical Germans generally marked these mine fields with a wooden sign having a black skull-and-crossbones insignia and the words "*Achtung Minen.*" Yet we could never be sure that a mine field was marked, and possibly a lush green meadow was strewn with these treacherous mines concealed by the tall grass and the brightly colored wild flowers dancing in the breeze. The GI's called these mines "Bouncing Betties." They were activated by a trip wire setting off a spring which would bounce the mine waist high and then it would explode like shrapnel. The anti-personnel mines would not damage a tank, while the anti-tank mines could not be detonated by the weight of a man stepping on it. A few times I did cross an unmarked field, thinking it might be mined and yet not having the time to move cautiously and feel ahead, and this left me with my mouth very dry. The German machine guns and rifles were different; at least I thought I could cope with them and I had a chance. Behind each such weapon was an enemy and I might get him before he could get me.

Our men were not equipped or trained to breach the Atlantic Wall, although this was attempted several times, but we could attack German patrols sallying forth from their bunkers to harass the American flanks. Once or twice we did move up to the coastal bunkers only to find them deserted because the Germans had withdrawn to other positions. There were brief clashes but generally at a distance, with the retreating Germans stopping now and then to get off a few scattered rifle shots or a long-range machine gun burst. We fired back at shadowy figures fleeing through the woods or scrambling through the hedgerows. Except in some instances this was not heavy fighting, although of course anyone getting shot at, especially from close range, thinks the fighting is very hard. There were no body counts, and unlike the gun-slinger of the Old West I could carve no notches on the butt of my pistol, nor was I like a fighter pilot who could paint emblems on his fuselage to mark his kills. Before we started our patrolling I had thought of how satisfying it would be to get the drop on an SS officer—preferably a colonel with a dueling scar and wearing a monocle—and keep my forty-five pointed at him as he raised his hands in surrender. Perhaps I hoped he would make a break for it and this would give me an excuse to gun him down. But this is not the way it was.

Some of our men were killed and I suppose they are now buried in little village cemeteries next to old, weather-beaten churches, and for several years afterwards, on the anniversary of the liberation of that village, the inhabitants would go solemnly to these graves and pile them high with flowers. Now this is probably no longer done, and only the family visits the cemetery, for time gradually wipes out the memories and the feeling that these dead should be honored.

The fighting was confusing much of the time. It brought to mind the closing lines of a poem whose title I had forgotten, something about being "on a darkling plain/Swept with confused alarms of struggle and flight/Where ignorant armies clash by night." Here it was the Resistance forces who were the "ignorant armies." The Americans seemed to know what they were doing, and the Germans certainly did. The Maquis groups did not fight according to a set plan, for there was no set plan except that our general mission was to act as a buffer between the Germans on the coast and the Americans on our left who were driving west and would then swing north towards St. Malo. The Germans were pulling back to their strongpoints. Sometimes the Americans punched north to smash a few fortifications and then would move west again. I tried to maintain liaison with the Americans, but without radio communications this was not easy. Military commentators sometimes describe a situation as being "fluid," which generally means that the enemy has broken through and your army is taking a beating. For us too the situation was fluid, not that our Maquis forces were being overrun, but because no one, not even Jeanpaul, could keep daily track of each Maquis group and neatly plot the next moves on a war map.

In giving orders for patrols Jeanpaul had to improvise, using his worn and soiled Michelin map, sifting sketchy and often contradictory reports of enemy activity, and finally relying largely on his military intuition. Occasionally his orders did not reach the Maquis leaders in time, or when the orders were received the situation had changed. On some occasions the Maquis chief wouldn't wait for orders and would lead his group off on a venture of his own. I would have thought that after commanding a battalion in Tunisia, Jeanpaul, with his precise, orderly mind, would have found this disorder intolerable. But he did have a sense of humor and at times he found the situation funny. He was particularly amused by what happened to Bourret one day. Bourret had led his Maquis group to attack a small village reportedly held only by a German squad. For once Bourret had carefully prepared his attack, skillfully deploying his men in a flanking maneuver, all in a way which the most exacting Infantry School instructor would have approved. But due to faulty liaison and lack of communication, Bourret did not know that the Americans had taken the village several hours before. So when Bourret and his men arrived in the village square they found two jeeps full of GI's throwing gum and candy to screaming kids. One of the GI's spotted Bourret and tossed him a pack of gum, shouting "Here you are, buddy!" Bourret was still sputtering with rage when he reported this episode to Jeanpaul.

The reverse happened a few days later when a Maquis group on the way to their objective approached a village liberated by the Americans the day before. The *Maquisards* came marching down the road, singing at the top of their lungs, when a machine gun opened up and three men were badly hit. What the patrol leader hadn't known was that a German platoon had retaken the village a short time before when the street was still decked out with French and American flags. The German lieutenant thought it good to teach the villagers a lesson. He ordered the mayor shot.

Jeanpaul frequently used his bicycle to maintain command over the scattered Maquis groups and to reconnoiter. Sometimes he was in uniform while on other days he wore civilian clothes in order to have greater freedom of movement. He had bought a dark gray suit in Combourg, but he still wore his jump boots and had no identity papers although he would have been able to get them then with little trouble. He just hadn't bothered. Several times he accompanied a patrol on foot, generally wearing his suit and always carrying a stout walking stick which I called his marshal's baton. He would joke a little with the men and then say, "*Eh bien, les gars, temps de partir*—time to go," and he would set off with them down a lane with the self-assured air of a country squire starting on an inspection tour of his estates. When he went alone to make a reconnaissance he was always casual about these outings. "*J'ai fait une petite promenade près de Pleudihen,*" he would say on returning and then he would tell Drouant and me what he had observed and what should be done and by which Maquis units. Jeanpaul ignored Truffington to whom he referred as "*le héros de Gorron,*" and although he frequently consulted at length with Drouant he rarely asked my advice which annoyed me considerably. Several times I suggested a change in his plans and as he listened politely I could see the thought running through his mind, "Ah yes, and now we have to hear from the amateur soldier." But once or twice he listened to me intently, nodding his head, and turned to Drouant and said, "*Vous savez, André, B-e-e-l a raison. C'est ça. Bon.*" After this approval of my recommendations Jeanpaul would stride away while Drouant grinned at me.

It was a few days after we had gone into action that I led a patrol to the place called La Bastille. We had vague reports that this was an outpost of the main defenses covering the port of St. Malo. There was supposedly a cluster of farmhouses at this point and although the locality was too small to be a village and did not show on our maps it was known as La Bastille to the people in that region. When I heard Jeanpaul telling me to take a patrol there I smiled and thought of the people of Paris storming that famous prison during the French Revolution and how the fall of the Bastille on July Fourteenth had become the National Holiday. Jeanpaul stressed that this was to be a reconnaissance patrol only. I was to bring back information on any enemy activity in that area and I was not to go beyond La Bastille. "Is that quite clear?" Jeanpaul asked, and I replied, "Of course, I understand." Then, speaking rapidly in a clipped voice he had ticked off on his fingers exactly what he wanted to know. I nodded my head impatiently. I've been on several patrols, I thought, and I know what he wants and there's no need for him to be so damned explicit.

I had about fifteen men in my patrol, including Pépin and his kids and four or five Algerians and Senegalese. The Algerians and Senegalese wore old French khaki uniforms which were shabby and stained and the leather of their army shoes was cracked and the soles badly worn. Most of the younger boys in Pépin's group had been replaced by lads in their late teens, but I still thought of them as kids although I treated them as men and we got along very well. One of them was a tall, lanky boy wearing a dark blue sweater that was too small for him and the sleeves were halfway up to his elbows. His name was Pierre and he had a long, thin face with a sharp nose and a roguish grin. They were all carrying Sten guns or rifles except for one of the Algerians who had a German light machine gun and ammunition belts. This Algerian was a short, swarthy man with dark, flashing eyes. I was glad to have the Algerian and Senegalese veterans for they were trained soldiers on whom I could count, and having the machine gun made it even better. This high velocity weapon, an MG-42, could fire about twelve hundred pounds per minute and was far superior to our BAR (Browning Automatic Rifle) or our light machine gun, neither of which our men had. I was surprised to see that another Algerian carried an extra barrel for the gun, as well as more ammunition belts. The gun was designed so that when the barrel became too hot from continuous firing it could be quickly changed, and the thorough Germans even issued one asbestos glove to each machine gunner. I wanted to be sure the Algerian knew how to handle the gun and understood how to change the barrel by first cocking the weapon, pressing on the catch, turning the butt away and letting the hot barrel slide out. He could use his handkerchief or shirttail to grab the barrel. I started to explain this to him, but he assured me that he knew all about an MG-42. When I insisted he became very indignant.

"Tu vas voir, mon Capitaine," he said, drawing himself up. *"Moi, je suis mitrailleur."*

"Bien," I said, pleased to learn that he was a machine gunner. *"Alors, ça va."*

We set out in the early morning of a gray and somber day. The mist had rolled in from the sea. I remember this very well, just as I remember everything that happened on this patrol, even little details of no importance such as the German Army belt worn by Pépin. Things did not go well that day, and for a long time afterwards I wished I could forget all of it, especially the tortured expression on the peasant woman's face. It is true that nothing really terrible happened. Many a patrol has gone out and never returned, or only one bloody survivor staggered back to his own lines. It was not like that at La Bastille. Yet when I was back in France in 1951 I drove past the wide stretch of open ground we had crossed seven years before and got out of the car and wandered into the field, and then I noticed that I was walking with my shoulders slightly hunched, squinting at that stone wall we had to reach, and it seemed that the Germans were still there, firing in quick bursts. I could hear again the sharp crackling of their machine gun, like someone ripping a piece of fabric, and I could see the spurts of dirt and dust kicked up by the bullets. La Bastille left a scar which I tried to hide. Had I been in combat for weeks before the action at La Bastille, what happened there would probably have seemed just part of one day in the war, no more than that, and even the peasant woman would have been only another victim, like one of many I had seen. But on that gloomy day in early August of 1944 I was not ready for all that happened on the patrol to La Bastille.

Our patrol left the fields and entered a forest. The tops of the trees feathered away in the mist and it was hard to tell what lay ahead. As I walked slowly and peered around I couldn't see that any lanes had been cleared through the woods to give machine guns a good field of fire. This should mean that there weren't any enemy positions within range, although of course we could bump into a German patrol. Coming to the far edge of the woods I saw a stone cottage with its thatched roof and a farmer sitting on a small bench with his back to the wall. When he caught sight of me he got up and started to go inside but I called out to him and he hesitated and stopped as I walked up to him. He was an old man with bushy eyebrows and deep wrinkles in his leathery face.

"*Bonjour*," I said, smiling at him. "Dreary day, isn't it?"

"*Bonjour*," he said gruffly without any change of expression. He turned to glance at my men. "More fighting, eh?" he grumbled. "And when will it end?"

"Oh, soon, very soon. Any Germans around here?"

"No. Today, no."

"Are the Germans still at La Bastille?"

"I don't know," he replied and shrugged his shoulders.

I was going to ask more questions when a skinny little girl in a black dress came slowly out the door. She was holding a slice of bread covered with jam and I saw that her other arm had been cut off above the elbow. She stopped when she saw us and looked shyly at me. Her face had a long, ugly red scar which twisted her lips so that she seemed to be grinning.

"Come over here and tell the American soldier hello," the old man said.

She walked slowly up to me, limping a little, and gazed solemnly in my face. "*Bonjour*," she said finally.

"*Bonjour*," I said. "What's your name?"

"Anne." She began to eat her bread, keeping her eyes on me. She turned to look at a brown puppy chasing the chickens in the farmyard, and I heard her shrill laugh while her mouth had that scar-twisted smile which never changed.

"That's my dog," she told me, and pointed toward him with her little stump of an arm. I stared at her as she ran awkwardly to catch the puppy, and the old man was watching me.

"A mine did that to her," he said.

I was going to ask the location of the minefield but I stopped.

"You keep telling the kids to stay away from anywhere near

the beach," the old man said sullenly. "Sometimes they don't obey."

"The beaches will be cleared of mines very soon," I said. The old man gave me a hard look and went back to sit on his bench. He rubbed his hand slowly over his stubbly chin. "She was lucky," he said in a low, toneless voice. "There were three other kids with her that day. They were killed."

I didn't say anything and I went over and sat next to him on the bench. The little girl came to us and looked me over thoughtfully for a moment as she put her bread down on the bench. At last she put her one hand in her dress pocket and brought out three small sea shells. She held them in the palm of her hand and studied them. Then she gave me one of them. I thanked her and said it was very pretty. I stood up and tried to smile at her, looking down at her mutilated little face.

"It will bring you luck," she said. "Isn't that right, *grand-père*?"

The old man grunted. I wanted to get away and when I said goodbye to Anne I made an effort not to stare at her twisted lips and the stump of her arm.

We moved out across the fields and through the hedgerows. From far off to my right came the sound of distant shelling. Now the mist had lifted a little and a fine drizzle came down from the slate-gray skies. Our patrol reached a farmhouse next to a narrow road. The farmyard was empty but I could see there had been fighting there because the windows were broken and the stone wall of the house was chipped, especially next to the open door. A wagon lay smashed on its side, broken boards and splinters littered the ground, and I saw an American rifle with its butt shattered. I called out but no one answered. Some American patrol must have pushed this far, I thought, and then was beaten back. We left the farm and went into an apple orchard across the road and walked alongside a hedgerow for a few hundred yards. When I looked back to the road I saw Jeanpaul in his civilian clothes pedaling slowly on his bicycle and glancing around. I was surprised for he hadn't said anything about joining us later. Apparently he hadn't seen us and he kept going until he disappeared behind a line of bushes and then I saw him coming back.

We had only gone a short distance further when I saw the dead American soldier next to a narrow slit trench. Probably he and the others in his patrol had been caught by surprise when they were digging in after reaching this advanced position. The soldier lay on his back so bloated that he looked as if he would burst out of his combat jacket. His face was puffed and yellowish-green and the smell of the body was very strong. I saw a deep gash across his throat and dried blood. At the same time I noticed something that puzzled me. One hand clutched a rosary while his other hand held a first-aid gauze pad. There was no blood on the pad. I wondered whether when this soldier was hit he had grabbed first for the gauze pad in the small pouch attached to his belt. And then, somehow realizing that this was hopeless, had he fumbled desperately in his pocket and brought out his rosary? No one would ever know. It could not have taken him long to die. The sharp stab of pain, his blood spurting, terror, the rosary, and then death.

My men gathered around the body and no one was talking. The light rain was still falling and tiny drops trickled off the dead face. Right now he was an unknown soldier because whatever had hit him had knocked off his identification tag and I was unable to find it. I could not leave him there like that. I decided to bury him in the slit trench and I asked Pépin to see if he could find some spades in the farm across the road. Pépin came back with two spades, and a cross made of two small boards he had wired together. Until I remembered that Pépin had no doubt been brought up as a Catholic I thought it strange that a Communist *Maquisard* would want to provide a cross. Pépin put up the cross at the head of the slit trench and said we should hang the rosary around the cross, but I said no. I wanted this soldier buried as he had died, with the rosary in his hand. We lifted the body into the trench, putting it down very carefully, and my kids shovelled in the dirt while the Algerians and Senegalese stood off by themselves. When we had finished I thought something more should be done. I was going to recite the Lord's Prayer in French while we gathered around the grave until I realized that I no longer knew the words I had learned as a boy. I did remember the phrase "*Endormi dans la paix du Seigneur,*" or "At rest in the peace of the Lord," and those words, particularly in French, had always suggested to me the tranquil feel of eternity, but I was uncertain about saying them now. So I took off my helmet and my kids bared their heads as we stood there for a minute. The distant rumble of the guns had died down and the rain fell gently. It was very quiet.

"All right," I said finally. "Let's go, back to the farmhouse across the way." When we got there I noticed for the first time that there was a long stone wall to one side of the large farmyard, about chest-high. Looking out over that wall I saw a bare field stretching at least two hundred yards in front of me and extending far to the left of the country road on my right. The field looked as if it had been plowed some time ago but nothing was growing. At its far edge and directly ahead the German barbed wire was strung out, row after row, and beyond the wire and half-hidden in a grove of trees was a cluster of two or three farmhouses. This was La Bastille. A farmhouse stood just this side of the barbed wire with a stone wall a good twelve feet high enclosing it. There were a few dead cows close to the farmhouse, all lying on their sides with their stiff legs sticking out. They must have been caught in the crossfire of the recent fighting. Getting to that farmhouse was my next objective. I climbed over the wall and motioned my men forward and we crossed the field and reached the protection of that high wall. Now I had the farmhouse and its back wall between me and La Bastille. We found an iron door in the wall but it was bolted shut and when I pounded on it there was no response.

The visibility was poor and I wanted a closer look at this enemy position. I wished I had my field glasses with me but I had left them behind because I wanted to travel light. Very likely the Germans had pulled out and so we could push on beyond La Bastille and go farther, much farther than Jeanpaul had ordered. The narrow road curved around to the right of this farm and apparently led straight to those farmhouses on the other side of the barbed wire. I knew better than to use the road. Even though we hadn't been fired on as we crossed the open field, and I had seen no sign of enemy activity, there was a chance, a very remote chance, that the Germans were still there. If so they would certainly have a machine gun trained on the road. The only other way was to skirt around to my left, keeping very close to the side wall of the farmyard on my right and sneak straight to the barbed wire where I would have a better observation point. "You stay here," I told Pépin, "and keep the men right here. I'm going ahead up to the wire. I'll be back."

I stepped out into the open, away from the protection of the rear wall. A sudden gust of wind brought the odor of the dead cows. I had only about a hundred feet to go and when I came to the barbed wire I saw a short scraggy bush and I got down on one knee behind it. The stretch of barbed wire was about fifty yards deep and the cluster of farmhouses was only a short distance beyond. I peered at La Bastille. The place was deserted, there wasn't a sound, so I was sure that the Germans had pulled out just as they had from the coastal bunkers I had reconnoitered yesterday. I lit a cigarette and studied the terrain to my left. Perhaps there was a gap in the wire farther down, or a gully or a hedgerow which might give us the passage we needed. I didn't know what lay beyond La Bastille and I was still afraid of the road. I was taking a last puff on my cigarette when I heard a noise and jerked around. Pépin and Pierre, the boy in the blue sweater, had joined me.

"Get back!" I said in a low voice. "I told you to stay behind. Now get . . ." It happened just then. There was a quick burst of shots from the other side of the wire and I heard the sharp, crackling sound and saw the puffs of dust kicked up by the bullets just ahead of us. We jumped up and ran in a crouch for the back wall of the farmhouse. There was another burst. I was running as hard as I could but it didn't seem fast enough. Then we were there and threw ourselves around the corner of the wall. I was panting with my chest feeling very tight and my heart was pounding. Pépin and Pierre were alright and I stared at Pépin. "Jesus Christ!" I gasped. "That was close. Holy Jesus Christ! The bastards are there!" I was looking for my Algerian machine gunner. "Where is our machine gun?" Pépin, puffing hard, appeared puzzled and I realized that I had been speaking in English.

Then I saw the gunner standing with his back pressed against the wall and his dark eyes darting back and forth. The machine gun was at his feet. "Swing that gun around!" I yelled at him. "Cover that road!" I turned back to face Pépin and the others. Only seconds before I had felt the kind of fear that churns way down in your guts and then climbs in your throat to strangle you. But now I was calming down a little even though I was still breathing heavily. And then, as if someone had given me a deep whiff of oxygen, my mind felt clear and sharp and I was thinking ahead. It must have been one of these *Schmeisser* burp guns, I thought, and not a machine gun. They wouldn't have missed at that range with a machine gun. No, but they shouldn't have missed with a *Schmeisser* either. Whatever it was, my men were not going to be pinned down by one automatic weapon. Pépin and Pierre were both speaking at once. "We can go back to that other farm," said Pépin, "and then circle to our left, get behind them and . . ." "*Oui, oui, bien sûr!*" exclaimed Pierre. "I know that," I said. "That's what I'm thinking about. But I want another look first. Try to see where those shots came from. Stay back. That's an order. Understand?" They both nodded.

That German gun was aimed right now at that corner of the wall, I thought, and they're hoping we'll come out again to fire at them. But the German gunner would probably be zeroed in on the corner at shoulder height. I got down low on my hands and knees and poked my head out. I peered hard but I couldn't see any sign of a gun or movement of any kind. I was still looking when there was another quick burst of shots followed by screams. Pierre had pitched forward and lay beyond the wall. He was trying to work his legs but he couldn't get up. I reached out and dragged him back as another volley crackled just over my head and chips of stone flew off the wall. As I was pulling Pierre back I could see Pépin out of the corner of my eye. He was clutching his wrist and his right thumb, half ripped off, dangled from his hand. I bent down over Pierre to see where he had been hit and at the same time I saw the Algerians and Senegalese huddled against the wall like frightened animals in a storm. The Algerian gunner was trembling. "Cover that road, man!" I shouted. "I told you! Cover the road!"

"I can't! I can't!" he shrieked, with his lips quivering. "I don't know how! I don't know how this gun works!"

It was the first time I had seen a man paralyzed with fear and I was unprepared for it. I looked again at Pierre and saw he'd been wounded in the chest near the shoulder and his blue sweater was soaked with blood. His face was white, his eyes half-closed, and he was moaning.

"Look!" the Algerian screamed at me. "Back there! Look!" With a shaking arm he pointed to the farm back of us, the one we had left to get here. "That's where they're shooting from! Ai-i-i-i-!" His voice ended in an eerie screech.

In that one awful moment I knew that the Algerian was right and I had only seconds to live. Holy God, I thought, we're pinned against the wall. That was why Pierre and Pépin had been hit. Done for! Jesus Christ! No, no, that can't be! And then looking back and at the same time using my combat knife to cut away Pierre's sweater I was sure the Algerian was wrong. I understood why my two kids had been hit. When I got down to look around the corner they had not stayed back. Without my knowing it they had been leaning out too, but standing up, and the German had been right on target. They were lucky to be alive.

I cut away Pierre's sweater—he wore no undershirt—and saw the bullet hole and the blood flowing but not spurting so I didn't think an artery had been cut nor that the bullet had pierced his lung. I got out my gauze compress and put it over the wound and attempted to tie it tightly in the back under his shoulder but it was a hard wound to bandage. Still trying to draw the bandage tight and stop the bleeding I kept glancing at the other corner of the wall towards the road. What if the Germans came charging around that wall with their *Schmeissers* blazing? Eight French kids was all I had left. The Algerians and Senegalese were worse than useless. Two of my kids were crouching by our machine gun working desperately to load and set up a weapon they had never used. They were getting in each other's way. Before starting out that morning I should have spent a little time teaching them something about the gun instead of relying completely on that goddam, terrified Algerian gunner. But how was I to know he'd crack? Again I was thinking of the Germans. What if they just crept along that wall on the side of the road and, before reaching the corner, tossed some of those "potato masher" fragmentation grenades? You can't think about that now, I told myself, you're a medic now. That's what comes first. But maybe the Germans had a mortar. A few mortar shells lobbed over the farmhouse and we'd be wiped out. Never mind that. Finish with Pierre and then take care of Pépin. Besides, if they had a mortar they would have used it by now. Yes, of course, but you were awfully sure they weren't there at all. How can you be so sure they don't have a mortar? Christ, I don't know. This is all I can do for Pierre now. Pépin next.

Pépin, pale and tight-lipped, held out his hand with the dangling thumb. "It's only my thumb, Captain," he said in a steady voice, trying to be very matter-of-fact. It looked as if his thumb would just drop off if he shook his hand once or twice. There were no more gauze pads. I hadn't reminded my men to carry them this morning. I wrapped my handkerchief around Pépin's hand, carefully tucking in the thumb. I added strips I cut from his shirt as though with this extra wrapping the thumb had to remain part of his hand. He thanked me, holding up his bandaged hand and taking his Sten gun in the other.

Pierre was on his feet now propped up by one kid on each side. Another one held up a small flask of Calvados to give him a drink and kept repeating in a high-pitched voice, "You're all right, Pierre. You're all right, Pierre."

"How do you feel, Pierre?" I asked him hurriedly, trying to look him over and also watch that far corner of the wall. "Think you can make it back to that other farm if we help you?"

He wobbled forward a few steps with the two kids holding him up and took another swig of Calvados. "Oh sure, sure, Captain," he replied weakly. "I'm just a little woozy. Doesn't hurt much."

No, I thought, but it sure as hell will when the shock wears off. His color was better though, and his eyes had less of a glazed look.

"Hey! All of you," I called out. "We're going back to the other farm." I had picked out a tall tree in the left corner of the farmyard and thought if we made straight for that tree we would avoid the grazing fire of the German gun as much as possible, and for at least part of the way we would be shielded by the farmhouse we were leaving. I pointed to the trcc. "Move in the direction of that tree, don't veer to the right. We'll make it all right. Let's go!" I tried to sound very confident, as though I were just giving a routine order.

"Captain," said a square-faced, chunky lad. "Why can't we leave Pépin and Pierre here with one man and then the rest of us can swing back and around . . ."

"Sure," interrupted another kid. "The Germans won't expect . . ."

"Shut up!" I snapped, suddenly feeling angry and tense, and knowing we had to get back as fast as we could. "Get going!"

The Algerians and Senegalese hesitated. They're afraid to cross that field again, I thought, otherwise they would have taken off long before. Then one Senegalese threw down his rifle and started running. The others followed him. "Hey! Stop!" I yelled at the Algerian gunner. "Come back and get the gun!" He didn't even turn around. One of the kids picked up the machine gun and we left. Ahead of us I could see the Algerians and Senegalese about half-way across, running hard, and then there was the crackle of automatic fire, and just off to their right the bullets kicked up the dust. Pierre was plodding unsteadily, supported by the two kids, with the other six boys walking behind. Occasionally one of them would glance over his shoulder at me as if to reassure himself. It was very slow going and although we only had about two hundred yards to travel the distance seemed much farther. When we were still only half-way there the Germans fired again and the burst tore into the dirt. At that range it had to be a machine gun, I thought, and not a *Schmeisser*, but the Germans did not have a perfect angle of fire. They would have to move their gun to sweep the area we were crossing. That machine gun could be shifted very rapidly.

Walking last, with my eyes fixed on Pierre's back as he edged forward step by step, I knew he could not go any faster but under my breath I kept saying, "Faster, Pierre! Faster, Pierre!" My fear came back then and I licked my dry lips nervously, breathing hard with my chest feeling tight again. Glancing to my right I suddenly saw a camouflaged bunker about four hundred yards off. I should have picked it out before. The shooting couldn't be coming from that bunker where they would have had a straight line of fire at us. Probably it was a bunker for an 88 and it was unoccupied. But the dark aperture of the bunker looked ominous, like an evil eye following us. The Germans fired again and again, in quick, angry bursts and the last onc came very close as we finally reached the stone wall.

We eased Pierre over the wall and stretched him out. My Algerian gunner was cowering against the wall with his arms crossed over the back of his head, shaking violently. I fought down a furious impulse to kick him. I knelt down beside Pierre and then looking up I saw that back of the farmhouse and away from the road there was a big clearing. Beyond that open space was a patch of woods which hid the German barbed wire curving in that direction. Here was the danger point now. They might send a patrol through the woods to outflank us. Checking Pierre's wound I noticed that he was bleeding less but the bandage needed tightening again and as I did this I sent the two kids with our machine gun to cover the open clearing. Two other kids crouched behind the wall with their Sten guns trained on the road. One of them was the square-faced boy who had spoken up before; now his jaw stuck out and he looked as if he was daring the Germans to come down the road. The two kids with the machine gun, unsure of where they should set it up, were looking back at me and I pointed again towards the clearing and yelled, "Farther! Down there!" At the same time I heard the Algerians and Senegalese babbling and then they ran off again. I didn't even call out to them.

I was still working on Pierre but my eyes kept searching through the drizzle and into the dark woods. In case I saw Germans dodging their way past the trees I would have to dash over to our machine gun and fire it myself. When they tried to cross that clearing my gun could rake them and I might even get enfilade fire.

If my two kids passed the ammunition belts properly at the start I was confident that from then on I could hold off a German patrol by myself. But only for a while, I thought, only for a while. Yes, but long enough for my two wounded kids and the others to get away, provided I handled the gun well. All right then, I told myself, I'll be the rear guard, I have to do this but I'll never make it out of here. The hell I couldn't; the thing to do was to keep cool and not panic like the Algerian gunner. I had finished with Pierre now and as I stood up it was so quiet that all I could hear was my heavy breathing. Then out of the stillness came the sudden singing of birds. It sounded very loud and out of place. I saw Pépin, holding his bandaged hand close to his chest and gripping his Sten gun with his good hand, and he too was listening to the birds. We looked at each other for several moments and then I relaxed a little and gave him a tight-lipped smile. All at once, and without knowing why, I was sure we were safe and that no patrol was coming after us. We could head for the American lines and somehow I would get my two kids to a first-aid station.

"We've made a little visit to La Bastille and found we're not welcome," I said to the men, trying to be funny and ease the tension. A few of them grinned. "We're leaving, but we'll make another visit here some time soon."

"*Ah çà, oui, bien sûr,*" said Pépin.

"Let's get moving," I said and I walked ahead slowly followed by the others.

We crossed several fields and then swung over to the road where Pierre could walk more easily. He seemed to have gained strength and was trudging steadily with his good arm around one kid. I thought we were now beyond the operating range of any German patrol. But then to my left I heard the crunching of shells, either mortar or artillery, and I wondered what was happening there. We had not gone much farther when a middle-aged peasant woman came running towards us waving her arms. "*Au secours!* Help!" she cried out. "My husband! My husband!" She stopped in front of me out of breath, her face contorted as she tried to speak. She was incoherent and only scattered words came out, "His legs . . . half torn off . . . bleeding . . . come right away . . .

help me! Help me!" I guessed that her husband had been caught in the shelling I had heard a few minutes before, or maybe his legs had been torn open by an anti-personnel mine. The woman grabbed my arm and started tugging.

"Where?" I asked. "Where is he?"

She pointed frantically towards a grove of trees not far off to our left. "Over there! . . . Right by our farm! . . . Ah, *Bon Dieu!* . . . Please hurry!"

I told her that I was very sorry but I couldn't come because I had two wounded men to take back. "Try to get a doctor, Madam," I said.

"A doctor! Where? No, no, you come! . . . I beg you! It's not far! . . . This way!" She was pulling harder on my arm.

I repeated firmly that I was *desolé*, very sorry, but I couldn't leave my men. Her arms dropped to her side and she began to sob, her eyes fixed on me with a look of terrible reproach.

I turned my back on her. "Let's go," I said to my men. We started again and when I glanced back a few seconds later she was running down the road again and I could hear her calling out, "*Au secours! Au secours!*" Even as I had spoken to the woman I knew down deep that the reason I had given for refusing help was not the true one, but it was only later that afternoon that I faced up to this.

We kept walking slowly down the road. I noticed that Pierre, who had looked better before, seemed to be getting weaker. I stopped and got the kids off the road and into a pasture where he could lie down. He insisted he was all right but his voice was feeble and he was very pale. I knew he should not walk any more so I left the kids in charge of Pépin and, taking one boy with me, I set off at a jog to look for the American lines and a first-aid station where I hoped to find an ambulance to send back for Pierre. We took a road to the right and were lucky for in about a half-hour we met an American company marching up to the front. They had a headquarters jeep and the company commander, a friendly-looking first lieutenant, listened to me for a few seconds and then ordered the driver to take us back to pick up my wounded kids and take them to the aid station a few miles in the rear. "You'll find Captain Dupas there," the lieutenant told me. "Doc is a fine guy. He's from the base hospital. Asked to be assigned to that first-aid post." We drove quickly to where I had left the patrol and Pépin climbed in the jeep while Pierre had to be assisted. I sat next to him in the back so I could hold him up. "Drive like hell," I told the driver.

We reached the aid station located in a vacant farmhouse. Captain Dupas was a dark-complexioned man with a kindly expression. Two medical staff sergeants put Pierre on a stretcher while the captain walking alongside and smiling spoke a few words of French. Pépin carefully put his Sten gun down by the entrance and grinned while even Pierre, his eyes half closed, smiled faintly. I looked at Pépin and Pierre. I wanted to say something to them. "You two men," I began, feeling self-conscious, "out there today you were great and I feel that . . ." I didn't know how to finish.

Pépin gazed down at the ground and mumbled something. Then he slowly raised his head and looked me squarely in the eye. "*Merci, mon Capitaine,*" Pépin said firmly with a touch of pride.

"*Merci,*" murmured Pierre.

"Well, now that you're here," I continued. "Well, everything is going to be all right."

The doctor asked me to wait outside. In a short time he came out and told me that Pierre would probably pull through but he had lost a lot of blood and was in partial shock. "He will never have the full use of his shoulder," the doctor said. "Muscle damage." As to Pépin, they would have to amputate his thumb. Both boys were being given tetanus shots and Pierre was getting plasma.

I stared at him. "They're Maquis kids," I said, thinking perhaps an explanation was necessary.

"Sure. I know. We've treated others before. They're always so appreciative."

"Please do everything you can for them," I went on. "You see it was . . ."

He put his arm around me. "Of course we will, Captain." He looked at me in a searching yet compassionate way which was partly that of a doctor observing a patient and partly that of a man eyeing a close friend. "How about you?" he asked. "You all right?"

"I'm O.K."

"Anything I can do for you? How about some chow?"

"No thanks." I didn't feel like eating. I wanted to get back to our headquarters and give Jeanpaul my report. And then I wanted to be alone for a while.

The jeep driver said he could take me back to our headquarters and we started off. The driver was a corporal who had recently been busted down from sergeant and wanted to explain all of this to me and how unfair the army was. He had an annoying way of ending most of his sentences with, "See what I mean, sir?" I wasn't really listening, for my mind was back at La Bastille, the cowardly Algerian gunner and the others who ran. I hadn't been ready for that. I remembered hearing that in the German Army, and probably in the Russian Army too, if a man tried to run away —which couldn't have been often in those armies—an officer would shout, "I order you to stop or I'll shoot!" and then, if the man kept going, the officer would gun him down. That was iron discipline, and it took a lot of guts for an officer to do that. Or was that really guts? Maybe. But I had no authority to do that, and if I had I wouldn't have shot them. Not under those circumstances anyway. Those bastards couldn't even be court-martialed, for this was only the Maquis and not a regular army unit.

"See what I mean, sir?" the driver was saying again. I just grunted and the corporal looked over at me and stopped talking. But by God, I thought, my kids had been great, particularly the wounded boys. Of course those two boys had disobeyed orders but after being hit they had accepted the pain and the danger without flinching. I was proud of all of them, and that was one thing I could feel good about. They were reckless, too brave, they had too much élan, but better that than the other way around. I used to think of them as my Boy Scouts, yet compared to the Algerian and Senegalese veterans my kids had been like the Emperor's Old Guard standing fast at Waterloo. They had only pulled back when I gave the order. These kids were a ragtag bunch all right, but they had one quality which any good infantry outfit always has, and that is courage.

The driver was talking again, droning on about "B" Company having been pinned down for quite a while earlier that morning by "some of them friggin' Kraut machine guns." Too bad for "B" Company, I thought, yes and too bad for me too, but "B" Company probably had about one hundred and sixty men, and no Algerians and Senegalese, and so evidently they had been able to push on. When we were fired on a few hours ago I had been determined at first that we were not going to be pinned down by one sub-machine gun, nor by a machine gun either. Now I realized that this fixed purpose stemmed, at least partially, from a confidential lecture given at Fort Benning in 1943 by an American colonel just back from the Allied campaign in New Guinea. He described how an American division attacking in a narrow valley had been stopped cold by two Japanese machine guns. The officers and men would not or could not go forward. Finally an Australian regiment had been leap-frogged over the American division and, accepting casualties, had quickly overrun the Japs and the advance had been resumed. As I listened to the colonel I had thought of the galling shame and humiliation suffered by the company commanders and platoon leaders of that American division. And so then, at a safe distance of at least three thousand miles from the nearest battlefield, I had made up my mind that this would never happen to any men I commanded. At La Bastille I had no time for such recollections, but the moral of that incident had become part of my credo of an officer's duty. A troop commander did not allow himself to be pinned down by an automatic weapon, and such decisions did not have to be weighed.

We arrived at our headquarters, a summer villa near a rocky promontory overlooking the ocean. No one was in the villa. Whoever lived in the house had left before the fighting started and all the furniture had been removed except the dining room table and a few straight-back chairs. The floor was covered with dust, and one window facing towards the sea had only one-half of a broken green shutter which banged loosely back and forth with a clanking sound. A copy of a painting, probably by one of the French Impressionists, hung tilted on the dining room wall. It was a bright picture, a field of tall yellow grass caressed by the wind, splashes of red poppies and a clear blue sky. Between the villa and the ocean were the German pillboxes and bunkers, some of which had been evacuated earlier by the Germans, while the others still held by the enemy had been pounded into silence by the big American guns. Like any headquarters we'd had, whether a manure-splattered barn or elsewhere, this villa was called by Jean-paul the "P.C." or "*Poste de Commandement.*" I was not thinking of it then as a command post but as a refuge where I could think back over what had happened and why things had gone wrong so that tomorrow I would not make the same mistakes. Other mistakes probably, but not the same ones.

But I could understand it very plainly now. The Germans at La Bastille had seen us when we reached that first farm before we crossed the open field to the next farmhouse in front of the barbed wire. They had not fired then because they hoped I would bring my men forward where there would be a clear field of fire. They also thought I might swing over to that narrow road leading to La Bastille. So the Germans had remained very quiet, letting me come into a trap. And now, as I reviewed what must have happened, I could imagine a German lieutenant crouching next to his machine gunner in one of the stone farmhouses clustered there. I still thought of the Germans as men with tough faces and hard, cold eyes, and this lieutenant was like that. He and his gunner were at an open window hidden by the trees. The gunner had his light machine gun with the muzzle propped on the wide window sill, or maybe with the gun's bipods braced on the sill. The lieutenant was watching us through his binoculars.

Then we had moved across the field to the farmhouse just opposite the barbed wire. The lieutenant had watched in disbelief as I skirted the farm and knelt on one knee behind the little bush while I took a smoke. "Look at that fool!" the lieutenant had muttered with his glasses fixed on me. "Unbelievable! Hold your fire. I can see him very plainly." Pépin and Pierre had joined me then. "Fire!" the lieutenant had ordered. I could imagine the gunner, squinting through his sights, and firing the first burst.

"Missed! Fire! Fire!" the lieutenant had shouted. The gunner, surprised at not hitting us, and determined to get us before we made it to the back wall, had jerked on the trigger instead of giving it a steady squeeze. That had been enough to throw the gun off by inches. The machine gunner knew he had fired poorly at an easy target. Probably he had not seen me poking my head around the corner close to the ground, but then he had caught sight of what he was waiting for when Pépin and Pierre had leaned out. His next burst had been right on the mark.

I got up and straightened the painting on the wall, lit a cigarette and sat down again. At least here I could smoke without being foolish. I thought of Farley and Cambray and Martel and what they might have done had they been at La Bastille. Despite his experience with the International Brigade Farley was impetuous, and maybe he too would have gone as far as the barbed wire. Certainly the cool and calculating Jack Cambray wouldn't have made that mistake. And probably Martel also would have known better.

It would not have consoled me then if I could have seen into the future and known that about a week later an American battalion reinforced by tanks would spend an entire afternoon battering its way past La Bastille. I suppose that my tactical mistakes would have seemed all the worse had I known then that the German position was much stronger than I thought. All I was aware of now was that little had been gained and two of my men had been hit, one badly. But if they had not been hit, and if the veterans on whom I counted had not panicked—every war, every combat action has its "ifs"—then I would have tried to outflank what I thought was a weakly held position, and things would probably have been much worse.

The swinging and banging of the half shutter was getting on my nerves and I got up to try to close it. As I stood by the window the wind shifted and I could smell the heavy stench of decaying bodies, the peculiar half-sweet odor which is like no other. This came from the nearby bunkers which had been smashed by American artillery a few days before. The German corpses lay under the rubble. The smell also came from the dead cows lying in a pasture just beyond our villa. I moved away from the window and sat down again.

I got out my combat knife and saw there was some dried blood left on it from cutting open Pierre's sweater. I scraped the blade against the sole of my boot. It was then that I remembered the peasant woman. I think that I had tried subconsciously to bury this memory down deep while reviewing the other things. But the memory would not stay down, and again I saw her tear-stained face and heard her panting, "My husband . . . his legs . . . bleeding . . . help me!" And I knew now, as I did at the time, that the real reason I had turned my back on the woman was that before meeting her I had seen enough of death and blood and panic, heard enough screams and groans, and I could not force myself to go and help a peasant with shattered legs. Perhaps there was little or nothing I could have done for him, and I had my two wounded kids to look after—they were my first responsibility—but I hadn't even tried. By the time we saw the peasant woman, La Bastille had done something to me and I was a tired, beaten man.

I had to stop brooding about the woman and her husband and get my mind on something else. I was sitting there, staring off into space, when Jeanpaul walked briskly into the room. He was still in civilian clothes but he had that military bearing, an air of command, so that I stood up although I knew no such military etiquette was necessary here. I gave him a brief account of our patrol, but I didn't mention the mutilated little girl, or the burial of the American infantryman, and I omitted the peasant woman. These things were of no military importance. I admitted that I had not brought back much of the information he had requested. Jeanpaul kept staring at me as I talked and I had the uncomfortable feeling that I was going to confession without the privacy of the confessional. I finished by saying I was sorry, much as a penitent would recite an act of contrition.

"Where is that first-aid station?" he asked immediately. I gave him the exact location and he said he would go see my two kids later.

"So you took a smoke right in front of the Germans?" he said with a little smile that I found irritating.

"Yes. I told you that."

"You should have stopped at that first farm when you spotted La Bastille. You know that now, I suppose?"

"Yes."

"And from there, behind that wall, you should have used your binoculars to study the position. But no, you had to push ahead right away. And you hadn't brought your binoculars. You should have been observing and listening, on the qui vive for any sign of enemy activity. Right?"

"Yes."

He was whistling under his breath and looking out the window. I asked what he had been doing when I had seen him on the road to La Bastille, and he said he had been taking a quick look before joining Taureau's group.

"Why did you turn around?" I wanted to know.

"I saw the barbed wire and, well," he shrugged his shoulders, "It was too quiet. I had a hunch the Germans were there."

He looked at me like a professor about to explain something to a student who is a little slow. "Bill, I think the Germans are at La Bastille in strength. More than one machine gun in all probability. Perhaps some heavy guns too. They're expecting an American attack there soon. Maybe they didn't want to disclose their gun positions prematurely."

"Maybe so."

"Now when you lit a cigarette under their noses, well of course, that was too much. You were asking for it. They felt they had to accommodate you." He smiled his peculiar lop-sided grin.

"O.K. So I was wrong."

"*Vous étiez un peu trop gonflé, n'est ce pas, B-e-e-l?* Too eager. Panache, eh? That sort of thing went out with cavalry charges." Again the little smile which annoyed me.

"I wasn't trying to have panache," I retorted angrily. "I made some mistakes. I told you I was sorry. I thought I could push beyond La Bastille." And besides that he's wrong, I said to myself, panache didn't go out with cavalry charges and he knows that very well.

He walked slowly over to the table. Leaning on it with both

hands, he gazed at me thoughtfully. "*Bon, bon, B-e-e-l*," he said finally in a gentle voice. "*Je comprends*."

He started pacing up and down the room. "I'm afraid I misled you about the Algerians and the Senegalese," Jeanpaul said. "I should have known better. It was not bad leadership on your part. They've lost their will to fight."

"I found that out."

"Yes. But remember those men were caught up in the retreat of 1940. I know what that was like. Then they were prisoners for nearly four years. When they escaped, where could they go? They're homeless men. So they joined the Maquis. At least they got food and shelter there."

"I don't want any more of those guys in a patrol," I said firmly. "Especially some bastard who swears up and down he knows all about German machine guns."

"No, naturally. But you know, those poor devils deserve our compassion."

I was surprised to hear him speak of compassion when he was so demanding of his own men, and especially of himself. Jeanpaul left then, giving me a friendly pat on the back. I sat down again but then outside I heard Truffington's refined voice. I was in no mood to put up with Truffington so I slipped out the back door and walked to a cliff overlooking the ocean. Although the rain had stopped there were patches of mist and dark clouds and the sea was gray and heaving with the breakers crashing against the rocks. I reached into my pocket for a pack of cigarettes and felt something small and hard. I knew right away what it was. It was the sea shell the little girl had given me for luck.

CHAPTER XV

The 'Liberation' of Dinan

During the next few weeks I led a group several times on free-wheeling, rambling patrols. The group included Algerians and Senegalese, but not the same ones I had with me (part of the time) on the patrol to La Bastille. At first I was not happy about having them, but I discovered that they had extraordinary eyesight, especially the Senegalese. So at times I would motion to a Senegalese to join me at the head of the column and point to a clump of trees off in the distance and ask what he saw. Sometimes he would spot Germans I hadn't noticed. I think that once or twice what the Senegalese took for Germans were cows glimpsed behind a hedgerow a few hundred yards away, and then before I could stop them a couple of my kids with rifles got off a volley. Whether these were cows or Germans, the kids missed, and I never had to explain to an irate farmer why we had shot his livestock.

The African soldiers were also very good at escorting prisoners to the rear, leaving the rest of us free to go on. There were never more than five or six prisoners at any one time, generally older men with haggard, grimy faces and dirty uniforms. The Germans did not like to be guarded by their former prisoners, but I thought the Senegalese and Algerians were due this small reward after their long years in prison camps. They gloried in escort duty and while the Germans shambled in single file along the edge of the road the Algerians and Senegalese marched proudly down the center of the highway like the color guard of a crack infantry unit parading before a reviewing stand.

I accepted these Algerians and Senegalese now because, unlike the day of the La Bastille patrol, I was no longer dependent on them as veterans. By this time I had about twenty young Maquis fighters on whom I could count, kids who had learned much in a short time. They knew how to handle machine guns and other automatic weapons and so if one or two of the Algerians or Senegalese should suddenly break for the rear we wouldn't miss them. After hearing Jeanpaul's explanation of their low morale I sympathized with their strong desire to keep a good distance between themselves and any soldiers of the dreaded *Wehrmacht* unless, of course, the Germans were disarmed.

Pépin was back with us after four days. His right hand, with the thumb gone, was heavily bandaged but he managed very well and had insisted on returning to action. Pierre was still recuperating from his chest wound. Pépin was now a hero to the other kids and he enjoyed it. "*Tu sais,*" he would tell a lad who had just joined our band, "*quand le Capitaine et moi nous étions à La Bastille, eh bien, ça bardait sec, hein, mon Capitaine?*" I would agree with Pépin that we had caught a little hell from the Boches that day and add that Pépin was a *sacré baroudeur,* a real fighter. Then I would change the subject. For while there were bloodier encounters afterwards, none affected me like that day at La Bastille.

One day I set out alone on a reconnaissance, slipped past two German strongpoints, and came to a ridge from where I could see the heavy black smoke billowing from the port of St. Malo. The town and its outskirts had been converted into a vast fortified zone by the Germans whose commanding officer, Colonel von Auloch, was determined that his garrison of ten thousand men would obey Hitler's orders to fight to the last man. With the Americans closing in slowly on the outer defenses the first shells had landed in the city. And then the Germans, gradually retreating to the old Citadel and the area just below the city, had set fire to the town because, as we later learned, von Auloch had decided that if he couldn't hold St. Malo the Americans would find nothing but ruins. St. Malo was an ancient town going back to the Twelfth Century. From there Jacques Cartier had sailed to discover Canada; in the old days corsairs had made it their home port; and later on fleets of fishing schooners used to put out to sea after the traditional blessing of the fleet, and head across the Atlantic towards Iceland and the Grand Banks off Newfoundland. The thick stone ramparts and battlements encircling the town had withstood assaults through the centuries. Now St. Malo was under siege again.

The previous morning we had seen the first refugees from St. Malo trudging wearily towards Combourg. They had two or three farm wagons, piled high with whatever they could take, including one wagon containing only a few mattresses and pots and pans. Jeanpaul and Drouant had been with me then, but they barely looked at the refugees. Standing on high ground, their faces grim and *la rage au coeur,* they had stared for a long time at St. Malo and watched fourteen centuries of French history going up in smoke.

Several days before the arrival of the Americans we had reconnoitered the approaches to Fort Lavarde which was situated on a rocky cape and formed one of the strong points of the defenses around St. Malo. When the Americans finally got there the fort was surrounded; it was impossible for the garrison to link up with the main German forces some four miles away. Drouant and I sat on a ridge with a clear view of the concrete bunkers and watched the infantry deploying along the routes we had shown them. One company was moving past us and plodding to the lower edge of the cliff where they would be safe from grazing machine gun fire. I wondered how they could scale the rocks but evidently Jeanpaul had a plan for he was walking alongside the company commander, gesturing and pointing as though these were his troops and he was impatient with their slow advance. Up to this point the Germans hadn't fired a shot, which made the attack remarkably similar to the demonstrations I had seen in the Shell Creek area of the Fort Benning Infantry School. There a battalion of the 300th Infantry, using live ammunition, would attack Hill 212 which was defended only by dummy targets. Everything always worked out neatly in these demonstrations—the machine guns zeroed in with tracers and pinned the "enemy" down; mortars hammered away; one company would make a feint from one direction while the main assault came from another; and at the end Hill 212 would be captured, the dummy targets shot full of holes, and the "School solution" would have been proven correct once more to the officer candidates.

Suddenly a voice boomed out in German from a hidden loudspeaker. Drouant, who understood a little German, told me an American officer was calling on the Germans to surrender. This surprised me for the 300th Infantry had never resorted to a public address system in winning the battle for Hill 212. The Germans answered the Voice with a few machine gun bursts which caused no casualties. Then the Americans cut loose with a heavy barrage of 81mm mortar phosphorus shells which can cause a nasty burn. We could see the white puffs of the phosphorus shells exploding inside the enemy positions, and after that the Voice came on again, not in a coaxing way, but in a loud impersonal tone. No doubt the Voice was telling the Germans that since they were hopelessly surrounded and the Americans had an unlimited supply of phosphorus shells a brave commander could surrender without losing his honor.

Instead the Germans opened up with a heavy gun. The first two shells landing just behind us were duds. Drouant and I scrambled to the open patio of a small villa as the third shell exploded. The Germans were shelling the infantry column and the villa. Some of the shells smashed into the patio wall while others tore through a hedge which was so close to us that I could have reached out and touched it. When a shell ripped through the hedge the bushes were bent back sharply, as though swept by a hard gust of wind, and twigs and leaves were sheared off, and the next second I would hear the explosion. I told the two GI's crouched beside us not to worry, the German gun couldn't shoot around a corner. They didn't seem reassured. Drouant hollered that this was a 75 and not an 88, although how he could tell I didn't know. I was less interested in the caliber of the gun than in the thickness of the patio wall and how much of this pounding it could take.

During the firing of the German gun which lasted about ten

minutes the Voice was silent, either because it was disgusted with the Germans for being so unreasonable or because it couldn't make itself heard over the din. The moment the gun stopped the mortars really plastered the position. When we peered around our wall the fortifications were completely hidden by the white puffs of smoke. Then the Voice sounded again, still in an even, dispassionate tone. In a few seconds a German staggered out from a bunker with his hands up, a few others followed him and next the whole garrison of some seventy men surrendered. It was a triumph for the Voice, with some help from the mortars and the phosphorus shells. As I watched this capitulation I remembered Father Melançon a few weeks ago shouting himself hoarse in a vain effort to persuade scattered Germans to surrender. I saw that, while he might have been daft, his theory could work, provided there were enough men and the proper weapons and equipment.

A few days later Drouant and I went on a reconnaissance accompanied by a Maquis kid of about sixteen. After moving cross-country for a few hours we stopped to rest at a small, isolated farm. The owner, a grinning, toothless old peasant, wanted to celebrate the occasion so he brought out three dusty bottles of absinthe he had kept hidden from the Germans. This was real absinthe which was very hard to get now because its manufacture had been forbidden many years ago when medical experts discovered that wormwood, from which absinthe was distilled, damaged the brain. Since that time you could still buy absinthe, but it was synthetic and only made you drunk. We added a little pump water to our glasses of liquor and had a number of drinks while the farmer grinned and mumbled happily. The absinthe had a greenish color, a pleasant licorice taste, and was very strong. When at last we decided to leave I saw that our young guide was *hors de combat,* his face as green as the absinthe. He couldn't get up although he tried hard. I laughed at him good-naturedly but I had the odd sensation that my laughter was coming from someone else. We left the kid with the farmer and headed out again.

Sometime later I found that Drouant and I were walking along an exposed beach. It was a bright day with a good breeze and the whitecaps flashing in the sunlight. That was when the shelling started. A shell landed in the water, sending up a big spray, and then off in the distance I heard the blast of the gun. More shells came, several of them close, but we kept walking and I was unconcerned though curious in a hazy way. Far in the back of my mind I realized that they wouldn't use artillery against only two men on a beach, so probably they were testing the gun and adjusting the range for eventual targets. Yes, but why were they testing the gun now? I knew that since the Americans had swept through most of this area the previous day there should be no machine guns to rake us out in the open. Although there could still be pockets of Germans left, and maybe a machine gun or two, it seemed to me this was nothing to worry about. I do not feel drunk, I thought, absolutely not, yet I am floating in a strange and lovely fashion and maybe this is what wormwood does to you. Drouant was just as unconcerned and when a spume of water shot up and caught the sunlight he pointed vaguely and said, "*C'est joli,*" and I said slowly, "*Oui, très joli.*" Somehow, without hurrying, we followed the curve of the beach and then turned inland.

After a while we came to a crossroad where, as usual, the Germans had installed posts with road markers, the pointers aimed in different directions and giving distances to various installations and headquarters. All of these markers had long German words, such as *Kommandatur,* followed by more German. Drouant stopped in front of the road marker and stared at it like a tourist in a foreign country trying to get his bearings. Ever since we had been dropped I had ignored these markers; they meant nothing to me, and I thought we were wasting time. Later I suppose we finished our reconnaissance and had supper at some farmhouse although I remain foggy about that afternoon.

Next I remember that a Maquis chief suggested that we could find shelter for the night in a nearby château. He told us the proprietor was a Count who had helped the Resistance in many ways even though he was a little old for active duty. Rounding a bend in the road we saw a small château which looked like a manor house with two round towers at either end and a pasture in front where cows were grazing. Drouant knocked at the massive door which was opened by an old, stoop-shouldered housekeeper who threw up her hands and shuffled off when Drouant told her we would like to see the Count. In a few minutes a tall, elderly man came to the door and gave us a quick, searching look. The Count had close-cropped gray hair, grizzled eyebrows, and a fine aristocratic face. When Drouant mentioned the name of the Maquis chief the Count motioned us inside with a courteous gesture and said gravely that we were most welcome. Showing no surprise he acted as though he were greeting visitors who were paying a formal call.

The Count led the way to a large drawing room with book cases on one side and a huge fireplace on the other. The only light came from a kerosene lamp on the library table. Above the fireplace was an old painting of a French grenadier of the Napoleonic era, a soldier with a bristling, upturned mustache and a fierce expression. Evidently one of the Count's ancestors, I thought. The Count went to his chair by the lamp and invited us to be seated. Stroking his chin, he listened calmly to Drouant's explanation of who we were and what we were doing here.

"Very good," the Count said quietly when Drouant had finished. He leaned towards me and said that some day he would like to visit America. "But not in the same way you're visiting Brittany," he added, smiling a little.

The Count asked Drouant about the Allied campaign and when he thought the war might end, and after hearing Drouant's views the Count turned to me.

"Your army has an incredible amount of matériel," he said in his polite tone.

"Of course," said Drouant before I could answer, "and that's exactly why they're winning the war." Drouant, like the other French officers, liked to believe that the success of the American Army was due almost entirely to their crushing superiority in tanks, guns and planes, and that the French would have done just as well—or even better—had they had the tools.

"Oh, I agree with you," the Count replied, with a fleeting ironic smile. "But then no doubt the Romans said the same thing about Hannibal when he crossed the Alps with his elephants."

Drouant grunted and then asked about the damage in St. Malo. The Count looked at him thoughtfully for a moment and replied that most of the old city was in ruins and that the Hotel Dieu had its spire knocked off. He reached on the table for one of those unbound French books whose pages have to be cut. The Count picked up a letter opener and began to cut the pages in a deliberate way. No one spoke and the only sound was that of the letter opener slitting the pages.

We were all thinking of St. Malo and I was reminded of the little village of Fleury at the site of the Verdun battlefield which I had visited when I had gone over in 1934. I remembered the desolate stretch of wasteland seen under a somber sky, the earth so battered by the shells that nothing grew except a few tufts of dried grass, the old trenches caved in, bits of barbed wire and rotted stakes. What had struck me was the silence which hung over the rolling countryside like a shroud. No birds sang. One could almost smell death there. For miles around there wasn't a house or any sign of life in that whole dreary landscape except for a small group of tourists some distance away. Then I had come to Fleury. The only thing there was a little pile of rubble with a wooden sign reading, "*Ici était le village de Fleury.*" (Here was the village of Fleury.)

I thought I saw a melancholy expression pass over the Count's face as he looked at us in the soft glow of the lamp. Drouant muttered that the Americans could have by-passed St. Malo. The Count nodded in agreement.

"Conquest, occupation, you have never experienced that in America," he said, "so I suppose it's very hard for Americans to really understand these things."

"Yes sir, I guess it is." I leaned back in my chair thinking this over. "But that's not quite true," I went on after a few seconds. "It happened in the South during our Civil War."

"Yes? Ah yes, in the Confederate States. I had forgotten. You're from the South?"

I replied that I was from New Orleans and told him a little about the occupation of the city by Northern troops, including General Butler's famous order that any New Orleans woman caught snubbing Union officers would be treated as a whore. "Well, actually he didn't use the word 'whore,'" I said, grinning a little. "As I recall, the order said 'a woman about town plying her vocation.'"

The Count seemed amused at my French translation. "General Butler must have been a very unpleasant man," he said with a faint smile.

I remembered an old newspaper clipping I had at home telling how my grandmother was caught secretly making a little Confederate flag, but since she was only sixteen my great-grandfather was held responsible. When I told the Count about that he raised his eyebrows. "They shot him?" he asked.

"No, no. But he was fined twenty-five dollars and got a reprimand. He was lucky they didn't throw him in jail."

"Ah yes. A fine and a reprimand." The Count smiled politely. "Here the Germans, when they use punitive measures, they go somewhat to extremes."

I realized that he was right; it would be hard, very hard, for the Americans—even the combat troops—to truly understand what four years of German occupation had been like. A newspaper article here and there, a radio broadcast, a few photographs in some magazines, that was as close as most people would get to it. Yes, but what did the Count know about our Civil War? Of course, the Northern troops were not the Nazis, still in telling him about my grandmother and about General Butler's order I had given him a mere vignette, a couple of incidents which gave a false picture of what the South had been forced to endure. To the Count the Civil War was hazy and remote, something that happened nearly a hundred years ago and thousands of miles away. But twice within his lifetime France had been invaded by the Germans. Even now as we sat in his drawing room we could hear the thunder of the guns at St. Malo.

The Count sat there with his legs stretched out, looking pensive. He began to reminisce about the occupation and said that for quite some time he had been sure that the British were doomed and that a German victory was inevitable.

Drouant reminded him that with the exception of General de

Gaulle and a few others, the high-ranking French officers had felt the same way.

"They were being realistic," said the Count. "Or, as we like to say, logical. And once in a while that's a mistake. General de Gaulle did not make that mistake."

Drouant glanced at him sharply and seemed about to say something but then changed his mind. Watching Drouant I thought of how many French officers had been torn between their allegiance to the recognized government of old Marshal Pétain at Vichy and their desire to continue the fight under de Gaulle. As Drouant had told me at Milton Hall only generals and colonels could make such a decision for their troops; younger officers could do nothing.

"But sometimes even calamity can be a friend," the Count went on. "Simplifies things."

"I beg your pardon?" said Drouant.

"What I mean," the Count replied, "is that with no hope of victory, failures didn't really bother me. But it seemed to me that helping the Resistance was the right thing to do." He shrugged his shoulders. "Nothing mattered anymore. So you did what you could."

I remembered the curé of Courcité telling us that from the beginning he was convinced, against all reason, that the Germans would lose the war, and this faith had sustained him. But the Count had a different point of view in 1940, a sort of noblesse oblige; all was lost, but you resisted because it was right.

The Count said his feeling of hopelessness changed suddenly on June 22, 1941—he remembered the exact date—when a haughty German captain, who had come by to requisition his horses, said he'd just heard the wonderful news that the *Wehrmacht* had invaded Russia, and so the Fuehrer's prophecy that the Third Reich would last for a thousand years was certain to be fulfilled.

"But I knew better," he added, "And I was sure that the Russian winter would swallow up the Germans just as it had Napoleon's Grand Army."

I offered the Count a cigarette and he said, "Thank you so much," lit it slowly and took a deep drag.

"I invited the captain in," he went on, "got out my best cognac, and we drank a toast to the invasion of Russia. I have never enjoyed a toast so much." The Count laughed quietly.

Drouant and the Count talked on and on about the war until finally the conversation began to lag. "I've enjoyed this visit immensely," the Count said as he stood up. "Now let me show you to your rooms."

He walked very erectly as he climbed the stairs and first took Drouant to one bedroom and then showed me my room across the hall. It was very large with a high bed and the usual French bolster rather than pillows.

The Count was smiling a little as he stood in my room. "I believe that there are only a few Germans left in our vicinity," he said. "Still, to be on the safe side, may I suggest that you keep your pistol on the night table. I hope that you enjoy a good rest. *Bon soir, Capitaine.*"

I thanked him and checked my forty-five which I put on the table within easy reach. I stripped to my shorts and climbed into bed. I hadn't slept between sheets in a long time and as I stretched out I had no worries about engaging in a running gun battle while clad only in my underwear.

At breakfast the next morning the Count told us of unconfirmed reports that the Germans were preparing to evacuate Dinan and retreat north to join the forces at St. Malo. Dinan, a town of about twelve thousand at the time, is situated on the west bank of the river Rance some thirteen miles below St. Malo, which is on the east bank and at the mouth of the river. Drouant and I had heard yesterday that an American armored column was pushing towards Dinan, that the Maquis there was harrassing the Germans, but that the enemy was in a good position to cut the American lines of communication. We wanted to make a patrol to Dinan, so after telling the Count goodbye and thanking him we got the St. Pierre de Plesguen group together and with about fifty men we set out towards Dinan.

It rains often in Brittany but this was a clear morning with a bright sun and blue skies and the tang of salt air blowing in from the sea a short distance away. Drouant was in fine spirits. Unlike

Jeanpaul André Drouant was easy-going and occasionally broke out in an engaging smile just when Jeanpaul was scowling over something that had gone wrong. Now Drouant was telling me about Dinan, saying he'd heard that like St. Malo it was an old town with quaint stone houses and narrow twisting streets and that there was a lane there called, "Promenade de la Duchesse Anne" in honor of Anne de Bretagne who had married a French king but remained Duchess of Brittany. Coming around a sharp turn in the road we saw the burned-out hulls of two American tanks in the ditch, and in a meadow beyond the road several bodies were sprawled, but they were too far away for me to tell whether they were Americans or Germans. Evidently the Americans had penetrated to this point before being smashed by the 88's, and now more armor was supposedly on the way. Off in the distance we heard a few sharp bursts of small-arms fire. I looked back at our men who were straggling in single file. A small group stood off to one side arguing.

Before leaving that morning Drouant had cut himself a willow stick which he was using as a cane, or maybe a swagger stick, and he was striding along with his carbine slung over his shoulder, swinging his stick like a boulevardier. In a low voice he started singing the folk song about Anne de Bretagne, "*C'était Anne de Bretagne avec ses sabots . . .*" and the men near us joined in but not loudly. One of our kids grinned and, pointing to Drouant, said, "*Il veut faire le Zouave,*" meaning he wants to be a daredevil. This mention of the Zouaves, formerly a crack French outfit noted for their colorful uniforms and especially for their élan, was not to my liking. I thought that while there were times when acting like a Zouave was the thing to do, now was definitely not such a time. I grabbed Drouant by the arm. "Look, André," I said, "this is a patrol and not a goddamned Sunday outing. Let's get the hell off this road and cut out this stupid singing."

"*Oh merde, B-e-e-l,*" he said pleasantly, and he sauntered off singing again, "*C'était Anne de Bretagne . . .*"

The hell with it I muttered to myself, and I impatiently signalled for the men in the rear to catch up with us. In a short time we reached a rise in the road and from there we saw the valley of the Rance, with the river curving away towards the north. Across from us was the town of Dinan on a ridge whose side dropped steeply to the water's edge. The top of the ridge was heavily wooded and above the trees I could see a church spire and some houses barely visible through the trees. We got out our binoculars to study the opposite bank where a low rampart, about waist high, ran along the side of town facing the Rance. There was no sign of Germans and no more sound of firing. The river was about fifty yards wide, and I saw that an old stone bridge had been destroyed. The center arch had been neatly blown, leaving a gaping space. It had been an excellent demolitions job, one that our instructors would have approved. That rumor is true, I thought, the Germans have apparently pulled out, but they're tricky bastards and I've been wrong before. One of the Maquis kids said he could lead us to a dike across the Rance a little below town. Drouant and I decided to make a reconnaissance alone and followed our guide. We crossed the dike, walked down a narrow road screened by tall hedgerows and arrived at a street stretching ahead of us with the houses next to the sidewalk forming a wall on each side. We were in Dinan. The street was deserted, the shutters of the houses were closed, and there wasn't a sound.

Drouant stopped for a second and took a long look. Then he squared his shoulders and began marching down the street as though he were taking possession of the town in the name of France. Watch it now, I said to myself, it's all very well for Drouant to stride in as a conqueror, and maybe the Krauts have gone, but did they leave a few snipers behind, or a machine gun? And why was everyone inside? I didn't want to be gunned down stupidly. I moved ahead close to the wall, with my carbine at the ready, peering down the street and scanning the opposite side. We had only gone a short distance when a door opened and a man poked his head out. He saw us and quickly pulled his head back and slammed the door. He's taken us for Germans, I thought. After we had walked a little farther another door opened and a young woman stood in the doorway and watched us coming. All of a sudden she threw up her hands, yelled "*Les Américains! Les Américains!*" and ran towards us. She threw her arms around Drouant and kissed him and shouted again, "*Les Américains!*" When Drouant smilingly told her he was a French officer she kissed him again and screamed, "*Les Français! Les Français sont ici!*" By that time doors had opened all the way down the street and people were running towards us and yelling. Within a few minutes we were surrounded by a jostling, screaming crowd. I couldn't understand how the word had spread so fast. Drouant's handsome face was glowing. Ever since the humiliating French surrender in 1940 he had been waiting for an occasion like this. In the past few weeks we had entered hamlets with only a few inhabitants, but this was a town and Drouant was the first French officer to walk down a street of Dinan.

All at once French flags appeared everywhere, and one faded American flag hung from a window. Hastily made bouquets were tossed at us while we were handed flowers from all sides, and I was carrying great bunches of flowers in one hand and my carbine in the other. There were many women in the crowd, and also lots of children. All of them surged around us, patting Drouant and me on the back, trying to shake hands, and screaming in our ears. Babies were held up so they could touch us. One red-faced woman held her little boy up to my face and kept telling him, "*Dis merci! Dis merci au soldat! Merci! Merci!*" Over on the sidewalk I saw a thin old woman wearing an old-fashioned bonnet. She was stooped over leaning on a cane and feebly waving her hand. I shoved my way towards her and I put my arm gently around her shoulders and kissed her on the forehead. "*Vive la France, grand-mère!*" I said, and she smiled back with tears running down her cheeks. Two very pretty girls had linked arms with me and I kissed them and handed each one a bouquet saying, "*Pour les deux plus jolies filles de Dinan!*" They exclaimed, "*Mais vous êtes Français!*" and I said, "*Non, non. Américain. Je parle français.*"

By now I felt completely carried away and I had forgotten all about the Germans and where they might be. I was only aware of the excited faces, the frenzied gestures, the tears and smiles, and the wild shouts of "*Vive la France! Vive l'Amérique.*" Dimly, amid the noise and confusion, I realized how the people of Dinan felt. They had hoped desperately for liberation, but they also had dreaded a battle which might destroy their town, and they had feared savage German reprisals. Now when it seemed to them that they were safe and free their emotions had erupted in a wild display. What they didn't know was that the nearest American forces were still miles away.

In a few minutes a stocky young man shoved his way to us and said that his name was Paul and he was with the Resistance. Motioning to Drouant and me, he elbowed and pushed through the crowd and led us to a square jammed with people yelling "*Les voilà! Voilà les Américains!*" He took us to a café and when we got inside Paul curtly ordered the customers out and bolted the door. Only he and six or seven Resistance men were left. Drouant asked Paul where the Germans were and he told Drouant with a sly grin that they weren't here anymore. Drouant drily said that he had figured that out but would like to know which way they had gone. Then the Resistance men all started talking at once and asked how far away the Americans were and how soon they would get here. From all this babble I learned that the Germans' rear guard had been pulling out at one end of town, headed north, at about the same time that we had come into Dinan at the other end. Outside the café a few men had begun singing the *Marseillaise*, and then all the people joined in and the ringing, full-throated chant of "*Allons enfants de la Patrie . . .*" rang out and reverberated in the square. The men in the café were quiet now. The crowd roared out the refrain, "*Formez vos bataillons . . .*" in a pulsating, crashing crescendo. I put my carbine down on a table, swallowed hard once or twice, and glanced over at Drouant. His jaws were clenched but he was impassive, looking straight ahead as though he were seeing something that no one else could see. The people had finished singing the *Marseillaise* and still none of the men moved or spoke. Finally the café owner got out a bottle of Calvados and poured drinks for everyone. Drouant put his glass down untouched and so did the others. The men were watching Drouant and they must have noticed, as I did, that he was fighting hard to master his emotions.

But Drouant had great self-control. "Comrades of the Maquis," he said in a steady voice. "I honor the memory of those men,

Frenchmen, Englishmen, Americans, who died—*tombés au champ d'honneur*—so that today Dinan might be free. May we never forget them."

He drained his glass in one gulp and all of us did the same. Again there was complete silence in the room as Drouant stood there, very straight, eyeing the *Maquisards*. Then he began speaking in a crisp, clipped voice like Jeanpaul did when he gave orders. The Americans, he told them, should reach the Rance in a few hours. They would either repair the bridge or throw a pontoon bridge across the river, and it was of the utmost importance that he and I find out where the German positions were, especially the anti-tank guns, so that we could bring this information back to the tank commanders. "You first," he said, jabbing his finger at Paul. "What do you know?"

Paul snapped to attention like a Guardsman and replied that the enemy was retreating along the main highway, and also on secondary roads, and would no doubt fight a delaying action before trying to cross the Rance near St. Malo so as to join the main forces there. He had no exact information yet, but perhaps some of the other men did. Drouant tapped his watch, tersely said we didn't have much time, and went on to question the next man. Oh hell, I thought, André is right of course, we have to get these reports of enemy activity right away. But I sure would like to go out in the square, mix with that wild crowd, receive bouquets, drink Calvados, and get hugged and kissed by the girls.

Drouant's sharp voice jarred me out of this reverie. "B-e-e-l," he was saying. "Listen to Zuzu."

"Zuzu? What?"

"This young guy here. He just came in. They call him 'Zuzu.'" Drouant grinned for a second. I looked up and saw that a lanky, awkward kid was talking to Drouant. Zuzu had a flat, stupid face with buck teeth and he lisped. His head was cocked to one side and he was scratching his behind. Paul called me aside and whispered that Zuzu was often able to get valuable intelligence because the Boches thought he was a harmless imbecile and let him wander around as he pleased. I hoped Paul was right, for it was certainly easy to see why the Germans had a low opinion of Zuzu. But the information he relayed to us was amazingly complete. He marked German positions on our maps, and even drew sketches to show the location of the 88's. Drouant fired questions and Zuzu, with a cunning gleam in his eye now, gave precise answers most of the time. After questioning other men and putting the pieces together we had as clear a picture as we could get. Drouant and I spent over an hour in the café and then left by a back door to avoid the mob in the square.

One of the men escorted us down a tree-shaded lane leading to a garden overlooking the river and told us that there should be a rowboat moored to the bank below so that we could cross there and not make a long detour by way of the dike.

We rowed across the river, and as we clambered up the bank and moved into a patch of woods we ran into an American patrol edging forward cautiously in what the American Jeds called "the National Guard Crouch." When I told the patrol leader that we had just come from Dinan he said, "Jesus! I mean, yes sir!" and then brought us to his officer, a lieutenant colonel in command of a tank destroyer outfit strung along the same road we had used to approach Dinan. There were some tanks in the column, the lead vehicle being stopped just below a rise in the road. I could tell that this column was advancing carefully after having seen the two burned-out American tanks. The lieutenant colonel sized me up as I gave my account, shook his head, and said, "You've been to Dinan? I'm a son of a bitch!" Then he asked me sarcastically if I knew we had rowed across the Rance practically under the muzzle of a German machine gun, and I said "No sir." He pointed to a farmhouse on the opposite bank and told me to take a good look at the chicken coop because that's where the machine gun was. "All right, now watch," the lieutenant colonel said. His 37mm guns opened up and I could see the red tracers zinging into the target. This did cause a great commotion in the chicken coop, but as far as I could tell these were only chickens madly flapping and hopping up and down. Loose feathers were swirling all over, chunks of wood and stone were blasted in the air, and puffs of dirt were spurting all around the coop. I didn't catch sight of any Germans and there was no return fire.

The guns clattered for a good five minutes and when they stopped the lieutenant colonel grunted, "That fixed those bastards." And I said, "Yes sir. It sure did." But it seemed to me that the 37mm guns had only killed some chickens, and of course scared the hell out of the other chickens and the farmer too. A few minutes later Drouant pulled out Zuzu's sketches to show the lieutenant colonel. "I'll be goddamned!" he exclaimed, and sent for his officers. They gathered around us, studied the sketches, drew lines on their maps, and asked many questions. The lieutenant colonel said, "Great poop you brought us. Real help, Captain." His staff was very cordial and also most curious about what they called "this cloak and dagger stuff." One or two of them spoke pidgin French to Drouant who smilingly replied in pidgin English. It was a happy little gathering. We rejoined our men, for now we had to make a sweep up the right bank of the Rance, opposite Dinan. We would not return to Dinan, and even if we did the town would have other heroes as soon as the Americans got there.

A few days later I went to Combourg to try to get more supplies. At a café I ran into Taureau who had just attended a funeral Mass for a gendarme killed in the Resistance. By that time I knew Taureau well and had grown fond of him so that we could tease each other without taking offense. When I needled Taureau about having gone to Mass he smiled and said in his soft voice that while he would not presume to discuss religion with such an eminent theologian as myself—*un vrai philosophe,* he called me—he wondered if, by chance, I'd heard of Anatole France's remark upon seeing the grotto at Lourdes, "Yes, I see lots of crutches and canes hanging on the wall," Anatole France had supposedly said, "but not a single wooden leg." I grinned but didn't say anything. Back at Milton Hall I had soon found out that I was no match for the French officers in one of those interminable discussions the French so dearly love. With their much wider vocabulary, and what may have been Cartesian reasoning, they invariably left me floundering and sometimes closed the argument by saying in an irritatingly courteous manner, "*Donc vous voyez bien, B-e-e-l, c'est la seule conclusion.*"

Taureau stirred his coffee slowly for a few minutes, looking pensive. Then, to my surprise, he began to tell me the story of his First Communion. It seemed that this had taken place when he was about seven years old. An old nun at the school he attended had explained to him that when he received the Host, "little Jesus will talk to you." He believed the nun absolutely and had been greatly intrigued for he not only wanted to hear "little Jesus" but he thought he himself might have a chance to ask a few questions. On the great day, all dressed up in his Sunday best, he had swallowed the Host and eagerly waited. Silence. He waited some more. Still complete silence, followed by more silence. He didn't say anything to his parents about this afterwards. But in bed that night he had thought about the whole thing for a long time and finally decided he'd been had. Gradually, he said, his skepticism grew until now he no longer believed in God. Taureau looked at me with a half-smile, as though waiting to see what I had to say. I smiled back at him, not knowing just what I could tell him.

"Well," I said, trying to make a joke of it, "well, anyway, if you get knocked off I'll get Father Melançon to say Mass for you. And give a sermon too."

Taureau chuckled at the thought of Father Melançon orating from the pulpit on the virtues of the "deceased."

Within the next few days we could tell that our mission was petering out, and it was then, on what probably would have been his last patrol, that Taureau's luck ran out. I was supposed to go with him that day to maintain liaison with the American infantry, but instead Jeanpaul had asked me to go to American headquarters—I've forgotten why—and when I got back to our command post in a farmhouse I saw that Jeanpaul looked grave. Speaking quietly, he told me that Taureau and two of his men had been wounded by anti-personnel mines and that Taureau, whom he had seen at the aid station, was very badly hit. This news jolted me, as though Taureau had just been cut down beside me, and at the same time I knew that I wasn't thinking only of Taureau and our friendship but I could see myself lying mangled or dead in that minefield.

Jeanpaul didn't say anything for a few minutes and then he sat down and started scribbling in a little blue note book. "Making a few notes for a citation," he explained. "When we get back to London I'll propose Taureau for the Croix de Guerre. Of course he's not in the regular army. Some staff guy may object. But he deserves it. *Chic type.*"

Jeanpaul read to me what he had jotted down but he seemed to be talking more to himself. French is a language ideally suited for military awards; somehow French citations have a ring like a bugle call. What struck me was that this one said something about Taureau's "*belles qualités d'officier*" (the fine qualities of an officer), for with these three words Jeanpaul was paying Taureau a very high tribute. It went on, measuring life and deeds in terms of his officer's code.

The next day the Operations Staff in London sent us a dispatch, relayed through American headquarters, telling us that we could now return to London. But what we wanted was to take part in the liberation of Paris by attaching ourselves to whatever Allied division would be heading for the capital. Our plan was to work closely with the advance units and contact Maquis groups en route to obtain intelligence and coordinate their efforts with the Allied drive. It was not a bad idea, but we made the mistake of proposing our plan to London, and back came the order, "Return at once." When I suggested that we forget the order, and later claim that due to the general confusion we had never received it, Jeanpaul and Drouant reluctantly overruled me.

Before returning to London I wanted to see Taureau and went to the base hospital. He was lying in bed looking pale and weak but when he saw me he forced a smile. I thought again that with his gentle expression he had the face of a poet, and yet when he was on a patrol, and at other times too, the face would reveal his underlying toughness. One of his legs was in a cast and the other was under the bed cover, and where his foot should have made a hump under the blanket there was nothing. The leg seemed to end below the knee, but I was afraid to ask how he was. I found it hard to say the right things, and mumbled that I had come to tell him goodbye and that we were proud of him and wished him a speedy recovery. He murmured something I couldn't catch and I leaned close to him and heard him whisper, "*Au revoir. Merci, mon Capi-*

taine." He was looking me straight in the eye, still with that faint smile. The nurses appeared very busy but I stopped one on my way out. She was a thin woman with a sallow complexion, a nervous twitch to her lips, and she looked disagreeable. "That Frenchman," I asked, "the one over there, is he going to be all right?"

"All right? Maybe," she snapped. She gave me an odd stare and looked down at my jump boots. "But not as healthy as you seem to be, Captain."

I flushed and started to say something, but she hurried away.

That same afternoon we visited the medieval abbey at Mont St. Michel located on an islet just off the shore and about twenty miles east of St. Malo. The Germans had withdrawn from this area a few weeks before and no fighting took place there. We were driving along the lowlands bordering the ocean when, through the haze, we glimpsed the abbey's tall and slender spire looking as though it were suspended between sea and sky. In a few minutes we reached a causeway and then saw the old abbey ahead of us at the summit of a massive, great mound of rock jutting some three hundred feet out of the water. The battlements and ramparts below the monastery seemed to have been carved out of the granite. For nearly eight hundred years the abbey of Mont St. Michel had weathered the lashing gales of the Atlantic and war and revolutions, and now after still another war it towered majestically above us.

Leaving our car by the causeway we walked through the portal of the ramparts and climbed a steep and narrow street winding to the entrance of the abbey. We passed two or three little restaurants and a souvenir shop with a terrace where a few G.I.'s were taking each other's pictures with Brownie Kodaks. At the end of the street there was a flight of stairs cut into the rock and after that another portal which opened into a small courtyard. We were standing there when a guide such as you find in museums hurried up to us all out of breath. He was a small man with a drooping gray mustache and a sad look in his deep-set eyes. The left sleeve of his blue denim tunic hung empty at his side and a medal with a yellow ribbon was pinned to his chest. I recognized that this was the *Médaille Militaire* which is awarded to enlisted men and then only for extraordinary valor. While on vacation in the summer of 1934 I had seen disabled World War I veterans employed as guides by the French Government (*La Patrie est reconnaissante*—The country is grateful) and at the time I had paid little attention, but looking at this guide now, after having seen Taureau that morning, reminded me of visiting the blind veterans as a little boy and of my father speaking about the cost of bravery.

I guessed that this man had watched us coming up the street and had hastily put on his medal before rushing out to catch up with us. He wanted the French officers to see him with his decoration, and I thought that anyone with an arm missing and the *Médaille Militaire* was surely entitled to this touch of pride.

Stopping in front of Jeanpaul the guide asked in a low voice if he might have the privilege of showing the abbey to the major and his party. Jeanpaul nodded—it was almost a half bow—and said that we would greatly appreciate the guide's help since none of us had been here before. When we followed him into the abbey no one else was there and the only sound was that of our boots resounding on the old flagstones. We walked slowly through somber vaulted chambers and then came to a lofty room with peaked Gothic arches and tall graceful columns bathed in the soft light diffused by the apertures. Here the guide paused to tell us the history of Mont St. Michel, beginning in the eighth century with the apparition of St. Michael the Archangel to Saint Aubert, Bishop of a nearby town, whereupon the good Bishop had started the stupendous task of constructing an abbey on the peak of this rocky islet. And then the abbey had been consecrated to St. Michael.

I had never heard this story, and I knew very little about St. Michael the Archangel (I didn't think anyone else did either) except the old prayer recited at the end of Mass, "St. Michael the Archangel, defend us in battle . . ." As a boy I had liked that opening line because, unlike so many cloying prayers, it had a martial quality. But it was a little late to be calling on St. Michael now, and anyway the prayer was a call on St. Michael for help against the Devil.

After listening to our guide I stepped out on a gallery and stood gazing towards the sea. There are very high tides in the Bay of

Mont St. Michel, and now the tide was at low ebb so that the flatness of the pale yellow sands stretched out far in the distance before meeting the sea, and beyond that, half-discernible in the mist, I could see the line of the horizon where the sea joined the sky. Sand, sea, and sky, and the old abbey, all this had a haunting beauty, but sadness too, and maybe this was because one could never really possess it. Our guide's expression had been solemn and his tone reverent when he told us the history of the abbey. Quite probably he seldom goes to Mass, I thought, but he's steeped in the mysticism of the Celt and believes in St. Michael just as surely as he accepts the rise and fall of the tides in the bay below me. If I said to him that I had some slight reservations about St. Michael and his dialogue with the good Bishop Aubert he would get indignant and ask me how I could explain all this, the magnificent abbey perched on a gigantic chunk of rock, if I did not believe in St. Michael, and I would have to agree politely and admit to myself that faith—at least the faith of the Middle Ages when men felt much closer to God, and especially to the Virgin—could aim for the impossible and succeed. So let our Breton guide hold fast to St. Michael, and skeptics discount the story as I did, but no skeptics had ever created anything like the abbey of Mont St. Michel. As Victor Hugo had said, in the Middle Ages men had no great thought that they did not write down in stone. And I remembered Henry Adams writing many years ago that all the steam power in the world could not, like the Virgin, build the Cathedral at Chartres. What is interesting about Adams, I thought, is that he was a sophisticated New Englander and not a Catholic and yet he had probably written more passionately about the Middle Ages than anyone else. Henry Adams, writing in 1907, had closed his *Education of Henry Adams* by saying that on his centenary in 1938 perhaps he would be allowed to come back from the grave and find a world that sensitive and timid minds could contemplate without a shudder. But since then World War I had come, and in 1938 Hitler was on the march.

I left the gallery and went back inside. The idea came to me of how strange it was that in a way our mission had begun in the church rectory at Courcité and ended at the abbey of Mont St.

Michel. Jeanpaul and Drouant were still there, gazing up at the arches, turning their heads to admire the columns and finally glancing down at the old flagstones worn into uneven hollows by the tread of countless feet. Now I understood why they had been so determined to visit Mont St. Michel. To me it had seemed just an outing, a chance to see a well-known tourist attraction. But to them it was a pilgrimage, not to the abbey as a religious shrine, but to Mont St. Michel as one of the glories of France, a symbol of her traditions and of her place in history, all of those things which the French have in mind when they use the proud phrase, "*Toutes les gloires de la France*." After we left Mont St. Michel Jeanpaul and Drouant were lost in thought and did not speak for a long time.

Later that afternoon we set out for the Normandy coast to board an LCI bound for England. On the way we passed through a village demolished by heavy artillery and bombers. The main street, clogged with rubble, was being cleared by an Army bulldozer which raised a choking cloud of dust. Because of the one-way traffic we had to stop and wait our turn while a long truck convoy rumbled past headed in the other direction. On our right I saw the wreck of a church with two broken and jagged walls left standing, and next to the church a small cemetery where the tombstones had been smashed and broken slabs lay on the ground. One tombstone was tilted almost all the way over and I tried to read the epitaph. All I could make out was the date "1847" and the word "*Mort* . . ." The rest of the words had been gouged out by shell fragments. With the roar and throb of the passing trucks in my ears I stared at the tombstone. Who was buried there? But what difference did it make? And still I kept looking. With my thoughts slowly drifting, I suddenly remembered that some Irish poet had composed his own epitaph: "Cast a cold eye/On life, on death/ Horseman, pass by!" Not bad that, I said to myself, and the Count at the chateau would have liked it. And then I wondered what went through a man's mind when he sat down to write his own epitaph. Was he resigned and serene, was he mocking death, or what? I looked up and saw that the M.P. directing traffic was signalling to us. Our car moved away slowly, jolting over the debris.

It was night by the time we reached the embarkation point. Truffington met two officers from a British unit with whom he bargained for the sale of our car. Handling these negotiations with great skill, he got more than the car was worth. We unloaded our gear and set out for the LCI. The beach was crowded with trucks and half-trucks, their engines growling and straining, and GI's were milling around as they loaded the trucks. We shoved our way through men and past stacks of supplies, hearing the occasional grunts and curses of the men toiling in the blackness and the hoarse commands of the NCO's.

We went aboard and met the skipper, a young clean-cut Navy lieutenant with a crew cut. This was only his second trip as master of the vessel and on this dark and foggy night he was nervous about keeping in the narrow channel cleared through the mines. Standing in the wheelhouse, his feet braced apart and his eyes squinting, he gave commands in a high-pitched voice. When he wasn't giving orders he chewed his gum furiously like the lanky, freckled kid who had been the despatcher on our drop into France. Jeanpaul and I had coffee and then while the ship nosed out slowly we went over to the rail and stood there together. This had certainly not been a hard day and I was not tired but I felt hollow and drained inside, with the emptiness of nothing to look forward to.

My mind went back to our briefing in London, the V-1's puttering overhead and Colonel Girard slapping at the map with his broken pointer and talking in staccato bursts, "Twelve bridges to be destroyed . . . the Germans are then bottled up in Brittany . . . *Bien* . . . Difficult, not impossible . . . *Bien* . . ." We had left with high hopes, accepting the risks, anticipating gallant deeds, bridges blown and convoys ambushed. I saw myself again in the converted B-24 bomber approaching the dropping zone and watching for the despatcher's hand signal and the green light on the panel, and then jumping into the darkness and the unknown. And now this was the way our mission was ending, in an LCI heaving slightly in the swells. "*Eh bien, B-e-e-l,* . . ." Jeanpaul started to say and he stopped. There was really nothing to say. We stayed at the rail a long time staring at the darkness and the fog.

CHAPTER XVI

"But what we tried to do was correct"

When we got off the train in London the next morning we were met by a staff major who greeted us with a brisk manner. "Good show, you chaps," he said. "Good show. Follow me this way, please. Righto." He walked ahead rapidly, his heels clicking on the platform alongside the train. After taking us to our quarters in a comfortable flat he asked that we prepare our report which should be submitted to headquarters the next day. Drawing up a terse summary of our operations didn't take us long, although Truffington insisted on including his own account of what had happened to him at Gorron when, as he put it, "We were scattered by a German patrol and I and one partisan were unable to rejoin our group." Our report concluded with a sharp criticism of the staff for the poor planning of our mission. On the following morning when I handed in our report to headquarters I was told to come back at three o'clock sharp to see Colonel Ormley-Dykes.

As I sat at headquarters waiting to see the colonel I watched the staff officers bustling back and forth. One of them, a solemn looking captain, stopped to say he thought he recognized me, and wasn't I a Jed back from France? I told him I was. He shook hands with me and told me how grand it was to have me back. I didn't say anything. The captain asked me if I'd heard about Dick Lacorde's team and when I replied that I hadn't he said that their dropping zone turned out to be behind our own lines, a regrettable fact that was not really the fault of the staff.

"Naturally not," I said.

He went on to explain that after Lacorde's team was briefed an American armored column spurted ahead and overran the dropping zone.

"We got word to Lacorde last night just as they were boarding their plane," he said. "A near thing, believe me. Dick Lacorde is rather upset about the whole business. Pity, wasn't it?"

The captain rushed off saying he had to smooth over a row with the French staff. I waited a long time until finally a British WAC came to take me to Colonel Ormley-Dykes. The colonel sat smoking his pipe behind a big desk in a spacious corner office. He was a ruddy-faced man with pale blue eyes and thinning hair slicked back. "Read your report, Captain," he said. "You chaps did a first-rate job. Under rather difficult circumstances, I should say.

"Thank you, sir."

"Quite an escape you had in the car."

"Yes sir, it was. We were awfully lucky."

The colonel had a faint trace of a smile as he asked for more details of that episode. Then he interrogated me at length while his eyes were fixed on the door behind me. His face with no expression whatever was like a mask. I found this a little disconcerting, especially since his questions though seemingly asked at random were sharp and pertinent. He had been taking notes; now he paused, began doodling on his pad, and cleared his throat with a loud, "Harum." "Captain," he said, looking at me directly, "I gather from your report that you're, ah, a bit critical of the staff for poor planning."

"Yes sir. That's right. Not just me, but the others, too."

"I understand," he said calmly. "But if you'll remember your briefing, no one, I believe, ever said this was going to be a piece of cake."

I tried to hold my temper. "No sir," I said, "but I don't see what that has to do with it." I told the colonel in detail why we thought the planning was poor. "What got us, sir," I added, "was not so much that our reception committee had no contacts with Brittany—that was bad enough—but as it turned out it looked as if they had orders not to let us get in touch with the F.T.P. there. Major Jeanpaul was really burned up about that."

The colonel had listened to me impassively, still doodling.

"We were supposed to blow twelve bridges," I said, my voice rising. "Sir, do you know what would have happened if we had?"

There was a gleam now in the colonel's pale blue eyes but he didn't say anything.

"We would have been court-martialed and shot, that's what. Because by that time the Americans were using those bridges."

The colonel looked at me for a moment while he re-lit his pipe. "Have you quite finished, Captain?" he asked in an even voice.

"Yes sir. For right now."

"Good. Now let me tell you a few things about your mission. First, at one time a second landing in Brittany was contemplated. That was changed. Second, the Americans got there much sooner than anticipated. Third, when they did get there they found a lot more Jerries than expected. O.K.?"

I didn't answer him. With his eyes shifting to the ceiling he explained that in planning such a mission the objectives and concepts of the Americans, the British and the French all had to be coordinated, not an easy thing to do. He had spoken slowly, articulating each word, like someone patiently explaining something to a child. Leaning back in his chair as he puffed on his pipe the colonel said that headquarters had been somewhat disturbed by our working so closely with the F.T.P., a Communist group. "You see, Captain," he said, still not looking at me, "if your reception committee had instructions not to let you get in touch with the F.T.P. such orders, of course, came from the Free French Organization here and well, after all, you were jumping into their country, weren't you? Strictly a matter between the French, wasn't it?"

Oh, Jesus Christ, I thought, to hell with this high-level politico-military strategy. With my ground-level view of *Schmeissers* and 88's, I thought that fighting Germans was what the war was all about, and anyone, Communist or otherwise, who felt the same way, was our ally.

"Of course you get my point, don't you, Captain?" the colonel asked.

I glared at him for a moment. "Maybe Churchill wouldn't get your point, sir," I said, straining to keep the anger out of my voice."

The colonel jerked up in his chair and gave me a startled look. "Eh? What are you . . ."

"Churchill was asked whether England would support Russia," I interrupted, "and his answer, as I remember, was 'if Hitler invaded hell England would be on the side of the Devil.'" Colonel Ormley-Dykes drily reminded me that I had not been asked to report to him in order to quote the Prime Minister. After a long silence he told me that another mission was being planned for both teams. Then he stood up. "That's all, Captain," he said. "Get a good rest."

Stepping out in the corridor I saw at the far end the husky figure of Major "Plug" Dillworth who had been our conducting officer, or "bird dog," during our briefing. When I called out to him he rushed over and threw his arm around me. "God damn it, Bill," he exclaimed. "Am I glad to see you! Heard all of you just got back."

I noticed that he wasn't chewing tobacco and asked him why. With a big grin he said that the Limeys at headquarters were stuffy about that sort of thing.

"I'll tell you this," he said. "When I saw you guys get on the plane that night I thought, Jesus, there go six good men. Bitch of a mission, wasn't it?"

"Yes, in a way it was, 'Plug.' Didn't work out the way we expected."

"No? Hell, I had a hunch it couldn't. But why tell you that? I wasn't in charge. Just a frigging staff flunky. And you guys—that Jeanpaul especially—were acting like you were off on some goddamn crusade."

When I got back to our flat I told the others about my debriefing *tête à tête* with Colonel Ormley-Dykes, and the possibility of another mission.

"We'll have to capture some more 88's for the French Army." Jeanpaul said with a sardonic smile.

"Look," I grinned. "This bird is a Britisher. Pukka sahib type. He doesn't give a damn about the French Army."

"Right now, I don't give a damn about the Army either," Larue said suddenly. "I want to go home, sit at a café with a tall glass of cold beer in front of me and watch the broads go by. *Ah çà, alors!*" Larue burst into a loud laugh at this happy prospect.

Jeanpaul lit a cigarette and looked coldly at Larue.

"Anyway, this goddam war is almost over," Larue went on. "I was talking to an Air Corps major in a pub this afternoon, and he says the Boches are getting the hell bombed out of them. They're on the run. Kaput. So there won't be another mission. I'll be out of the army and . . ."

"Larue!" Jeanpaul said sharply.

"Yes sir."

"You won't be out of the army for some time. The Germans will re-group, either this side of the Rhine or on the Rhine. They'll fight like hell. Look what they did at Cassino. The fly-boys always have these distorted views of the war. Bombs away! Convoy smashed. Enemy panics. *Merde!*"

I didn't want to contradict Jeanpaul but for once I thought Larue might be right. The newspaper reports, which were giving a vivid picture of the German rout in the Falaise gap, had me wondering how much more the Germans could take before divisions and even army corps surrendered as had happened at Stalingrad and in North Africa.

I got to bed late and did not sleep well that night. The V-1's were coming over again and the air-raid siren sounded constantly. Our flat was on the top floor so that from time to time I could hear the puttering of a V-1's motor, then the engine would cut off as the bomb glided down and crashed some ten or fifteen seconds later with a blast that rattled the window panes. Although I tried hard to ignore the V-1's, lying there in the total darkness with my eyes closed, I couldn't help listening to the engine and trying to figure out how close the flying bomb was when the motor stopped.

I thought how ironic it would be to come back from Brittany only to have a V-1 smash into our flat.

The next day when Jeanpaul and Drouant asked me to have lunch with them they both looked so serious that I wondered if anything was wrong. Each had one apéritif while I caught up on the Martinis that were unavailable behind the lines. Several times I tried unsuccessfully to start a conversation. After we had finished our lunch Jeanpaul, looking at me steadily, said he was going to ask for a short leave to see his wife and children in North Africa after which he would rejoin his battalion somewhere in France. He added that he hoped I understood, paused a few moments with a pensive expression, and said in a low voice, "But what we tried to do was correct."

Before I could say anything Drouant, speaking as if on cue, said that he had learned of Jeanpaul's decision that morning. He didn't want Truffington as a partner for the second mission and he had told him so. "Considering the changed circumstances," Drouant went on somewhat stiffly, "I should like to know whether you would become my partner. I hope that you will accept, B-e-e-l, for I think you and I and Descartes would make a fine team."

I looked at them for a few seconds, taking all this in, and then held up my glass of cognac. "All right," I said, "here's to our new team. And by God, here's to me too, for I am beautiful and desirable." Drouant chuckled while Jeanpaul's face twisted in his quick, lopsided grin and then he laughed very hard, a rare thing for him.

I went back to my room in the apartment and sat down to mull things over. Teaming up with Drouant suited me fine, and his radio operator, Descartes, was a good man in the clutch, which was more than could be said for Larue. I felt confident about going on a second mission, providing the staff planned the operation properly this time so that we didn't land on top of an SS division, or behind the Allied lines as Dick Lacorde's team almost did. But I certainly would ask a lot of questions at our next briefing; I wasn't going to be mesmerized by a briefing officer jabbing at a map to point out all sorts of tempting targets in our zone.

Jeanpaul came into the room, paced up and down a few times,

then stood gazing out the window. He turned to face me, frowning a little.

"I hope you realize my decision wasn't easy," he said. "I wouldn't want you to think that . . ." he seemed ill at ease.

"Sure," I said. "I understand. Don't worry about it."

He looked as if he wanted to say more but changed his mind and walked out. It was true that Jeanpaul's decision had come as no great surprise to me. I remembered one of those rare times when he had let his feelings show, telling me almost wistfully that he hadn't seen his family in a long time. Behind the lines I had noticed how the hard lines of his face would soften when he got down on one knee to talk to little kids. I could also understand his wanting to go back to his battalion. The company commanders would listen to Jeanpaul's crisp orders, snap a salute, reply, "*Bien, mon Commandant,*" and hurry off to execute those orders. Jeanpaul had seen chaos during the campaign in North Africa, and particularly during the German blitzkrieg of 1940 in France, but somehow this was, at least to him, still within a recognizable military pattern. What was not in this military pattern was making long bicycle trips, dressed in shabby civilian clothes, in repeated efforts to establish contacts blocked off because of the bitter rivalry between the F.F.I. and the F.T.P.

Perhaps for me, an amateur officer, it had been easier to adjust to the rambling, freewheeling, shoot-and-run Maquis operations, and especially to the lack of discipline. Maybe the ideal was to adopt a "so what the hell" attitude to some of the things that went on. Yes, maybe so, but I sure didn't have a "so what the hell" attitude at La Bastille when the Algerians and Senegalese took off, nor at some other places either. But what about Drouant? Like Jeanpaul he was a career officer and yet sometimes it seemed to me that he was determined to fight his own individual war, like the actor on stage who constantly improvises because he doesn't want to be bothered by a hopeless script. Once I had seen him strolling towards the beach on a reconnaissance with two Resistance men, one of whom had an old World War I rifle while the other, a stout red-faced farmer, was unarmed and carried a bottle of Calvados by the neck. Jeanpaul could joke and banter with the men, but anyone showing up like that with a bottle of Calvados would have been sent back at once with a few blistering words.

I got up to stretch and went to the window where I saw Jeanpaul leaving the building. He generally walked fast, regardless of where he was going, but this time he was moving slowly with his head down, probably still pondering the choice he had made. For some time now I had thought that Jeanpaul had volunteered for the Jeds because of a pledge he had made to himself, a fierce resolve to be among the first French officers returning to France. Since he wasn't sure that his battalion would land with the forces making the second invasion on the southern coast of France he had decided to jump in, just to be sure. Then I remembered his saying at lunch that what we had tried to do was correct. I knew what this French word meant to him. One's goals and conduct were either decent and honorable, or they were not: "*Correct*" or "*pas correct*"; there was no in-between. You lived and died by certain simple words, "*honneur et patrie*," "*le devoir*," "*la tradition*," "*belles qualités d'officier*," "*tombé au champ d'honneur*." Not that Jeanpaul used these words often, but they were so deeply rooted in him that one could not think of him without also thinking of "*honneur et patrie*" and all the rest of it.

Sometimes I wondered whether Jeanpaul saw life as really the acceptance of death—or maybe a defiance of death. Life was short, and better to die on the battlefield than live on into old age and gradually rot to death. We never talked of such things for Jeanpaul was a quiet man, but if we had I would have told him I could understand that point of view but some career officers did not get killed with a clean bullet hole through the head: they ended up mutilated or blind, while still many others became retired colonels and generals who died in bed.

I went into the next room where Drouant was changing into another pair of boots. "André," I said. "I've been thinking about Jeanpaul."

"You mean the 'divorce?' " he grinned.

"No, no. I'm serious. Do you ever get the idea that he really expects to get killed? See his family once more and then bang! Right through the head."

Drouant went on lacing his boots as though he hadn't heard me. When he finished he turned to me. "That doesn't concern us," he said quietly. "Come on, let's get out of here. Let's go to that pub around the corner."

A few days later word came from headquarters that our mission was delayed and that Drouant, Descartes and I were to report to Milton Hall to wait until we were alerted. Jeanpaul was not leaving for North Africa for several weeks. When we returned to Milton Hall some other Jeds were back from their missions, including Major Hartwell who had been slightly wounded and limped about with his bulldog once more trailing him. Then Major Dick Whitley came back, not quite as debonair as before, but still with a zest for life. On the night of his return he borrowed a motorcycle, although he had never ridden one before. Roaring at high speed on his way to a pub where no doubt he would meet Rosalie, he hit a bump in the road, went sailing off into the night, and broke his leg. I could have warned Whitley that riding a motorcycle for the first time can be a rather tricky thing. A number of Jeds had been taught how to handle a motorcycle at about the same time we were learning how to run a steam locomotive and also how to pick locks, the latter being a course that fascinated a few of the Americans to the point where the sedate British instructor became visibly worried.

Gradually word came back about more of the Jeds. Two of them got away from an ambush but their radio operator was critically wounded. One Jed, whom I knew only slightly, was missing in action. Another had been grabbed by the Gestapo. One had been gunned down when the Germans raided the barn where he was hiding. Another was killed covering the retreat of his Maquis group after they had blown up an ammunition dump. I kept thinking about Bob Farley, Jack Cambray and Pierre Martel, but there was no report on them. One day I heard about Captain Atherton, a British Jed who had been a good friend of mine. Atherton was getting his guerrilla band together for a night attack on a command post. While they were at their assembly point and starting to move out one of the men stumbled in the dark. His Sten gun, always a treacherous weapon, had gone off and the bullet hit Atherton in the thigh, severing an artery. First-aid measures couldn't stop the bleeding. The Maquis was unable to sneak a doctor out to Atherton until the next night. It was too late. Atherton bled to death. But even though bad news trickled in from time to time the casualties had not come anywhere near the point of "maximum casualties," that vague and ominous phrase mentioned by the OSS recruiting officer in Washington.

One of the Jeds who returned was an American captain named Hebert. He gave us an account of what happened to the village of Oradour-sur-Glane which was located within his zone. It seemed that when a Panzer division was rushing towards Normandy the Maquis kidnapped an SS officer near the village. Evidently the division commander was a decisive man who knew exactly what to do in a situation like that. He had issued a short order. On June 10 a company of his troops wheeled into the village just when school was letting out and the mothers were picking up their children. The Germans first rounded up the men in the main square and methodically machine-gunned some two hundred. The Germans next herded all the women and children into the church, set it afire after barring the doors, then gunned down those who tried to claw their way out through the windows. It was all over in a short time and the Germans drove away leaving behind about six hundred dead. Five villagers had somehow managed to survive. Captain Hebert said he'd seen Oradour-sur-Glane a few hours later; it had made him sick to his stomach. There was another point of interest mentioned by Captain Hebert: as it turned out the SS officer had not been kidnapped by the Maquis of Oradour-sur-Glane, but by another group from a nearby village.

Then one day Jack Cambray came back, rolling up in a jeep as we were leaving the mess hall. "Hi, you near-sighted bastard!" I yelled.

He waved back half-heartedly. When I got close I saw that he looked older. Farley in his sharp, teasing way had once told him that "the Krauts will chew up a Boy Scout like you," but if Farley could have seen him now with his boyish look gone he never would have said that. Cambray told me hello with a tight-lipped smile, his face drawn and a hard look in his eyes. His French partner was with him but their radio operator had been killed a few days before their return. Cambray asked about Martel, Farley and a few others before reporting to the camp commandant.

By now what had seemed to be a German rout two weeks ago was turning into fierce fighting. A war map was kept in the lobby at Milton Hall with the Allied lines shown in blue and the German positions in red. Blue arrows showing the direction of the Allied thrusts were moved each day to show another deep advance. But then the blue arrows slowed down and almost stopped. For the first time red arrows were drawn to indicate enemy counter-attacks. A battle was raging around Metz in northeastern France where Patton's armored columns, running low on supplies and especially on gasoline, were being held back by repeated German assaults. This gave me a mixed reaction; I wanted to see the Germans smashed but I also hoped for a second chance.

The stiffening German defenses made our second operation look like a certainty, although this mission was still postponed. I felt that on our first mission the Germans definitely had the better of it. They had scared the hell out of me at Gorron and at many other places. And what had I done? Very little except survive. The next time it would be different. Now I had experience of what it was like to be behind the lines so I could prepare myself ahead of time for unexpected situations—some of which I had already encountered—and think of what I might do then. I remembered one evening in a Peterborough pub that May when one of the American Jeds had said that guts, and that alone, counted. Martel's French partner, Delbecq, was there listening. With his aristocratic bearing and his twisted, crippled left arm Delbecq stood out, especially when he gestured with his bad arm. At one time I wondered whether he did this to call attention to it, but I had decided that this was unworthy of him. Perhaps he did this as an unconscious way of reminding himself that his left arm was still at least partially functional. It was right after the American had mentioned guts that Delbecq had spoken up, talking quietly as he always did, and making that awkward horizontal motion with his bad arm. He had said that the whole knack was to be able to anticipate (unless you were either stupid enough or lucky enough not to realize the danger) for otherwise even a brave man's courage could fail him. But if before going into action a man had thought of all the things that might happen, including his being hit, and had accepted these risks, then he stood a better chance of having guts.

I was still thinking of Delbecq when the commandant sent for me. He looked grave. "Good morning, Dreux," he said. "I know you and Bob Farley were very good friends. Thought you'd want to know about the report I just got."

"Yes sir." I braced myself.

He must have noticed my expression. "Oh, he's all right," he hurried on. "Well, that is, he's alive. But apparently he was shot up rather badly, I'm afraid. Should pull through, though."

"Yes sir. Where is he?"

"Some hospital in France. But you know, Dreux, the doctors do wonders these days. They'll patch him up pretty well, I dare say."

"Yes sir."

The commandant offered me a cigarette and watched me light it. "The report on his team is a bit sketchy," he went on. "His French partner, you know, the Foreign Legion chap, well, he was hit too. Radio operator O.K. Seems Farley was in command of a Maquis force holding a bridge until the Americans got there. The Jerries tried like hell to get the bridge back. Farley's men took quite a beating. When our tanks finally got there one tank commander says there was Farley, covered with blood, still firing his machine gun and it was going like the hammers of hell."

I thought of Bob Farley and all his push-ups, the long cross-country runs he took bundled up in sweat clothes, and Jack Cambray kidding him about his "Cyrano complex."

"Of course these tales grow in the telling," the commandant smiled a little, "but it seems Farley had mostly older men in his group. Anyway, when he was hauled off on a stretcher the story is that he said the Germans thought his old men would run away but they were too old to run so they stayed where they were and fought till they died." The commandant again smiled a little. "Does sound a bit like Farley at that, doesn't it?"

"Yes sir. It sure does. He was one hell of a guy."

"Yes, yes. Of course. Fine chap. If I hear any more I'll let you know. By the way, your mission is still postponed. But you should be alerted within a fortnight, I'm sure."

The commandant walked with me to the door, saying something about his bloody fool of a batman not having his tea ready otherwise he'd invite me to have some.

By that time most of the other Jeds were back, except Martel's team and two or three others. Martel was still on my mind, particularly late one night when there were only a few of us left in the officers' mess and a Scottish officer sang, "*Auld Lang Syne*," in a soft, clear tenor which reminded me of that night in Scotland when Martel had sung, "*A la Claire Fontaine*," with its hauntingly beautiful tune.

The following weekend Drouant and I went to London and just before catching the train back to Milton Hall we went to see Jeanpaul who was leaving the next day. We gathered on the sidewalk to tell him goodbye while a cab waited to take us to the station. Jeanpaul shook hands with us, smiled a little, and wished us well. Although I wanted to say something more to him—just what I didn't know—this was one of those times when Jeanpaul intimidated me a little. Since our return to London he had changed from a combat jacket to his khaki French Army tunic with its rows of ribbons, including the Legion of Honor, the Croix de Guerre and the British Military Cross. Above the ribbons were his jump wings. He looked very military, standing there erect, wearing his kepi and holding his gloves in his right hand. Now he was no longer smiling. He stepped back a pace, looking at us as though he were inspecting junior officers under his command. I thought, oh Lord here it comes, he's going to make a farewell speech to the troops in his sharp, clipped tone. But I was wrong, for when he spoke his voice was low and gentle and he said very little. "Our mission was a failure," he said and paused a few seconds. The only sound was that of the cab motor idling. "Partially at least. No bridges blown, B-e-e-l," he smiled at me briefly. "But we have nothing to reproach ourselves for. *Au revoir.*" He nodded his head, flicked at the visor of his kepi with his gloves in a sort of half-salute, turned on his heels, and walked briskly back into the building. I never saw him again.

CHAPTER XVII

Farewell to Milton Hall

Back at Milton Hall the days dragged by while Drouant and I waited to go on our mission. Then one morning the commandant sent for us. We were excited as we hurried over to his office. At last, we thought, this is it, we're going to be alerted. But after greeting us the commandant said that he had just received some bad news, our mission was cancelled. He explained that the plan had been to drop us near the Vosges Mountains in northeastern France where two Jed teams had gone in. A four-man team, composed of four senior officers from London headquarters, was to be dropped with us. But the Germans had rushed reinforcements to that area and the Gestapo was carrying out savage reprisals. The two Jed teams, badly mauled, had been forced to go into hiding and their operations were drastically curtailed. Radio contact with them had been lost for several days. Although there was a good D/Z in that sector, dropping us there was considered too risky now.

When the commandant had finished Drouant and I looked at each other. Our bitter disappointment must have shown on our faces.

"Sorry," the commandant said softly. "I know what this meant to you."

Drouant started to plead with him, saying we were used to tough situations, but the commandant shook his head. "No, no," he replied firmly. "It would be suicide."

There was a long pause while Drouant, his jaws clenched, stared at the commandant. He opened his mouth to say something, but changed his mind, saluted briskly, and marched out. I hesitated a second and then followed him.

That afternoon I sat in Drouant's room while he was packing to rejoin his infantry outfit in France. He took off his combat jacket and for a few moments, a sort of distant expression on his face, he fingered the parachute badge.

"Well, we'll have the 'liberation' of Dinan to remember," he said at last with a faint smile. "I can tell my grandchildren about that."

"That was quite a day," I said. "You were like Napoleon coming back from Elba."

Drouant chuckled a little. "I guess I felt that way. But I'll have to tell those kids the whole truth. Dinan was not liberated by their grandfather but by American tanks. Naturally before I get to the point of talking to my grandchildren the Germans will have to cooperate. So far they have."

"Maybe you'll end up marrying one of those Dinan girls," I said.

He laughed. "Still, you know B-e-e-l, Dinan is a pleasant memory, isn't it? So we must keep it that way, hold on to it but not let it get worn out by constant use. Then when you and I get old, when it's better to look back than look ahead, you know, when the future has shrunk to almost nothing, that will be one of the memories we'll smile at, sitting huddled by a fire with a blanket over our knees."

"You're a cheerful bastard," I said. "I suppose someone will be serving us a hot cup of chocolate then, or maybe a *camomille tisane*."

He grinned. "Why not?"

And then from out of nowhere a picture came to me, very sharp and clear, and I saw the old peasant woman sobbing and pleading in vain for my help on the way back from La Bastille.

"André, you're making it too damned easy. There will be painful memories also," I said.

"No, no. Not then anymore. You see, the trick is to try drawing the curtain on those right away."

He had finished packing. I thought he was taking a long time adjusting the straps on his gear, tightening them then loosening a buckle and slowly fastening it again. Finally he turned towards me to shake hands. It was not the usual polite and perfunctory French handshake, but a firm clasp and for a second neither of us wanted to let go. Then Drouant walked out without either one of us saying a word.

About a week later American headquarters in London notified us that all American Jeds would get a month's leave back in the States pending re-assignment to the Far East or other duties. Cambray and one or two others turned down the leave to stay in Europe. Cambray had succeeded in getting a special combat assignment to Italy which he refused to talk about. The rest of us returned to London to wait for space on a convoy to America. Several times I went by headquarters to ask about Martel and the few others who had not returned but were not listed as casualties. All I got was the evasive answer that no information could be disclosed at this time as to teams still in the field. "Security, you know," the staff officer added. As time went by I wondered more and more about Martel.

Walking back to my quarters late one night I saw a thin streak across the sky, like a falling star. Some seconds later there was a dull explosion far off in the distance. Although the same thing happened twice the following night I thought these were meteors and the explosion was just an odd coincidence. Clearly these had not been V-1's, for the streak had been much too fast and the air raid hadn't sounded. A few days later the British government announced that the first V-2's had dropped on London and that these were rocket missiles traveling at thousands of miles an hour. Most of the V-1 launching sites had been overrun by the British Army. Now the V-2's were starting. The Londoners didn't mind the V-2's as much as they did the V-1's; you were killed by a V-2 before you knew what hit you. No listening to a puttering motor and trying to guess where the bomb was. Warfare was becoming much more sophisticated; either way you were dead, but technology was replacing cruder methods. It did make me realize that the development from the Sten gun to a rocket missile represented an enormous leap forward in human achievement.

Pierre Martel didn't make it. I learned it the day before we sailed. Right after his area was reached by the Americans the report had come in, pieced together from the accounts given by one farmer and several Resistance leaders. All three men of Martel's team had been killed and later buried by the French in temporary graves. What had happened to Martel was not much different from my experience in the car outside Gorron. The three men, dressed as peasants, were on a country road at night, walking alongside a horse-drawn haycart when a German squad, thought to be SS, stumbled on them by accident. Their radio and weapons as well as extra guns were under the hay in the cart. Unlike the Germans at Gorron the SS reacted with murderous efficiency. A few questions, a search of the haycart, and Martel and the two others were marched to a farm wall for quick execution. They made a break for it. Delbecq and the radio operator were killed instantly, but Martel, although badly wounded, stumbled off in the woods. The SS hunted him down and one quick burst of a *Schmeisser* submachine gun finished him off. The farmer had found two of the bodies after the SS had gone. At daybreak he had found Martel's body. As I heard the story I could picture all this vividly, Martel lurching off in the dark and reaching the woods, then the barking of sharp gutteral commands. Perhaps when the SS got to Martel he was crawling on hands and knees, spurting blood and already dying.

The next morning I told Jack Cambray goodbye before catching the train to our embarkation port. He knew about Pierre Martel. We did not say much to each other. It was late November now and a cold, raw wind was sweeping down the street. By the time I got a cab the rain had started. At the station I found a vacant compartment in our train and settled down hoping to be left alone. This station was like others I had seen during the war, ugly, grimy, crowded with soldiers. I heard the locomotives puffing and hissing steam. Staring out the window I could see the rain slanting down hard, the black clouds, and the drab, gray tenement buildings on the other side of the tracks. The boarding ramp beside our car was streaked with patches of soot and littered with dirty, wet scraps of paper and torn bits of wrappers. Sometimes as one of the soldiers tramped by my window one of these bits of paper would stick to his heel and get carried off out of sight among all the moving legs and feet.

A few seconds before the train pulled out two young French WACS rushed into my compartment, laughing and chattering. They sat down after I assured them that I was not saving these seats for anyone. From what I overheard they were reporting for duty somewhere in Normandy on their first trip to liberated France. One of the girls was very pretty, a brunette with flashing brown eyes and an easy smile. The other was a pudgy blonde whose uniform was too tight. After a while they kept glancing at me and the pretty girl whispered something to the other one.

"Pardon me, Captain," the pretty girl said in English with a strong accent. She paused a second then went on quickly, her voice shrill. "Did you jump in?"

"Yes, I did."

"Oh! You see, I told you!" she said to the pudgy one. "What was it like? What did you do after you landed?"

"I went to see a priest."

"A priest? No! But why? Where?" She was very excited.

Speaking in French I told them briefly about the curé of Courcité. The pudgy one, moving over to sit next to me, asked how it was that I spoke such good French. I thought of all the times I'd had to answer that question behind the lines and said that I came from New Orleans, located in the former French colony of Louisiana, where most people spoke French and very few could talk English. They both nodded. I was beginning to enjoy myself. After that their questions came very fast, first by one, then by the other, often both together. The shorter my answers the more they pressed me, politely but insistently. Was I married? Yes. What did my wife think of my being a paratrooper? Wasn't she terribly worried? I told them I supposed so but she was a strong person. Was I in the regular army? No, I was a lawyer. Was I going back to the practice of law after the war? Yes, I was.

The brunette opened her musette bag, pulled out some sandwiches, and offered me one. While munching on it I thought, as I hadn't done in a long time, of what it would be like to practice law again. I could see myself in the library of the law firm where I was an associate, poring over a long draft of a contract handed to me a little earlier by one of the senior partners. He was a tall, gaunt man with cold gray eyes who believed that success in his profession came from power and power came from having the right contacts. When giving me a copy of the proposed agreement he would speak in a deep voice. Getting to the point always took him a long time, and a good ten minutes passed before I understood that he wanted me to check the contract to see if it violated the anti-trust laws. After reading and re-reading the contract, looking up the law, checking statute after statute, and reading dozens of cases, I would dictate an opinion letter to be sent to the client. But since I was only a lowly associate and this was an important client, the letter would have to be signed by this senior partner. He liked his letters well padded with jargon not because of the tenet (adhered to by some lawyers) that the longer the letter the more work had gone into it and therefore the higher the fee, but simply because that was the way his mind worked. Unless a letter for his signature was verbose he would glower and hand it back to you unsigned.

After the salutation the letter would read something like this: "I have given serious and careful consideration to all the complex facets and aspects of the problem . . . the fact that this specific situation is not unlike but actually similar to . . . For your further and fuller information it is my considered opinion that the penultimate paragraph of the proposed contract, namely the one commencing with the words . . . might be construed (the partner liked to hedge) as a violation of the law all as fully set forth in Title 15 Section 1 et seq. of the United States Code, as subsequently amended by the Statute of August 17, 1937." The letter had to close by saying, "If you have any further questions about the matter hereinabove discussed, please do not hesitate to call me."

That was the sort of thing I would be going back to. And after Brittany and whatever else was to follow—assuming my luck held out—the transition from a Jed to an associate in a law firm was not going to be easy.

Finishing my sandwich I noticed that the pretty girl was staring at me intently. She said she'd been thinking of my being a lawyer in New Orleans and that it seemed to her only right ("ce *serait juste*") if, after the war, I should be the lawyer for all French citizens there, corporations, individuals, and the French Consul too. She took down my name and the address of the law firm, saying she would speak to her father who was very influential. With a serious expression on her face she repeated emphatically that this was important to her and implied that it was important for France too. I had the impression that she saw a grateful France rewarding me for jumping in by providing me with many affluent clients. While I didn't want to discourage her I knew enough about the practice of law in New Orleans to see that things would not quite work out that way, even if her father was influential. It was true that, with or without her father's intervention, there would be a dribble of French clients over the years, but this would not be a clientele which other lawyers would envy.

I could picture a little old Frenchman in a worn suit coming into my office. Perhaps something in his face would remind me of some old peasant in whose barn I had hidden behind the lines, a man with whom I'd drunk Calvados while he told me of how a German patrol had raided his neighbor's farm the day before to search for hidden Sten guns. And now sitting there across from the brunette and smiling a little, I knew that those days behind the lines were gone forever. Even if I jumped in somewhere else, like French Indo-China, it would never be the same. That little old man in my office, say two years from now, might be a Basque from southwestern France—there were some Basques in New Orleans—who would ask me to draw up a power of attorney in French to be sent to his sister in France so they could sell the little family farm at the foot of the Pyrenees. After telling me all about the farm, his sister and her children, he would cautiously ask how much my services would cost him. I would tell him about fifteen dollars.

"So you see, Captain," the pretty girl went on, still with that serious expression, "this is something I will do for you."

"Thank you very much," I said. "That would be great."

Epilogue

Yet we'll go no more a-roving
By the light of the moon

Lord Byron

When my wife and I went to Europe in the summer of 1951, we rented a car to go to Brittany and then to the village of Courcité near where I had been parachuted. The car was a low-slung, racy looking Citroën sedan. Though small compared to a Ford or a Chevrolet of that time it was very fast and cornered beautifully.

From Paris we drove some thirty miles to the Château des Mesnuls, a lovely old castle dating back to the sixteenth century. The building and grounds were used as a center for the rehabilitation of boys, most of them orphans, who had been maimed and disabled in the war. They might have been caught in a heavy Allied air raid, or trapped in their village under fire from both sides, or crippled in numerous other ways. I'm not sure why I wanted to go there; certainly I wasn't drawn by any feeling of guilt. I hadn't been an Allied bombardier aiming for a railroad yard and releasing his bombs just a little before the target was lined up in the cross-hairs of his bomb sight. Nor had I been a gunner whose cannon was pouring shells into a village. But I was sure some of those kids must have been mangled by anti-personnel mines on the coast, and yet I'd had nothing to do with that either.

We went to the office where we met one of the therapists, a young man with a little mustache and a pleasant expression. He thanked us for coming and told us about the rehabilitation program, saying we were not allowed to visit the dormitories or the workshop. When I asked what sort of work the boys did he replied that they were taught to make various things, including toys. I could picture a kid with an artificial arm awkwardly sawing a block of wood to be made into a toy sailboat. Across the courtyard I saw a boy walking stiffly with an artificial leg. With him was a kid whose right arm was missing. They were too far away for me to see their faces. We did not stay long at the Château.

From there we set off for my area of Brittany, stopping overnight at Dinan and also at Dinard, across the bay from St. Malo which was being rebuilt. The new stones there contrasted sharply with the few ancient and weatherbeaten ones still intact. As we were having dinner in Dinan I thought momentarily of telling the old waiter that I had been the first American officer to enter the town in 1944. But this might sound like boasting. And anyway the waiter might have courteously replied, "*Ah, vraiment, monsieur?*" and then after making some polite comment he would have asked what we wanted for dessert. Or worse still, he might have responded enthusiastically, saying, "Ah! Monsieur was with those American tanks! How well I remember!" It was much better to say nothing.

During this trip I took many pictures in the usual attempt to give permanence to the past. When I saw the prints they were as I had expected, flat and meaningless, such as a bare field, a curve in a country road, a clump of trees, a cluster of farmhouses, a villa by the seashore. But my memories of what had happened to me at all those places leaped back at me furiously. When I stood in the open field in front of La Bastille taking pictures I found that I was unconsciously hunching my shoulders and peering ahead as if I expected the German machine gun to open up any second. I felt my heart pounding a little when I photographed the bend in the road near Gorron where the Germans had surprised us. I keep these pictures loosely in an old cardboard box and hardly ever look at them now.

Epilogue

On our way back from Brittany we headed for Courcité, getting there about five o'clock on a Friday afternoon. I drove through the square and parked by the rectory. Everything was as I remembered it, except for a monument to the dead of World War I near the entrance of the church. This had been beyond our line of vision from our room in the rectory. Dressed in slacks and a green sports jacket, I got out of the car and knocked at the door. It was opened by an elderly priest who gave me a surprised and questioning look. Although he had aged I was quite sure this was the same curé.

"Pardon me, Father," I said. "But weren't you the curé here in July of 1944?"

"Yes, I was." He looked at me very closely.

"Well, do you remember hiding out three paratroopers, and one of them was an American?"

"Yes! Yes! Of course!" Now as he stared at me I could see a glimmer of recognition in his eyes.

"And the American said if he got through the war, he'd be back. Do you recall that, Father?"

"Yes! Of course I do! But . . ."

"Well, Father , I'm the American, and I'm back."

He threw up his arms. *"Ah! Mon Dieu! Mon Dieu! Quelle surprise! C'est formidable! Entrez! Entrez!"*

"My wife is in the car, Father," I said. "She'd like to meet you."

"Your wife? Wonderful! Please ask her to come in." A broad smile spread over his face. "You must stay for supper. Yes, yes, and spend the night here." He kept rubbing his palms together and looked very excited.

I started to explain that we hadn't expected to spend the night in Courcité for we were due back in Paris.

"Ah no!" he exclaimed, holding up his hand. "I insist. You simply must." He chuckled, "And in the same room too."

I thanked him and as I turned back to get my wife I was a little surprised to overhear him calling out to his housekeeper that she'd have to get another can of sardines. When I returned with my wife the curé, still beaming, told her how pleased he was to meet her, what an unexpected honor it was to have me back and ended by saying, "*Vous comprenez, n'est ce pas, madame?*" Since the curé had spoken rapidly she had barely understood a word or two but she smiled, said "*Oui,*" and then added slowly, "*Je comprends un petit peu.*"

The curé's old housekeeper shuffled into the room puffing a little, her face flushed. Except for being a little stouter she looked the same in her black dress and white apron. With her came Casa, the Alsatian watchdog, or maybe now it was *Casa fils*. The dog sniffed, wagged his tail, and yawned. I started to shake hands with the housekeeper who was muttering, "*Ah, le Capitaine! Ah, le Capitaine!*" but she first wiped her hands carefully on her apron. She did the same thing before shaking hands with my wife.

We all sat down and looked at one another, the curé and the housekeeper fixing their eyes on me as though I were an apparition. I noticed that the curé's cassock seemed a little more worn and frayed but as in 1944 it was perfectly clean. The housekeeper timidly asked my wife if we'd had a good trip. My wife tried answering in French, groping for words, but in a loud voice as people often do when trying to speak a foreign language to a native. Although the housekeeper seemed to be having some difficulty in understanding she kept repeating, "*Ah oui, madame. Bien sûr, madame.*"

The curé leaned forward, still staring at me. "Well now, tell me all about it. What happened after you left here?"

I looked at him for a moment. "To tell you the truth, Father," I said, "I was a little disappointed about the whole thing. You see, in the First World War I was a fighter pilot in Guynemer's squadron."

The curé's face went blank.

Smiling a little, I told him how Guynemer had been my boyhood hero and how I'd played at being a fighter pilot, but that our mission had brought no dazzling victories such as those won by Guynemer.

"Ah!" he smiled back in a kindly way. "*La poursuite de la gloire, eh?*"

"No, Father, that's not really true. Not entirely true anyway. There were other things too."

"Naturally. I understand that. I was only teasing a bit."

I went on to tell him how we'd reached the St. Malo area and what we did afterwards, leaving out a great deal. He listened carefully, asked a few questions, and occasionally exclaimed, "*Oh, là, là!*"

When I finished he looked at me for a long time. "Well, even if your mission was not all that you expected," he said, "it seems to me that you certainly performed admirably. So you have nothing to reproach yourself for."

I thought that's what Jeanpaul had said too, "nothing to reproach ourselves for." I knew what Jeanpaul had meant; he was looking at our mission as a whole. But I could blame myself for tactical blunders, or an easy target missed, and yet I was not thinking of such failures now. It seeemed to me that there were other things you could reproach yourself for, unless war had truly hardened you and robbed you of all pity. Time had not erased the memory of the old peasant woman and her accusing eyes.

"Now, Captain," the curé said pleasantly. "You remember how I prayed for you—and for myself too—when you were hiding here, eh? Well, after you left I prayed every night to Our Lady that my three paratrooper guests should be spared. And, say what you want, those prayers were answered."

"I believe that . . ." I was going to say the wrong thing, that luck played its part and an eighth of an inch, or a second, one way or the other, could make all the difference. "I believe you're right, Father. That's the way my mother sees it."

I thought of my mother when I had come back to New Orleans on leave after our mission in France. She hadn't known that I was a paratrooper for I had only written to her that she would not be hearing from me for some time, giving her a rather far-fetched but seemingly plausible reason. And yet when she had learned what I'd done she was not at all upset and said that my father, who was long dead, would have been proud of me. Like the French officers I had known, my mother had rigid ideas of what was "*correct*" and "*pas correct*," and what her only son had done was "*correct*." What sometimes intrigued me about my mother was that, although of Irish descent and without a drop of French blood, she had grown to love France and it was she, rather than my father, who always insisted that we speak French so that I wouldn't forget the language. When it came to France her instincts were sure; my mother had backed de Gaulle from the start, with a fine disdain for the pro-Vichy coterie in New Orleans. Soon after reaching her house on the day of my arrival I could see that she had something on her mind. Looking at me thoughtfully for a minute my mother had told me quite calmly and firmly, in a way that made it clear that there was no room for discussion, that my safe return must have been due to her constant prayers to the Virgin. "Look, Mother," I'd replied jokingly, "how about giving me some of the credit? It took a little doing, believe me." She had given me a little smile and said nothing.

The curé and I had been talking for some time when the housekeeper said that dinner was ready. There was a big loaf of bread on the table, plenty of butter and a bottle of cider. We were served a watery potato soup, followed by sardines, and that was all. I was still hungry at the end and couldn't understand why the meal was so skimpy. The cuisine at the curé's in 1944, the rabbit stewed in wine, the plump chickens cooked with a delicious sauce, all this would have rated at least one star in the *Guide Michelin*. Later I understood why. In July of 1944 the curé had notice several days in advance that three men would stay with him. So by scraping together a few extra francs he had been able to get those fine victuals for us. Now, caught unprepared, he could only serve us his regular Friday fare, plus the extra can of sardines. What I liked is that he made no apology.

Halfway through dinner the curé suddenly put down his fork. "*Mon Dieu!*" he said. "It just occurred to me. We have not introduced ourselves." He stood and bowed towards my wife and me. "I'm Father Bourdin." So I got up, introduced my wife and myself, we shook hands self-consciously and sat down.

After dinner the curé sat back with a broad grin and put his hands on the table. "Now we have a little surprise for you," he said. "We're going to show you an American movie over at our schoolhouse."

I could read his mind: how do you entertain American guests?

A movie, of course. And they won't be expecting it; so much the better.

"That would be wonderful," I said, trying to sound enthusiastic.

But before we left for the schoolhouse the curé insisted on taking us out to his little garden in the back so that my wife could see the stone wall over which we'd climbed when we left the rectory that night. The wall was of no interest to me either then or now. Getting over that wall had been easy enough; the problem had been what lay ahead of us, on the other side.

On the way to the schoolhouse the curé told us that the movie projector had been obtained a few weeks ago and that Courcité was the only village in this entire region that now had movies. He took us to a classroom—I think it was the only one—where about seventy-five people, including some children, sat on long wooden benches facing a portable screen. All eyes were on us as we entered the room and I overheard several low voices, "Ah, there he is . . . the American paratrooper . . . came all the way from America to see Father Bourdin . . . he speaks French . . . that's his wife, look at that dress . . ." One woman told her little boy, "*Voilà, regarde, c'est le parachutiste Américain.*" The boy seemed disappointed at seeing a civilian. Kid, you should have seen me seven years ago, I thought. I had an idea that the curé, who looked very pleased with himself, would make a little speech about me which would call for my responding in some way—how I wasn't sure—but I would close by saying, "*Vive la France!*" always a good ending. Instead the curé led us to reserved seats in the center and we sat down. All the windows were closed so that the room was a little stuffy, with a faint odor of sweat and barnyards. As the evening wore on these smells became more noticeable.

The movie was an old, flickering film with French subtitles. I hardly saw any of it. My mind was back in our room at the rectory on July 14, 1944. What if atmospheric conditions had been bad when we were on the air that morning—one of those frequent disturbances in the ionosphere—or the operator in London had been a little slow and asked for repeats of parts of the message? Then we would have been sending for an extra minute at least, maybe several minutes. That might have given the D/F truck enough time to pinpoint our location. Had that happened, I probably wouldn't be here. Nor would the curé.

I remembered a book written about the OSS after the war. In the chapter on the Jeds the author said we "belonged to a strangely fatalistic organization where every moment was the last moment, and each man carried an undated death-warrant in the pocket of his jumpsuit." It amused me to think of how scornfully the Jeds would have reacted had they been told something like that before jumping in. And yet it was true that my mood was fatalistic on the plane, but that was because there was nothing I could do about flak, night fighters, or the pilot's navigation. Yet beginning with the moment I flung myself out of the bomber the rest was up to me—up to me and chance. It was not so easy to be fatalistic from then on.

After the movie the fresh air felt good. When the curé asked how we'd liked the show I said it was the first movie we had seen since leaving America—which was true—and we had enjoyed it all the more for that reason. "*Très bien,*" my wife said firmly. I wasn't sure whether she meant the movie or my reply.

Back at the rectory the curé got out a bottle of cider and poured drinks. He didn't say much and I think he sensed that I wanted to talk. There was something about the calm expression on his deeply lined face, the steady eyes, that encouraged you to speak freely and gave you the feeling—as you had with so few people—that he would understand. I told him I'd been thinking of those days behind the lines and that one of the qualities of that life was simplicity. All I wanted to know then, for example, was what lay around the next bend of the road, or whether that enemy machine gun in that clump of trees could cover the road to my left, or how soon it would be before I could stop and rest. Could I trust this Resistance leader? That barn we were hiding in, what was the best escape route if a German patrol came, and could we fight our way out? Most of the questions then were like that, basic and uncomplicated. There was no need to consider a compromise between integrity and money, between moral courage and popularity. The answers often were not easy, but you got them fast enough. You were not dealing with a lot of trivial matters, or if some of them were trivial they did not seem that way.

The curé listened to me, his hands folded in his lap. Of course there was more to it than that, I went on. I thought of that time when the American Jed had said that in combat guts was everything, and Delbecq had quietly replied that a knack of anticipating helped one to have guts. A few minutes after that Delbecq, looking pensive, had said he thought when it was all over he would miss the war, and others of us would too. Not really the war itself, he had added, but the camaraderie, the respect of your men, and fighting for a cause. "*Non,*" he had said with a half-smile. "*Après la guerre il n'y aura plus rien de beau.*" (After the war there will no longer be anything truly worthwhile.) Then, as if regretting having shown his feelings that much, Delbecq had turned to the barmaid, making that awkward gesture with his cripped arm to order another round of drinks.

When I told the curé what Delbecq had said he gazed at me thoughtfully for a few moments with a faint, tolerant smile, but he didn't say anything. I didn't add that Delbecq had been killed. There was a long pause, the curé still looking at me in a kindly way.

"Well, how are things with you, Father?" I asked him finally.

"Oh, pretty much back to normal, thank God." Then his face lit up. "Say, we just got a new altar. Italian marble. Beautiful! Come to six o'clock Mass tomorrow and I'll show you."

"That's fine. We'd love to come," I said with a forced smile. The curé continued to beam at the thought of his new altar.

"Father, I've been meaning to ask you, have you . . . I mean, in looking back on those days, did you find, well, a sense of purpose and . . ." I stopped, not knowing just how to put it.

"Purpose? My purpose then was to help boot out the Germans." He stopped to pour himself more cider. "But I hated the violence," he added vehemently. "Men—good men, men I knew and respected—were killed."

"Yes. But those that were killed, it isn't as though they died in an automobile wreck, and . . ."

"You speak of purpose," he interrupted as though he hadn't heard me. "My real purpose is here, right in the Church." He looked at me intently. "*Ad majorem Dei gloriam*," he said quietly. "I was reminded of that just the other day when the children made their First Communion." He went on to describe at length how the solemn-faced little girls, all dressed in white and in rows of two, each one holding a candle, had made their procession into the church.

"It must have been very nice," I said politely.

"Oh, yes indeed. And then I thought of how our village had been spared heavy fighting. It just shows that God has been good to us."

"Yes." There was no use in continuing this conversation, and I noticed that my wife, straining to catch the words, was frowning and looking a little bewildered. I glanced at my watch and stood up. "It's getting late, Father," I said. "If you'll excuse us, I think we ought to turn in."

"Why of course," the curé replied and led us upstairs to our room. Nothing had changed, the wooden crucifix, the gaudy holy pictures including the one of Saint Sebastian with arrows sticking out of his body, blood streaming from his wounds, and an ecstatic expression which showed clearly he was certain of finding a speedy entrance into heaven. The small, badly chipped statue of the Virgin still stood on the table. Seeing the room gave me a very strange feeling.

"Do you see anything different?" asked the curé as he stood in the doorway.

"No Father. It's just like it was."

"No, no!" he replied with a grin. He turned and pounded on the door of the room opposite ours. "Don't you see? No sign there anymore!"

He meant the sign, in French and in German, which gave notice that the room had been requisitioned as a billet for German officers. I recalled how the curé had told us then that if a German officer showed up to claim the room "this could be embarrassing."

I said this was a tremendous improvement. The curé chuckled

and said he hoped we would get a nice rest, a much better rest for me than the last time, He nodded to my wife, "*Bon soir, madame, bon soir, Capitaine.*"

"*Bon soir, mon père.*"

At breakfast the curé first shook hands with us—the French always did that in the morning as though they hadn't seen each other in some time—and then got out the Calvados to lace our coffee. I had an idea that he was doing this out of amusement, just to remind me of the custom among the peasants in whose barns I had hidden. Even though he only poured out a few drops for my wife she eyed her cup warily and later cautiously sipped her coffee. Afterwards the curé took us to call on the widows of the butcher and the veterinarian who had been on our reception committee. When the curé had told me that both men had been gunned down by the Gestapo a few days after we'd left Courcité I said that I would like to pay my respects to the widows. At first I found it hard to talk to them, but they were so grateful for my visit, so sincere, that eventually I managed to say more or less the right things. Each one made the same remark about her husband, "*C'était un brave homme,*" which has nothing to do with bravery but simply means, "My husband was a good man."

Then we went to see the mayor, a tall, sturdy man wearing a badly fitting dark blue suit and a starched collar for this occasion. With him was a little delegation of villagers, two or three of whom had been on our reception committee. They also wore dark suits with neckties which were knotted in a clumsy way and didn't match their clothes. The men were reserved and shook hands with me self-consciously, each one saying in a low voice, as if he had rehearsed it, that I had done their village a great honor by coming back. Then one of them, a chunky man in his early thirties with the pushed-in face of a professional wrestler, stepped out in front of me and said he'd been one of the men who had located me as I waited in the field after landing.

"I had my Sten gun right on you, Captain," he said with a roguish grin, and he made the motion of pointing a submachine gun at me. "Just to be sure," he added.

"So you were the guy," I said. "I remember that very well.

Well, I had my forty-five out, ready and cocked—just to be sure."

They all laughed and we chatted pleasantly for a few minutes until one of the men spotted my Citroën. They left me to gather around the car and admire it. I suppose there were only two or three cars in the village, probably old, sputtering Renaults and the new Citroën created the same effect as if someone in the States wheeled up to the corner drugstore in a bright blue Rolls-Royce convertible. The men seemed a little disappointed to learn that I had rented the car and didn't own it, but they asked lots of questions about the Citroën, especially when I raised the hood so they could peer at the engine. I couldn't answer some of their questions but I did tell them that the car easily did one hundred and forty kilometers an hour. This produced a sensation and, I think, gave them an even more favorable impression of me.

One of the villagers wanted to know if I didn't want to take a look at our D/Z, only a short distance away, but I said we didn't have time. Afterwards I was sorry I hadn't gone, for while the field would have looked like any other field, it wasn't just any other field. Perhaps had I stood in the middle of that open space I could have recaptured a little bit of the feeling I'd had that night, the dark ground coming up to meet me as I swayed above it, and then the elation of a good landing, my bad ankle not hurt, and afterwards crouching in the field, forty-five in hand, watching, listening, waiting, all for what seemed a very long time, and then seeing two shadowy figures moving slowly towards me out of those dark woods, all of this barely discernible in the pale light of the half-moon, and I wondering whether they were French or Germans, feeling fairly sure they were men of the Resistance but not being positive.

Later that morning when we told the curé goodbye he gave me a photograph of himself on which he had written "*Amicals souvenirs du curé de Courcité. Heureux et fier de vous avoir reçu du ciel le 14 juillet 1944. R. Bourdin.*" (Friendly remembrance from the curé of Courcité. Happy and proud to have received you from the sky on July 14, 1944.) He handed me the picture with a little smile, half-shy, half-sad, and waved to us slowly as we drove off.

Epilogue

From Courcité we drove to Chartres where we spent a long time visiting the Cathedral. As I stood inside the vast church the same feeling came over me as when I had seen Notre Dame de Paris, a sort of reverence for the Middle Ages and its deep faith in God and especially in the Virgin. Yet this feeling was tinged with doubt; perhaps I was in a sense the unbeliever who wanted to believe. I realized that I had a tendency to romanticize that period, the Virgin and her miracles, chivalry and plumed knights, Francois Villon wandering through the crooked streets of Paris and scribbling the verse, "Where are the snows of yesteryear?" No one thought it unbelievable then that God—and especially the Virgin—could instantly heal the sick or make the crippled walk. When I looked back on the Middle Ages its rough and cruel edges seemed to disappear and the era had a glowing quality, a mellowness and stillness, which it did not have then and which only the passing centuries had given it. Here in the Cathedral were those tall, stained glass windows with their "*bleue de Chartres*," a shade and richness of blue never duplicated since, and the quiet beauty of the glass reflected this quality of stillness. I thought of the artisans who had toiled a lifetime to build this church in honor of the Virgin, and the other artisans after them. But I had to remind myself of the squalor and misery of those days, the callousness and hypocrisy, the ignorance. Yet we still had all of that—except that our ignorance had expanded with our knowledge. We also had Buchenwald and Auschwitz, and Hiroshima and Nagasaki.

The legends of those times appealed to me. I liked the tale of Our Lady's juggler who was making the only offering he could by standing on his head in front of a statue of the Virgin and juggling balls and knives like mad until suddenly the Virgin had stepped down from her pedestal and with a corner of her blue mantle had tenderly wiped the sweat from the poor juggler's brow. Now we knew that those legends were just that: only legends, however beautiful. Not for us Keats' view that "Beauty is truth, truth beauty." And yet, as Henry Adams had said, this medieval faith in the Virgin had created a mysterious driving force of incredible power, the force which had built these soaring cathedrals. Then with the scientific age came the certainty that the creed of the Middle Ages was false; it was intellectually unacceptable. But it seemed to me that this certainty had a kind of hollowness to it, and that we had only substituted another set of myths and legends. I could not say that we were living in an intellectually and spiritually more pleasing world, nor that we were really closer to truth. And the Christian who had lost his faith, didn't he sometimes retain a certain tenderness for it? Was he perhaps "haunted by the mystery he flouts," as Yeats said of George Bernard Shaw? Yet one thing was now sure: the once universal belief of the Christian world in the power and compassion of the Virgin was shattered, just as if someone had tossed a stone through one of the great stained glass windows, leaving fragments of colored glass, red, yellow, blue, scattered on the cold stone floor of the cathedral.

But all this thinking was like being in a mental revolving door, and I broke off these reflections while waiting for my wife. She was still looking up at the immense circular window, some forty feet in diameter, known as the "Rose de Dreux" and named after Pierre de Dreux, Duke of Brittany and a member of the royal family early in the thirteenth century. Of course the name had aroused her interest, but I'd told her that this branch of the family had died out many long years ago so that if by any chance she thought I might be a direct descendant of the Duke of Brittany she had better forget it.

Occasionally I indulge in a sort of odd speculation about my ancestors and try to imagine what one of them was doing five hundred years ago or two thousand years ago. Now I wondered just what one of these ancestors was doing on this very day in the year 1251. And who was he? What sort of person was he? When I was in Brittany had I spent the night in a barn where once stood my ancestor's home? This home, had it been a small farmhouse set in a clump of trees and looking out to the sea? Although there was no connection between me and Pierre de Dreux—unless possibly by way of some bastard offspring—could it be that this unknown ancestor had been, for example, a groom in the Duke's stables and that eventually he, or his descendants, had appropriated the name? I then imagined one of my ancestors cleaning manure out of the stalls and becoming accustomed to the stench just as I had when resting in a barn. And so, *"Plus ça change, plus c'est la même chose."*

We left the Cathedral and went to a café where I ordered two *cafés filtres*, probably the least objectionable way of drinking French coffee. Seeing that my wife looked pensive I assumed that she had the Cathedral on her mind. But she was thinking of Courcité. "I wasn't ready for that," she said. "The curé, the housekeeper, all those people, you know—how they felt about your coming back. It was all so . . . so touching. It made me want to cry."

"Well, I wasn't really ready either," I said. "But I'll tell you, I wouldn't trade that experience, going back there, I wouldn't trade it for anything. Of course not many exciting things happen for those people there. Way off the beaten track—say, did you notice how they admired the Citroën? Well, anyway, when the American paratrooper comes back, that's a big event. And I guess our story has grown. Probably they're saying that the curé was holding off the Germans at the front door, talking and stalling, while we were scramming out the back door and over the wall." We sat for some time saying nothing.

After a while we got up and left the café. There was one more thing I had to do before leaving Chartres, and that was to see the Jean Moulin monument somewhere near the Cathedral. Jean Moulin, former prefect of the district, had been General de Gaulle's deputy and one of the organizers of the Resistance in the early days of 1941. At that time, when the grip of the Nazi conquerors was slowly choking France, the French underground was only a scattered handful of hunted men, proud men, tough men, men who had made a pledge of their lives and their honor. Those were the grim days when beady-eyed agents of the Gestapo and the Vichy Milice spread like vultures across the land. When he was arrested by the Gestapo in 1941, Moulin was afraid that he might talk under torture. He had tried to commit suicide by slashing his throat but a German guard had prevented him just in time. Either Jean Moulin had been released by the Gestapo for want of proof, or he had escaped—I couldn't remember which—but his throat had a telltale scar which he concealed by always wearing a gray scarf. In June of 1943, Moulin was picked up again. This time the Gestapo had all the proof it needed. What the Germans wanted were the secrets locked in Jean Moulin's head, especially the names of the other leaders. Although the Germans tortured Moulin for days they couldn't break him; Moulin did not talk, and when the Gestapo finished they had a mangled corpse but no information.

After walking around a bit my wife and I found the monument located on a sloping plot of grass. A great stone hand, clasping the hilt of a broken sword, juts out of the ground. Many thoughts went though my mind as I saw this memorial. A short poem by Patrick Shaw Stewart came back to me. He had been a British infantry officer aboard a troop ship heading for the Dardanelles in World War I. These were the waters where Achilles and other Greek heroes had sailed on many an epic journey, and Stewart had jotted down these lines: "Was it so hard, Achilles/So very hard to die?/Thou knowest and I know not/So much the happier I." A few hours after writing this Stewart was killed leading his platoon in the assault on the beaches.

I thought of the soldier I had buried near La Bastille. It had not taken him long to die. Pierre Martel, only a little longer. But for Jean Moulin, and many others, dying had been very long and very hard. The whole story of the Resistance in those early days, when the shame of defeat hurt like a festering wound, was told by the sword, broken but defiantly held aloft.

Finally we got in the car, not saying a word. I had thought that in going back to Courcité I would, in a sense, complete my mission, and that there was something unfinished until I had done that. But now there was a feeling of emptiness; something still eluded me. Some day, perhaps, it would be made clear.

On the way to Brittany and Courcité I had driven fast, letting the car out on the flat stretches. Now as we left Chartres and went past the rolling fields of golden wheat I drove more slowly. Paris lay ahead—and after that New York and then New Orleans. I was in no hurry.

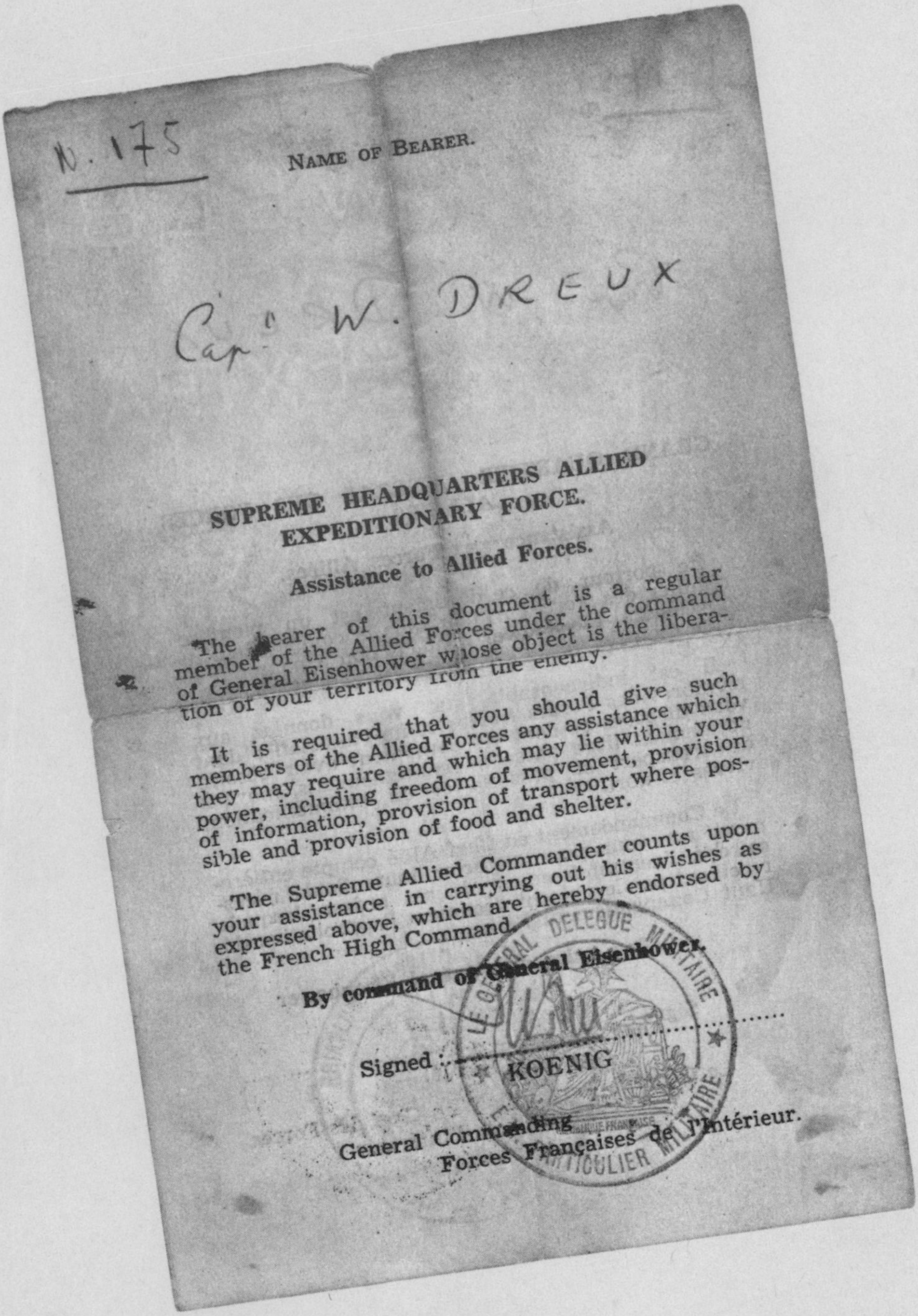

N. 175

NAME OF BEARER.

Capt W. DREUX

SUPREME HEADQUARTERS ALLIED EXPEDITIONARY FORCE.

Assistance to Allied Forces.

The bearer of this document is a regular member of the Allied Forces under the command of General Eisenhower whose object is the liberation of your territory from the enemy.

It is required that you should give such members of the Allied Forces any assistance which they may require and which may lie within your power, including freedom of movement, provision of information, provision of transport where possible and provision of food and shelter.

The Supreme Allied Commander counts upon your assistance in carrying out his wishes as expressed above, which are hereby endorsed by the French High Command.

By command of General Eisenhower.

Signed : ....

KOENIG

General Commanding
Forces Françaises de l'Intérieur.

LE GENERAL DELEGUE MILITAIRE
ETAT-MAJOR PARTICULIER MILITAIRE